RALPH
DOUBELL

RALPH
DOUBELL

RALPH DOUBELL

DO NOT WORRY, IT IS ONLY PAIN

MICHAEL SHARP

STOKE HILL PRESS

First published in 2018
by Stoke Hill Press
c/ 122 Wellbank Street
Concord NSW Australia 2137
www.stokehillpress.com
© Michael Sharp 2018

 A catalogue record for this
book is available from the
National Library of Australia

ISBN: 978-0-9945008-7-8

Edited & Produced by Geoff Armstrong
Cover Design by Luke Causby, Blue Cork
Internal Design & Typesetting by Kirby Jones
Printed in Australia by Ligare Book Printers

I tell my athletes that one day they will enter an Olympic stadium all alone, with thousands of eyes watching. They must prepare thoroughly for this moment.

I try to make their minds so strong that they are blessed with an inward feeling of complete superiority, for there must be no mental breakdown or all the physical training will be in vain.

I try to lift them above themselves — for immortality may be only a few minutes away.

Franz Stampfl

Contents

Mexico City, 15 October 1968

It's raining, but not enough to postpone competition at the Estadio Olimpico Universitario.

I'm not as nervous as I was before the semi-final yesterday, when I beat Wilson Kiprugut. He is the favourite and the Kenyans are keen to make a clean sweep of the middle-distance and long-distance events.

But not if I can help it.·

The final of the 400-metres hurdles has finished and the marshal takes us down to the track. Now I'm getting more nervous. I start jogging and hear someone barracking for Australia. It's good to know someone in the crowd is on my side. The marshal calls for us to take off our tracksuits and go to the start.

I settle at the starting line. The gun fires. But someone has broken and they're pointing at me. But it wasn't me, it was Walter Adams, the German in the next lane! I mustn't worry about that. I know what to do. If I break the second start, I'll be disqualified.

The gun goes again and Kiprugut races to the front. Good! He can use up valuable energy. I'm last at the first bend but that's okay and I soon move to fifth. I must maintain contact with Kiprugut.

This feels good. Don't panic, stay where you are for the moment.

I'm still feeling good. How fast are we going? Probably 50 or 51 seconds for the first lap. Okay, I must move up a bit so I don't get boxed in. That's good. There's the bell, one lap to go. I'm fourth on the outside, just where I want to be.

They're starting to move. Ben Cayenne of Trinidad and Tobago is dropping back and I race past him into third. Now Kiprugut is trying to break away. I must stay with him. I pass East Germany's Fromm in the back straight and I'm second. I must be in contact with Kiprugut with 200 to go. Keep the rubber band between us taut.

The others aren't coming with us. Okay, Kiprugut, it's between you and me. I'm still feeling good. Don't go too early. Remember what Franz said … leave it as late as possible. We've still got 150 metres to go.

He's flat out now. Don't let him get away. Wait for the straight. Wait for it. Wait. Wait. Okay, now! Eighty metres to go. Go! Go!

Hit it!

I'm past, I'm past him. But he's still there. I haven't broken contact. Come on, push it! He's still there. Fifty metres to go. Come on, push harder!

That's it, I've done it. I've broken the contact. The elastic band has snapped. Keep pushing, he's still right behind me but not threatening.

Thirty metres to go. He's still there! I think I'm going to win!

Twenty metres to go. I'm going to win! There's the tape. Keep pushing, he's still there. Ten metres to go. That's it, that's the tape, I'm holding the tape.

I've won!

I wonder what happens next.

CHAPTER 1

Inauspicious Beginnings

There were very few signs in the early life of Ralph Douglas Doubell that indicated he would enjoy success on the athletics track — or off it, for that matter.

He was born on 11 February 1945, six months before World War II ended and at the beginning of a new era in Australia's history. The country's population was 7.4 million when he was born, but it would grow by another 5 million over the next 25 years, largely through migration, as the Government decided Australia must 'populate or perish'.

His father, Douglas Clayton Doubell, was an immigrant who had come to Australia a quarter of a century earlier. Born in England in 1907, Douglas Doubell left his country of birth as a 14-year-old who dreamed of discovering gold on the other side of the world. He was over six-foot (183cm) tall and strong, but he didn't find his fortune prospecting and spent most of his life as a labourer. When Ralph was born, his father was working as a storeman and packer for Dunlop Rubber Company in Port Melbourne. The company made car tyres and Douglas was a shift worker, with the shifts being 7am to 3pm, 3pm to 11pm and 11pm to 7am.

Ralph's mother, Beryl Doubell (née Stanley), was born in Melbourne in 1914 and grew up in the inner-city suburb of Albert Park, about three kilometres south of the city centre. She came from a close family and always worked, including many years at the Kellow-Falkiner car retailer. Beryl was shy and not very social, and she was determined that Ralph and his older sister, Barbara, would have the education opportunities that she craved but never enjoyed. Beryl loved opera. She couldn't afford to go to a live performance but would on rare occasions spoil herself by buying a record. She adored *The Pearl Fishers*, an opera by the French composer Georges Bizet, and would sit and listen to that record for hours. She took great pride in the fact she could grow an orchid from seed.

Ralph Doubell's earliest years were spent with his father, mother, sister and their dachshund Cracker in a small house in the working-class suburb of McKinnon, 12 kilometres south-east of Melbourne's city centre. Young Ralph went to Ormond State School, which was in walking distance from the family home, and after school he would meet up with the local kids at the park at the top of their street, to play cricket or footy. For boys in Melbourne, 'footy' meant Australian rules football.

At the end of the day he would go home for 'tea'. Dinner was for posh people. There would be a roast on Sunday, meat patties made from the leftovers on Monday, and usually some kind of 'meat and three veg' for each day of the rest of the week. The meat was covered in copious amounts of gravy and the vegetables were overcooked, but Ralph thought it was just fine. Meat and three veg was his core diet throughout his running career.

Douglas Doubell wasn't around the family home as much as his wife and children would have liked because of his shift work. He didn't spend much 'quality time' with his children either, but that was quite common at the time. The Doubells could afford few privileges and Douglas and Beryl wanted their children to have a better life than they had. They worked hard and instilled a strong work ethic in their children. Their goal was to save enough money to build a house in East Bentleigh, a nearby suburb that had once been dominated by market gardens but was now being redeveloped as a residential area. When they moved there a few years later, they would have a small garden with a few chickens and an outdoor toilet. The 'pan' was collected every Thursday. Doubell remembers his father enjoying the new family garden, mowing the lawn and feeding the chickens.

The Doubell family wasn't religious at all, but Ralph's first organised sporting experience was with the Bentleigh Methodists cricket club. He had been mucking around regularly with his mates at the local park, and he was keen to play with a proper team in real games. When one of his friends invited him along to training at Bentleigh Methodists he gladly accepted the offer. Doubell became a wicketkeeper and batsman, and like so many Australian kids he dreamed of playing for Australia and wearing the baggy green cap. His heroes were Colin McDonald, the Victorian and Australian opening batsman, and then Bob Simpson, captain of the Australian XI during the 1960s. Doubell won his first sporting trophy at Bentleigh Methodists, for being most improved fielder. But while he loved playing cricket he wasn't overly talented and the baggy green would remain a distant dream.

In winter, Doubell switched to playing football with his mates at the park and supporting the family team, South Melbourne Football Club. His mother and her family were long-time and passionate fans of 'The Bloods', having grown up in the area, and Ralph would regularly go to home games with them. He watched the legendary Bob Skilton play his first senior game as a 17-year-old, the beginning of a 16-year career that would see Skilton play 237 games, kick 412 goals and win three Brownlow Medals as the 'fairest and best' player in the Victorian Football League. After years of financial stress, South Melbourne moved 700 kilometres north to Sydney in 1982 and the club is now known as the Sydney Swans. Doubell remains a keen Swans fan and is a proud ambassador of the club.

Cricket and Australian football were Doubell's only sporting interests in the years of his youth. He did compete in his primary school's athletics carnivals, and would usually finish with a place, sometimes first. But running wasn't a big deal to him.

CHAPTER 2

Melbourne High and Mr Woodfull

After finishing his primary education at Ormond State School, Doubell went to Gardenvale Central School. His most significant memory of his time there was getting 'the cuts' with a 15-inch ruler because he threw a ball that hit a window. 'I couldn't understand why I was punished so severely when I didn't even break the window!' he says with umbrage 60 years later. The pain from the punishment was bad enough, but it was the embarrassment that hurt more than anything else. He'll never forgive that teacher.

Gardenvale Central School was a feeder school for the prestigious Melbourne High School, which opened in 1905 and was the first State secondary school in Victoria. It was originally named the Melbourne Continuation School because its intention was to cover the gap between State schools, which finished at Year 8, and the University of Melbourne. At that time, secondary education after Year 8 was only offered by private church schools. Many boys and girls finished school at 14 and went to work. When it opened, Melbourne High School was located at the top of Spring Street in central Melbourne and was co-educational. The boys moved to a new campus at Forrest Hill, South Yarra, in 1927 and the girls moved to Albert Park in 1934. The girls' school was then renamed Mac. Robertson Girls' High School to recognise the substantial donation of £40,000 given to it by Sir Macpherson Robertson, founder of the MacRobertson's confectionery company that introduced chewing gum and fairy floss to Australia as well as creating iconic brands such as Freddo Frog and Cherry Ripe. In 1967, MacRobertson's was acquired by the Cadbury Group, which merged with Schweppes two years later.

Melbourne High School is a selective entry school for boys in Years 9 to 12, or Third to Sixth Form as they were then known at the school. Boys sit for an examination when they are in Year 8 and then wait to hear if they have been accepted. Doubell was reasonably clever but he wasn't at the top of his class at Gardenvale Central. He knew that his parents, and his mother in particular, wanted him to have the best education possible, so he applied himself and did well enough in the examination to be accepted into Third Form at Melbourne High in 1959. His mother was delighted. The change of school meant he now caught a bus for a three-kilometre journey from his home in East Bentleigh to Hughesdale each morning, and then took a 20 to 30-minute train trip towards the city centre, to South Yarra station, which was a short walk from Melbourne High. As he made his way from the station into the school grounds, he and his classmates would joke about the ghastly smell wafting across from the yeast factory in Claremont Street, South Yarra, and the more pleasant aroma of tomato sauce coming from the Rosella factory across the river.

Throughout Doubell's four years at Melbourne High School, an extremely important period in his development, Bill Woodfull was the Principal. Woodfull was one of seven children born to Reverend Thomas Woodfull, a Methodist minister, and his wife Gertrude. Bill Woodfull attended Melbourne High in 1912 and 1913 and was captain of the tennis team. He also played some cricket, but without distinction. After school, he studied at Melbourne Teachers' College and the University of Melbourne, and graduated with an Arts Degree and Diploma of Education. He became a teacher and it was while working at a school in Maryborough, 140 kilometres north-west of Melbourne, in 1920 and 1921 that his cricket began to improve substantially. Woodfull made his first-class debut for Victoria in 1922 and, after scoring consistently as an opening batsman, was selected for Australia's 1926 tour of England. He began teaching Mathematics at Melbourne High School in the same year. At the beginning of that 1926 Ashes tour, Woodfull was not considered an automatic selection in Australia's first XI. However, he performed well in the opening games and ultimately topped the tour batting averages, scoring 1672 runs at an average of 57.65, including eight centuries. As a result, Woodfull was named one of *Wisden*'s five cricketers of the year.

Woodfull would play 35 Test matches for Australia until his retirement from the game in 1934. He averaged 46.00 in Tests, 64.99 in all first-class matches, and captained Australia in 25 Tests, including during the infamous Bodyline series in 1932–33.

During that series, Woodfull refused to publicly criticise the English for their 'leg theory' attack, which directed short-pitched bowling at the upper body and head of Australia's batsmen in order to blunt the home-team's strong batting line-up, and particularly Don Bradman. He also refused to retaliate with similar tactics when Australia was bowling. While Woodfull contained his emotions in public and with the media, he did express his feelings clearly when the English manager, Pelham Warner, came to visit him after he had been hit by a bouncer: 'I don't want to see you, Mr Warner,' Woodfull said. 'There are two teams out there. One is trying to play cricket and the other is not. The game is too good to be spoilt.' Someone within earshot leaked the comments to the media and they have become an integral part of the Bodyline story.

Woodfull's behaviour during the Bodyline series highlighted his qualities as a cricketer and a leader. He was known for his strength of character, high morals, calmness under pressure and his respect for his teammates, the opposition and the game of cricket itself. He disliked any focus on individual averages, stressing repeatedly that cricket was a team sport. He was far from being a flashy batsman or radical strategist on the field, and was labelled 'The Rock' and 'Old Steadfast' by the media. A devout Methodist, he did not drink alcohol, but he did not impose any such restrictions on the other members of the team and would regularly buy them beer to help them rehydrate after a long day in the field. For all these reasons, he was an extremely popular captain who enjoyed great respect and loyalty from his teammates.

At school, as a teacher of Mathematics, Woodfull was a disciplinarian with high standards. He became Vice Principal of

Melbourne High in 1948 and then Principal in 1956. He regularly reminded boys of the school's motto, *Honour the Work*. Woodfull avoided talking about his cricket career whenever possible and did not become involved in coaching any of Melbourne High's cricket teams out of deference to the sporting staff. When he retired at the end of 1962, *Unicorn: the magazine of Melbourne High School*, paid tribute to his character and qualities:

> Few can rival this record of service, but Mr Woodfull's fame does not rest simply on his number of years at the school. Those who have worked with him, members of staff and boys alike, have never failed to be impressed by his sincerity, his determination, his great sense of justice and above all, by his unassuming, self-effacing nature. Any man who had led Australian cricket teams in Tests against England, South Africa and the West Indies could well be excused if, at times, he treated those around him in a condescending or patronising manner, yet such an action was completely foreign to Mr Woodfull's nature.
>
> Perhaps it was this trait more than any other which explains why the Principal was held in such high regard, and why there was such a spontaneous ovation when he left the Hall at the end of the final assembly on August 22.
>
> At a dinner given in Mr Woodfull's honour, the Prime Minister, Mr RG Menzies, referred to the Principal's qualities of leadership on the cricket field. Mr Woodfull, in reply, said that although he deemed it an honour to have captained Australia, he thought it a greater honour to have led Melbourne High School. Such was the man and such was his attitude to the school which owes him so much.

Woodfull set the tone for the Melbourne High School that Doubell experienced from 1959 to 1962. The school record for these years is a ledger the size of a brick, with a double-sided page featuring handwritten notes in black and blue ink for each pupil. It shows that in 1959 Doubell studied English, Algebra, Geography, Science, French, Modern History, Art and Mechanical Design. His marks were mostly around the pass level, except for Modern History for which he averaged 86 per cent for the year. Despite this strong result, he didn't continue with Modern History after Third Form. The summary of his year's performance in the school record notes that he 'worked reasonably well' but that 'some results were less than they should be'. It also observed that he 'works quietly' and 'would respond extremely well if a more personal approach was tried with him. Tends to be distant'.

There were seven classes in the 1959 Third Form and Doubell was placed in 'Form 3D'. The classes were not ranked and each had about 40 boys, which must have been a challenge for the form masters. The *Unicorn* of 1959 notes that a highlight of Form 3D's year was the week spent at Tecoma at the end of July. Tecoma Forestry School had been built a few years earlier and was used regularly by the school from 1958. It consisted of a classroom, a kitchen that doubled as the dining room, a teachers' annexe and an ablution block. Doubell, together with all the boys in Forms 3 and 4, spent a week there learning about forestry, geology, botany and zoology. They also worked on the plantation, helping to maintain and improve the buildings. The main aims were for the boys to experience community living and to learn to appreciate Australia's flora and fauna, including the local lyrebirds. The boys cooked their breakfast and dinner while a woman known as 'Mrs

Jayne' would cook lunch. The anonymous author of the 3D report wrote:

> On arrival there we were greeted by rain, slush and, for the boys on kitchen duty during the first day, smoke. The stove, according to the cook, 'never worked properly on the first day'. We had only one fine day, that being the last one. On our last night Roger (Elvis) Fraser rocked everyone with his songs. This trip was enjoyed immensely by the Form.

There is a note in the 'General' section at the bottom of the second page of Doubell's school record that briefly acknowledges an event that forever changed his life, and the lives of his mother and sister. It states simply: 'Father dead '59.'

Douglas Doubell died in the winter of 1959 after a long battle with cancer. He had been diagnosed with bone cancer, which is usually a secondary cancer, but they did not know the whereabouts of the primary cancer. He was extremely sick for the last 18 months of his life, his occupation being listed as 'invalid' in the school record, and Doubell remembers it being a terrible time. Three generations of male Doubells had died in their 50s, but Douglas' death at just 52 still came as a great shock to his wife and two children.

The Doubells didn't have much money before Douglas died, and now there was a lot of pressure on Beryl to take her children out of school and send them to work. Ralph was 14, and the law only required children to stay at school until they were that age. However, Beryl Doubell had always regretted not having more educational opportunities herself and she had great ambitions for her children.

She was not going to allow her son to be sent to work so young and stood up to the pressure she was receiving from family and associates to do so. She insisted Ralph would stay at Melbourne High School and his older sister Barbara would remain at Mac. Robertson Girls' High. To her children's eternal gratitude, she succeeded. She was clearly a remarkable and determined woman.

Doubell says that when his father died, the family just got on with life as best they could. They had never shown much emotion and this didn't change despite Douglas' early death. Doubell didn't realise it at the time, but his father's death must have had an impact on his academic performances. The school record shows that his worst mark in Form 3D was 34 per cent in the second Science exam. His teacher singled him out for criticism and shouted at him in the classroom: 'Doubell, this is one of the worst Science results I have ever seen!'

'I was extremely embarrassed,' Doubell recalls. 'I was humiliated in front of my classmates and I couldn't stop the tears from rolling down my cheeks.'

When he calmed down and the tears subsided, Ralph resolved that he would show everyone that he was smarter than the Science teacher thought he was.

Melbourne High only accepts boys who are above average academically, so for Doubell to be around the middle of the Third Form, apart from a rare bad mark in Science, was nothing to be ashamed of. Outside the classroom, he was not showing much sporting talent. He wasn't selected for the school cricket team but he did keep playing with his mates at Bentleigh Methodists. He had a go at Australian football, but while he possessed speed and some skill, he was literally a lightweight. The range in size and weight among boys of the same age was starting to make a real difference. One afternoon, a large boy named Colin Green came charging towards Doubell during a footy game. Doubell knew immediately it wasn't going to end well for him. 'Green basically ironed me out,' he says with a wince and a smile. 'Soon afterwards, I decided that Australian football was not the game for me.'

Green went on to play in the school's First XVIII footy team for two years and then became the leading goalkicker in the Under-19 Victorian Amateur Football Association. He also played in the First XI cricket team at Melbourne High and represented the school in field events during the athletics season. In his final year at school, Green won the Geography prize and he went on to become a Geography teacher at Melbourne High School for more than a quarter of a century. He has also had a strong involvement with the school's Old Boys' Association. Whenever Doubell sees Green at school reunions and other events he reminds him that he can take some of the credit for starting Doubell's athletics career.

However, Doubell wasn't having much success on the athletics track at this time. In fact, he didn't seem to have much athletic talent at all. There are four school houses at Melbourne High: Como, Forrest, Waterloo and Yarra. Doubell was in Como, the yellow house. The only event he qualified for at the school inter-house athletics carnival in third form was the C-grade hop, step and jump, and he didn't win or even finish with a minor placing in that.

The *Unicorn* reveals that a tragedy occurred during the 1959 inter-house cross-country run on 18 August. William Bruce Walker, who was described as 'one of the school's promising long-distance runners', collapsed and died. Like Doubell, he had come from Gardenvale Central School, but he was two years older, so Doubell knew him only slightly. The *Unicorn* reported:

> Bruce, an excellent student in all subjects and particularly brilliant in Mathematics, was holder of an RS Marr Scholarship, one of the most sought after and valuable scholarships offered in Victoria, and was expected to produce outstanding results at Matriculation level. His cheerful and friendly disposition, coupled with his sense of justice and loyalty, made him liked and respected by all who knew him, and his death, coming so suddenly and unexpectedly, deeply shocked and saddened the whole school.

Despite the complete absence of any athletic achievement at this time, for some reason young Doubell believed he could be a good runner. Somewhere inside, he thought he had talent. 'I was very effective in hiding it, but I just knew it was there,' he says. One thing supporting this view was that, while he wasn't having any success in track events, he did do comparatively well in cross-country races. Although he did not do any training, like the boys who qualified for the school's representative cross-country team, he would sometimes finish with a minor placing.

Pressed to explain where this mysterious faith in his own ability came from when he wasn't having any success in athletics, Doubell slowly shakes his head. 'I don't know,' he says softly. 'It was just part of me.'

In 1960, the 55th anniversary of the school's foundation, Doubell was one of 44 boys in Form 4G. His subjects were English, Algebra, Geometry, Geography, Science, French, History of Australia and the Pacific, and Social Studies. He achieved solid passes for all his subjects, including Science. At the end of first term, he was described as 'a quiet earnest worker who is doing his best' and by final term he was praised for 'continued excellent work with good results'.

Form 4G enjoyed another week in winter at Tecoma and, in a sign of the times, when they returned from the trip two boys, including the Form captain, left the school to go to work full-time. Doubell knew he was fortunate not to be following that path. He remembers the family washing machine breaking down and that they couldn't afford to pay for it to be repaired. His mother washed their clothes by hand for six months. 'That was just the way it was,' he says. While he continued to play cricket with Bentleigh Methodists on weekends, and thoroughly enjoyed it, Doubell didn't have any other interests because, he states matter-of-factly, 'We didn't have any money, so we couldn't afford it.' The Doubells weren't impoverished, but they were certainly struggling financially.

He did not have many close friends at Melbourne High School, although he is more accurately described as 'quiet' or 'reserved', rather than lonely. He was involved in the school's cadet corps for two years and was regularly singled out for public criticism. 'I was used as an example of how *not* to prepare clothes, webbing and boots,' he remembers. He switched to the Air Force cadets in his second year at the school because it meant he wouldn't have to clean webbing. Overall, he didn't enjoy cadets 'because of the way power went to some people's heads'.

While Doubell was not showing any particular talent on the sports fields, Melbourne High had a strong year in 1960 due to David Parkin's leadership and performances for the Australian football First XVIII and the cricket First XI. Parkin would go on to play 211 games for Hawthorn in the Victorian Football League between 1961 and 1974, and was a member of Hawthorn's premiership winning team in 1971. He became a coach and guided Hawthorn to a premiership in 1978 and Carlton to premierships in 1981, 1982 and 1995.

Doubell's subjects in Fifth Form were English, Maths, Physics, Chemistry, Biology and Social Studies. He was clearly focusing on an academic path that would help him prove his old Science teacher wrong. His marks remained in the solid pass category, although his first year of Physics provided a considerable challenge. At the end of first term, he was urged to make a greater effort in English, and by the end of the year it was noted he had worked well. Beginning in Fifth Form, the school record for each pupil at Melbourne High School includes comments under some broad headings. Doubell's Health was considered 'Good'; his Leadership was 'Average'; his Reliability was 'Excellent'; his Conduct was 'V Good'. Under 'General' is written: 'Quiet, well-adjusted boy.'

It has always been reported that Doubell did not make any sports team, even in athletics, until his final year at Melbourne High School. However, there he sits, third from the left in the front row of the *Unicorn's* photo of the 1961 school athletics team. His hair is parted neatly and he is slumped slightly in his seat, looking as if he doesn't really think he belongs. Doubell insists that, despite his appearance in this team photo, he did not represent the school when he was in Fifth Form. He suspects he was a reserve. To the best of his memory, he definitely did not compete against other schools until he was in the Sixth Form.

Doubell turned 16 in February 1961 and, as he matured, he was increasingly influenced by the culture at Melbourne High School.

He was one of thousands of boys who benefited from the leadership provided by Bill Woodfull as Principal, and the team of teachers that Woodfull built around him. Doubell was exposed to not just the core curriculum and the various sports on offer, but also his schoolmates' efforts in drama, singing and art. Doubell found himself among a group of young men who had gained their place at the school because they were above average intelligence — and this was an extremely stimulating environment.

The school captain in 1961 was a charismatic young man named Gary Evans, the son of a tram driver. Evans won the school History and Debating prizes, represented the school in football and produced a play for his House. In the years after leaving school, and now known by his full name of Gareth Evans, he graduated from the University of Melbourne with a Bachelor of Arts and Bachelor of Laws with First Class Honours. Evans won a scholarship to Oxford University and graduated with a Master of Arts with First Class Honours in Philosophy, Politics and Economics. He worked as a law academic and then a barrister before beginning an extremely successful political career that included terms as Australia's Attorney-General and, most notably, Foreign Minister.

Another great character in the year above Doubell at Melbourne High School was Ross Fitzgerald. He was known for his intelligence (he won the Economics prize), quick wit and the piles of books that seemed to always surround him. The *Unicorn* reported sarcastically that Fitzgerald was an all-round sportsman due to his four ducks for the Second XI and his selection as 'emergency' for his House C-grade football team. On the other hand, he had genuine success in the school's plays and revues. Fitzgerald became an academic, writer and political commentator and Emeritus Professor in History and Politics at Griffith University. He has written 40 books.

In his memoir, *Incorrigible Optimist*, Evans recalls that one of Fitzgerald's books was about his recovery from alcoholism 'to which he insists I drove him'. Evans continues, 'That might not be a complete exaggeration. We certainly had what might be described as confrontational, rather than complementary, personalities.'

The school captain in 1962, Doubell's final year at Melbourne High, was Leslie Rowe. He collected the Drama and Debating prizes and was also a member of the school's athletics team. Rowe would become a senior diplomat, serving as Australia's Ambassador to Russia. Alan Stockdale, who was also in Doubell's year, would become Victoria's Treasurer. Alex Wodak would become a leader in public health, most notably as Director of the Alcohol and Drug Service at St Vincent's Hospital in Sydney. Terry Smith, the son of a Geelong greenkeeper and a rebellious boy at school, became an esteemed art historian. He served as Power Professor of Contemporary Art at the University of Sydney and then as Andrew W. Mellon Professor of Contemporary Art History and Theory at the University of Pittsburgh.

These were just some of the boys who contributed to the life-shaping environment that Doubell experienced as he made his own path through Melbourne High School. They were taught not just to *Honour the Work*, but to enjoy a range of educational experiences and strive for excellence in whatever they did. Evans recalls:

Melbourne High during my time rivalled the top private schools not only academically but in the multi-dimensionality of the educational experience it provided. It was where I learned to debate ... It was where I learned to enjoy theatre, by watching slightly older contemporaries like Max Gillies find their wings, if not performing myself ... It was where I learned to enjoy — though again, performance skills were beyond me — both classic and contemporary music, as did Athol Guy, Bruce Woodley and Keith Potger, in the year ahead of me, when they started calling themselves *The Seekers*. It was where I learned, in the school cadets, that whatever other career I might follow it was not going to be in the military. It was where I learned that, while I enjoyed playing Australian rules football, I had peaked as a 12-year-old playing in the first ruck at Hawthorn West alongside the later legendary David Parkin, and that I was condemned thereafter to being a second eighteen battler.

In his final year, Doubell studied English, General Mathematics, Physics, Chemistry and Biology. He passed Matriculation and the handwritten notes in the school record describe him as a 'steady and reliable lad with good steady habits'. It also noted he had 'a mature approach to study and is improving his position'. His Health, Reliability and Conduct were all listed as 'Excellent' and his Leadership potential was 'Possible'.

CHAPTER 3

The Four-Minute Mile

As a boy with an interest in sport growing up in the 1950s, young Ralph Doubell was aware of the frenetic race taking place among the world's best runners to become the first to 'break' the four-minute mile. In Melbourne, as in many cities around the globe, the saga was frequently in the news. The three athletes leading the race to achieve this milestone were Roger Bannister from England, Wes Santee from America and John Landy from Australia. Journalists tracked the progress of the trio closely and speculated continuously on who would be the first to break the barrier and when. The Australian media reported on the story as regularly and enthusiastically as any of their peers because one of their own, John Landy, was at the centre of the story.

The concept of the four-minute mile captivated tens of millions of people around the world for a number of reasons. First, it was considered beyond the limits of human capability. It was an arbitrary time and distance, but running under four minutes for 1760 yards (1609 metres) had become viewed as a superhuman feat. Secondly, it was an extremely easy and symmetrical concept to understand — exactly four minutes to run four complete laps of an athletics track. Another reason for the fascination with this record was that there was a truly global competition to achieve the feat. A Frenchman, Jules Ladoumègue, was the first person to run under 4 minutes and 10 seconds when he ran 4:09.2 in Paris in 1931, breaking the record of the legendary Paavo Nurmi of Finland. Two years later, New Zealand's Jack Lovelock set a new world record of 4:07.6 while representing Oxford University at a meeting held at Princeton, New Jersey. One year later, America's Glenn Cunningham reduced the record to 4:06.8 on the same Princeton track. Cunningham's time was not beaten until England's Sydney Wooderson ran 4:06.4 in 1937 and this remained the world record for five years until two Swedes, Gunder Hägg and Arne Andersson, took it in turns to lower the mark on several occasions between 1942 and 1945. Hägg's time of 4:01.4, set in Malmö in 1945, was still the world record in the early '50s as Bannister, Santee and Landy focused on taking the time under the magical four minutes.

It cannot be overstated that all three young men were motivated not just by the prospect of making athletics history, but also to atone for their personal failures at the 1952 Helsinki Olympic Games.

Most people know Roger Bannister as the legendary athlete who was the first person to run faster than four minutes for the mile. He did so after studying medicine at Oxford University and St Mary's Hospital Medical School in London. He was feted for his achievement and knighted in 1975 for his services to sport and medicine. However, from late July 1952 he was pilloried by the British press for his failure to win a medal in the 1500 metres in Helsinki, despite being expected to win gold.

In the year leading up to the 1952 Games, Bannister had insisted on sticking to his own training regime. This involved hard workouts but virtually no racing at all. He didn't even turn up to defend his British mile championship. Many openly questioned his approach at the time and, when he didn't deliver on the Helsinki track, the media was remorseless. Bannister had been caught off guard by the late addition of a semi-final to the 1500-metres schedule in Helsinki, which meant he had to compete in three races instead of the two he had built his training program around, but the press was unsympathetic. The entire British team had performed poorly in Helsinki and Bannister, who had a high profile leading up to the Games and was considered Britain's best prospect, became the focus for public and media anger. He was going to retire from athletics after Helsinki to focus on his medical studies, but he decided to keep running for two more years to try to make up for his failure in Finland. His goal was to be the first person to break four minutes for the mile.

Wes Santee was a star athlete at the University of Kansas who, unusually for the time, was not afraid to speak brashly about his undoubted ability. Though only 20 years old in 1952, he held both the 1500-metres and 5000-metres national titles and, unsurprisingly, was intending to compete in both events at the American trials for the Olympic Games. He won the 5000 metres at the trials comfortably but then, the next day, the officials refused to let him run in the 1500 metres. They told his coach that Santee, at 20, was not strong enough to run against the Czechoslovakian champion and Olympic favourite, Emil Zátopek, in the 5000 metres and then back up to run the 1500 metres. Santee was furious. He was sure he could run both races, as he always had done, and furthermore his best event was the 1500 metres, not the 5000 metres. The officials wouldn't budge.

Helsinki was a disaster for Santee. He was eliminated at the heat stage of the 5000 metres after he went out unnecessarily fast in the first half of his race and then faded badly. He was embarrassed by his performance but also angry, because of what had happened during the selection process. He decided his revenge would be to become the first person to break four minutes for the mile.

John Landy was a late addition to the Australian Olympic team for Helsinki and not much was expected of him. He had only started taking running seriously in 1949, after he finished school; his main sporting focus until then had been Australian rules football. Now 22 years old, he had run some solid times for both the 5000 metres and the 1500 metres in early 1952 and the Australian selectors offered him the opportunity to represent Australia at the Olympic Games if he could raise the money needed to cover his travel expenses. The Geelong Guild Athletic Club held fundraising events and made a generous contribution, and his parents had to make up the difference.

Landy didn't progress past the heats in either the 5000 metres or the 1500 metres in Helsinki, and he felt he had let down his Geelong club teammates and his parents. Importantly, he learned a huge amount from the experience. He realised that Australia was a long way behind Europe when it came to training methods. He had watched Zátopek crush his opponents on the track and also had the privilege of listening to the great Czech athlete during training runs.

Zátopek was always happy to tell others about his latest program and what new things he was trying. Landy spoke to other Europeans about their training and methods of preparation, and when he returned to Australia he decided he would leave his enigmatic coach, Percy Cerutty, and increase the intensity of his training. He believed if he worked as hard as the Europeans and Americans he could take his running to a new level. At this stage, however, he did not even dream of running four minutes for the mile.

On 12 December 1952, only four months after adopting his more punishing training regime, Landy ran an extraordinary 4:02.1 for the mile at Olympic Park in Melbourne. The time was a shock to everyone, including Landy, and was regarded with significant scepticism overseas. Three weeks later, he ran 4:02.8 and this silenced the disbelievers. In fact, the media noise around Landy became increasingly loud and every race he ran was anticipated eagerly, attended by huge crowds and then analysed forensically. The paparazzi in Melbourne followed him while he trained at Central Park in Malvern East (now called John Landy Oval) and when he occasionally went to a restaurant or a social function. His life had changed forever.

This had occurred in the Australian summer of 1952–53. In Europe and the USA it was winter, the off-season for athletics, which meant there was a scramble to find out as much information about Landy and his latest race as possible. Bannister and Santee stepped up their winter training, as they sensed that time would be of the essence in the months ahead. Throughout 1953 and early in 1954, the efforts of Bannister, Santee and Landy to break the four-minute mile barrier in their respective countries made headlines around the world. This is no exaggeration. The media continuously and excitedly anticipated the possibility of the milestone being achieved, and thousands turned up to watch any of the three race in the hope of witnessing history.

EDMUND HILLARY AND TENZING NORGAY became the first people to reach the summit of Mount Everest, the highest mountain on Earth, on 29 May 1953. Hillary was a New Zealander and Norgay from Nepal, but the expedition was regarded as very much a British one. The excitement around the successful ascent was heightened when the news reached London on the eve of Queen Elizabeth II's coronation. It was a time of great British pride. Following this magnificent achievement, the media began comparing the scaling of Mount Everest to the challenge of breaking four minutes for the mile. Both were seen as being at the very limit of human endeavour and made front-page news around the world. The four-minute mile became known as 'Everest on the track'.

Bannister ran 4:03.6 in May 1953, his best time by four seconds, and the following month Santee ran 4:02.4, the fastest mile ever run by an American. The world's media wrote that it was a matter of when, not if, one of them would achieve Everest on the track before the end of the year. They were wrong. In November, Landy began the Australian summer with his first ambition to again run faster than 4:03. This he did on 21 January 1954, when in front of thousands of spectators at Melbourne's Olympic Park, he recorded 4:02.4. On times, he was the best miler in the world, having run less than 4:03 three times but, as he waved to the crowd, their disappointment was palpable. They had hoped for even better. Denis Johansson, an outstanding Finnish runner who had come to Australia, thought Landy was a magnificent athlete who would break four minutes if he had the opportunity to race on a better-quality cinder track than the ones available in Australia. He started to make arrangements for Landy to travel to Finland for the upcoming Scandinavian season.

Finally, and famously, Bannister broke the four-minute mile on the Iffley Road track at Oxford on 6 May 1954. In the winter of 1953 he had joined his University friends, Chris Brasher and Chris Chataway, at the training squad run by a mercurial Austrian coach named Franz Stampfl. The four of them had trained hard, harder than Bannister ever had before, and developed a plan for Bannister to break the four-minute barrier. At Oxford, Brasher and Chataway played critical roles in pacing Bannister for the first three laps and then Bannister surged home to cross the line in 3:59.4, almost two seconds faster than Gunder Hägg's world record and a crucial six tenths of a second under four minutes.

Six weeks later, in Turku in Finland, Landy ran a magnificent 3:57.9 for the mile to beat Bannister's time by a significant one-and-a-half seconds. Landy had set a new world record that would not be broken for three years, but Bannister had beaten him to be the first to conquer Everest on the track. Later that year, Bannister and Landy, still the only two men to have broken four minutes for the mile, competed in what was labelled 'The Miracle Mile' and the 'Race of the Century' at the 1954 British Empire and Commonwealth Games in Vancouver, Canada. The Commonwealth Games might not attract much global interest today, but it is estimated that 100 million people listened to this race on radio while millions more watched on the new technology of television. Landy was a front runner and led for almost the whole race until Bannister passed him with a well-judged finishing burst. The time was just outside Landy's world record. It later emerged that Landy had cut his foot on a photographer's light bulb the day before the race and had run with four stitches in the wound, but he refused to tell anybody about the injury or use it as an excuse for not winning the race.

Landy's popularity among the Australia of Ralph Doubell's youth was enhanced in March 1956 in the mile race at the Australian Amateur Athletics Championships. A promising junior runner, Ron Clarke, fell during the third of the race's four laps and Landy, who thought he might have spiked Clarke as he jumped over him, stopped and turned back to help Clarke to his feet. Landy apologised to Clarke and then set off after the rest of the field. Incredibly, he chased them all down and won the race in 4:4.2. If it weren't for his sporting gesture to help Clarke, many thought he would have broken his own world record that day.

So, although young Ralph Doubell's interest in sport was mostly focused on barracking for South Melbourne and following the Australian cricket XI, by the time of the Melbourne Olympic Games he knew that athletics was a major global sport and was very aware that an Australian, John Landy, was one of the best middle-distance runners in the world.

CHAPTER 4

Melbourne 1956

There was one person who had noticed that 11-year-old Ralph Doubell had some athletic talent. Ralph Holden, a teacher at Ormond State School, saw something in Doubell as he watched him play footy in the playground and compete, enthusiastically if unsuccessfully, in the primary school athletics carnival. Ormond State School had been given 10 tickets to the 1956 Melbourne Olympic Games and those who were interested put their name in a ballot. Like many Australian kids at the time, Doubell tried to imagine what it would be like to be an Olympian. For the first time, running races sometimes replaced games of cricket or footy up at the local park.

Doubell entered the school ballot for the Olympic tickets, but his name wasn't drawn. He was extremely disappointed at missing out, but then Mr Holden asked him if he would like to go. The teacher said he thought Ralph would enjoy watching some of the world's best runners while they were in Melbourne. Doubell accepted the invitation immediately, somehow Mr Holden managed to get 11 kids through the entrance with just 10 tickets, and they squeezed in to watch one of the greatest events in Australian sporting history.

The 1956 Melbourne Olympic Games was the first Olympics held outside Europe or the United States and the first in the southern hemisphere. In the final round of voting at the International Olympic Committee session in Rome in April 1949, Melbourne beat Buenos Aires by just one vote. In making its case to host the Games, Melbourne highlighted the fact that Australia was one of a select few nations to have competed at all summer Olympic Games of the modern era. Furthermore, Australian athletes had performed consistently well since 1896 and won many medals. Three of the nations that had been represented at all the modern summer Olympics — Greece, Great Britain and the USA — had received the honour of hosting.

As is almost always the case with Olympic Games, there was plenty of controversy about the choice of Melbourne as host city. One of the main concerns was the logistics and cost of transporting thousands of athletes and officials all the way to Australia. When finalising its bid in 1949, the organisers tried to assure the IOC, stating, 'Modern air travel has brought Melbourne at the present time within three days' travel of Europe, and four of America. Indications are that by 1956 those times will have halved. There are in addition a wide variety of well-serviced sea routes from which to choose.' Another concern was that the Melbourne Olympic Games would be held late in the year, in November and December, instead of July or August, and so not during the usual competition season for northern hemisphere athletes. Some commentators argued that these athletes would be unfairly disadvantaged.

In Australia, the Federal Government and the Victorian Government could not reach agreement on the financing of the Games, and in the early years of preparation this resulted in some confusion around construction of the venues and the Olympic Village. This was of great concern to Avery Brundage, the powerful President of the IOC, and he began considering whether Rome, which had been selected to host the 1960 Olympic Games, might be ready in time to host the 1956 Olympics instead of Melbourne.

The funding issues were eventually resolved and the enormous construction program was completed on schedule at an officially estimated cost of £8 million.

The Melbourne Cricket Ground was expanded and would be the main stadium for the Olympics, with a capacity of 105,000 spectators. Right next door, Olympic Park was redeveloped as a spectacular complex of venues for the swimming, diving and cycling, and as a training centre for several sports, including athletics, football and hockey. The Olympic Village, which would house over 6000 athletes and officials, was built in the northern suburb of Heidelberg. Importantly, from a domestic politics perspective, it was built by the State Housing Commission and would be used for public housing after the Games.

International politics also had a significant impact on the Melbourne Olympic Games. In fact, there were real fears at the time that the Cold War could degenerate into World War III. In late October, just a month before the opening ceremony in Melbourne was due to take place, the people of Hungary rose up against the country's Soviet-influenced government and demanded democracy. The USSR decided to crush the incipient revolution and on 1 November commenced an invasion of Hungary by land and air. Soviet power was restored by 10 November, and in those bloody few days thousands were killed and hundreds of thousands fled the country. The USSR's invasion of Hungary resulted in the Netherlands, Spain and Switzerland withdrawing from the Melbourne Olympic Games.

At the same time, the Suez Crisis erupted in the Middle East. In July 1956, Egyptian President Gamal Abdel Nasser nationalised the Suez Canal, which had been owned and operated by Britain and France since its construction in 1869. The Suez Canal revolutionised global trade routes because it reduced sea travel between the North Atlantic and Indian oceans by about 7000 kilometres. Attempts by the US to resolve the issue diplomatically were unsuccessful and on 29 October 1956 forces from Israel and then Great Britain and France invaded Egypt. The USSR demanded the troops withdraw. The United Nations, extremely concerned about the heightening tensions between the world's great powers, brokered a ceasefire by 8 November. However, Egypt, Iraq and Lebanon withdrew from the Melbourne Olympics.

Despite these boycotts, and the withdrawal of China because Taiwan was allowed to compete, more than 3200 athletes from 72 countries travelled to Australia to compete in 145 events across 16 sports.

As an 11-year-old boy, Ralph Doubell had no idea about the controversies and concerns leading up to the Olympic Games. Like most Australians, he was excited and proud that Melbourne had been selected to be host and he couldn't wait until the show came to town and Australia could prove to the world what it could do.

The excitement started to build significantly with the Olympic torch relay, a tradition introduced 20 years earlier by Carl Diem and Adolf Hitler for the 1936 Berlin Games. On the morning of 2 November 1956, in front of the Temple of Hera in Olympia in Greece, a flame was kindled by using a glass to concentrate the sun's rays onto wood shavings. The flame was used to light a torch and a girl dressed in classical Greek robes took this torch and handed it to the first of 350 young Greek athletes, one for each kilometre between Olympia and Athens, who carried it by relay to the ancient capital. A dedication ceremony was held at the stadium used for the 1896 Olympic Games before the torch was taken to Athens airport and placed on board a Qantas Super Constellation aeroplane, *Southern Horizon*. International air-safety regulations prohibit naked flames on aircraft, so the torch was used to light a flame in a specially designed miner's lamp. The flame was then flown to Darwin via Istanbul, Basra, Karachi, Calcutta, Bangkok, Singapore and Jakarta.

On 6 November the Olympic flame, still in the miner's lamp, arrived in Darwin to be welcomed by a crowd estimated at 3000, about a third of the city's population at that time. It was placed in a Royal Australian Air Force prison cell for safe keeping before being flown in a RAAF jet to Cairns. There, the local mayor lit the first official Olympic torch and handed it to the first relay runner, a man born in Australia of Greek heritage named Constantine Verevis. He ran for one mile before handing it to Anthony Mark, an Aborigine from the Mitchell River Mission on the Gulf of Carpentaria. They were the first of 2830 runners, one for each mile, who would carry the torch down the east coast of Australia to Melbourne.

For most Australians, seeing the Olympic torch would be their only direct contact with the Games. Huge crowds gathered to see it along the 5000-kilometre route that ran through Townsville, Mackay, Rockhampton, Bundaberg, Maryborough, Brisbane, Grafton, Newcastle, Sydney, Canberra, Albury, Bendigo, Ballarat and Geelong.

The crowds were sometimes so large that runners were blocked completely, even though police accompanied the torch each day on its journey. The organisers began to worry that such delays might jeopardise their carefully organised schedule that had the torch arriving in Melbourne just in time for the opening ceremony.

Prince Philip, husband of Queen Elizabeth II, had travelled to Australia to officially open the Games. When Melbourne won the right to host the event in 1949, King George VI was invited to perform this duty but he died of cancer in 1952. His daughter, now Queen Elizabeth II, and Prince Philip had visited Australia in 1954 and the Queen accepted an invitation to become Patron of the Melbourne Olympic Games. However, she could not justify another journey to Australia in 1956, and Prince Philip was sent as her representative. He arrived at the stadium in a Rolls Royce and, dressed in his naval uniform, waited until the President of the IOC, Avery Brundage, and Australia's Prime Minister, Robert Menzies, delivered their speeches. Then His Royal Highness stepped up to the microphone and said simply: 'I declare open the Olympic Games of Melbourne, celebrating the XVI Olympiad of the modern era.' Trumpets sounded, the Olympic flag was raised, 5000 pigeons were released and a 21-gun salute was fired.

But who would have the honour of carrying the Olympic torch into the main stadium and lighting the Olympic flame? The identity of the runner had been kept secret and this mystery added to the rising excitement among the crowd as the temperature rose toward 30 degrees Celsius.

The organisers had chosen 19-year-old Ron Clarke, a promising young athlete from Melbourne. Clarke was the junior mile world record holder and would go on to set 17 world records and compete at the 1964 Tokyo and 1968 Mexico City Olympics. If you had told the young Ralph Doubell that day that in the not too distant future he would become Ron Clarke's teammate at Commonwealth and Olympic Games, as well as on athletics tours to Europe and the US, he would have thought you were mad. Clarke was never told why he was chosen to light the flame, but he presumed it was a combination of having set some junior world records and because he was not competing in Melbourne.

Melbourne was the first Olympic Games to be extensively televised, which was particularly exciting for Australians because this new phenomenon had only been introduced into the country a few weeks before the Games began. The organisers wanted the opening ceremony to set the tone and standard for the television coverage and they were keen for the lighting of the Olympic flame to look spectacular. They therefore created a torch for the final leg of the relay that was different from the torch that had been carried from Cairns to the main stadium. It was much larger and sent bright sparks flying out of its crown. Clarke had only practised with an unlit torch, and now, as he ran around the track, he realised he had to carry it facing away from him so the sparks wouldn't blow back into his face. The ash-like material falling off the torch did, however, burn holes in his shirt. He had been told to wear a white t-shirt, white shorts, white socks and white shoes — and to buy them himself. He was never reimbursed. Clarke proudly wore his Essendon footy shorts from when he played in the club's under-19 team.

Clarke ran up the 85 stairs to the top of the Melbourne Cricket Ground, as he had practised, and stepped on to a specially placed stool before thrusting the flaring torch into the cauldron. During the practice, the gas in the cauldron had been turned down low. However, someone had decided to turn it up for the actual lighting to make absolutely sure it caught fire. No one told Clarke. In front of more than 100,000 people in the stadium and millions watching on television, Clarke stumbled off the stool as the flame blew up significantly higher than he expected. His arm was burnt and he had to seek treatment from the St John Ambulance volunteers. At the press conference, he rolled up his track suit sleeve to show how they had bandaged his arm up to his elbow.

While Clarke was dealing with his singed limb, John Landy stepped forward from the Australian team of athletes. The world record holder for the mile held the Australian flag in his left hand and raised his right hand to pronounce the Olympic Oath:

> We swear that we will take part in the Olympic Games in loyal competition, respecting the regulations which govern them, and desirous of participating in them in the true spirit of sportsmanship, for the honour of our country and for the glory of sport.

Landy had been in excellent form early in 1956, but unfortunately he agreed to an official request to travel to the US in May. This was part of a public relations exercise designed to counter negative publicity that had arisen out of concerns about whether Melbourne would be ready to host the Games. Landy was now an athletics superstar, and not just in Australia but also in the US where his battle with Bannister and Santee had been followed closely by sports fans. Despite Santee's best efforts, no one had yet run under four minutes in the US. Santee's best time was 4:00.6.

Landy performed strongly on his brief tour of the US, breaking four minutes in both his mile races. While he achieved the desired goals of positively promoting the Melbourne Olympics and running under four minutes before huge crowds and live television audiences, the tour had a very unfortunate downside: he injured himself on the hard tracks on which he raced. After he recovered, Landy was unable to run competitively, including in Australia's Olympic trials. He had lost fitness, form and confidence. While the public dreamed he would win the 1500 metres in Melbourne, those who knew the extent of his injury and the impact on his preparation were amazed he even made the final. Ron Delany of Ireland would win the gold medal. For Landy to finish third and take home a bronze medal was outstanding in the circumstances.

YOUNG RALPH DOUBELL HAD been soaking up the atmosphere in his home city during the lead-up to the Games and he couldn't believe that now, thanks to Mr Holden, he was sitting in the Melbourne Cricket Ground with his mates watching the greatest athletes in the world. His strongest memory is of watching the great Russian, Vladimir Kuts, who won gold in the 10,000 metres and 5000 metres. Kuts had burst onto the scene in 1954 when he broke the 5000 metres world record at the European Championships, beating the legendary 'Czech Locomotive', Emil Zátopek, and

Britain's Chris Chataway. Another British runner, Gordon Pirie, went into the Melbourne Olympics as the 5000-metres world record holder while Kuts held the 10,000-metres world record.

Kuts ran two superb finals in Melbourne, grinding Pirie and the other competitors into the ground. He became the first Russian male to win an Olympic track-and-field gold medal when he won the 10,000-metres final on the first day of competition in a time of 28:45.6. József Kovács of Hungary finished seven seconds behind Kuts while Australia's Allan Lawrence earned bronze in 28:53.6, about 30 seconds faster than his previous best. Five days later, Kuts won the 5000 metres by a substantial 11 seconds. The Melbourne crowd gave Kuts a standing ovation after both races for his gutsy running and his unconventional, even ugly style. It didn't seem to matter that he represented the country that had recently invaded Hungary and was on the other side in the Cold War. The track coach of the Yale University team, Bob Giegengack, summarised what many felt about the great Russian runner:

> Vladimir Kuts typified the spirit of Melbourne. I don't think anybody thought about his nationality. Everybody thought about the man. He led all the way and it seemed he might be exhausted at any time. Instead he ran the others blind. He was magnificent. Such times are what make the Olympic Games worthwhile.

Kuts inspired many athletes around the world, including 18-year-old Herb Elliott. who had taken a three-day train trip from Perth to Melbourne with his family to watch the Olympics. 'Of all my memories of the '56 Games,' he wrote in his autobiography *The*

Golden Mile, 'the one that burns deepest is of the unathletic looking Russian sailor Vladimir Kuts, his arms flailing and blond hair flapping, running his opposition into the red cinders during the 5000 metres and 10,000 metres. The ruthless determination in his hatchet face held everyone spellbound. We could see that he was tired and yet he tortured himself by continual bursts of sprinting.'

Elliott was a superb all-round schoolboy sportsman — he captained his school's athletics and hockey teams and rowed in the first VIII — but a bad foot injury at the end of 1955, caused by a dropped piano, led to a loss of interest in athletics and the picking up of some bad habits. 'I smoked thirty or forty cigarettes a day, I liked an occasional noggin of beer and I was bent on having a whale of a time – as far as one can have a whale of a time with a crushed foot,' he recalled.

The trip to the Melbourne Olympic Games, and Kuts' performances in particular, reignited Elliott's interest in running, and he decided to visit Percy Cerutty, the charismatic coach whom he had met when Cerutty visited Perth during the previous year. Elliott begged his parents to let him stay in Melbourne and train with Cerutty and they ultimately agreed, his mother reluctantly. From this moment in Melbourne, with Kuts as a key catalyst, Elliott began a journey in which he would dominate the world's mile and 1500-metres races from 1958 to 1960.

Melbourne introduced one of the great traditions of the modern Olympics. The closing ceremony at past Games had often been regarded as something of an anti-climax and the Melbourne organising committee had been wondering how to liven it up. Teams of athletes did not participate in the closing ceremony at that time; instead, one flag-bearer from each country would stand on the field in a semi-circle as speeches were made. Just a few days before the end of competition in Melbourne, the chairman of the Games' organising committee, Wilfrid Kent Hughes, received a letter from John Ian Wing, a young Australian of Chinese heritage:

Dear Friend,

I am a Chinese boy and just turned 17 years of age. Before the Games I thought everything would be in a muddle, however, I am wrong, it is the most successful Games ever staged. One of the reasons for its great success is the friendliness of Melbourne people. Overseas people would agree with me that Melbourne people are the most friendly people in the world.

Mr Hughes, I believe it has been suggested that a march should be put on during the closing ceremony, and you said it couldn't be done? I think it can be done.

The march I have in mind is different than the one during the opening ceremony and will make these Games even greater. During the march there will be only 1 NATION. War, politics, and nationality will be all forgotten. What more could anybody want, if the whole world could be made as one nation? Well you can do it in a small way.

This is how I think it can be done. No team is to keep together and there should be no more than two teammates together. They must be spread out evenly and THEY MUST NOT MARCH but walk freely and wave to the public. Let them walk around twice on the cinders and when they stop the public will give them three cheers.

I'm certain everybody, even yourself, would agree with me that this would be a great occasion for everybody and no one would forget it. It will show the whole world how friendly Australia is.

THE IMPORTANT THING IN THE OLYMPIC GAMES IS NOT TO WIN, BUT TO TAKE PART.

Kent Hughes liked the idea immediately and sought approval from his fellow committee members, as well as from Avery Brundage and the IOC. The green light was given. But it was already the eve of the ceremony, so there was no public announcement. The new closing ceremony, with athletes of the world marching together as a gesture of international friendship, was a surprise to the crowd … and a huge success.

The Melbourne Olympics, which became known as the 'the friendly Games', was a major milestone in Australia's history. The venues were superb, the events ran like clockwork, volunteers were outstanding and a wonderful initiative had been introduced at the conclusion of the competition. The Australian team performed magnificently, finishing third on the medal table behind the USSR and the USA. Australia won 13 gold, eight silver and 14 bronze medals. A number of Australia's greatest sporting legends emerged from these Games, including Dawn Fraser, Murray Rose and Betty Cuthbert.

Significantly for the young Doubell, Australia's track-and-field team performed very strongly. The women were outstanding, with Cuthbert winning the 100 metres and 200 metres, Shirley Strickland the 80-metres hurdles and the Australian team of Cuthbert, Strickland, Fleur Mellor and Norma Croker won the 4 x 100-metres relay. Marlene Mathews claimed bronze in the 100 metres and 200 metres. While not securing any gold medals, the male athletes impressed with their results. Silver medals were won by Charles 'Chilla' Porter in the high jump and the 4 x 400-metres relay team of Graham Gipson, Kevan Gosper, Leon Gregory and David Lean. Bronze medals were earned by Allan Lawrence in the 10,000 metres and Hector Hogan in the 100 metres.

Australians were thrilled to see that their athletes could not only compete with the best in the world, they could actually win or make the podium. They realised Australia was now a real force in world sport, and this had a major impact on Australians' view of themselves.

Young Ralph Doubell didn't realise it at the time, but some individuals involved in the Melbourne Olympics would have a major influence on his life. Mike Agostini, a sprinter from Trinidad, would soon immigrate to Australia and become his high school athletics coach. Franz Stampfl, who had coached Britain's Chris Brasher, the winner of the 3000-metres steeplechase, was already coaching in Australia. Doubell would join Stampfl's squad when he went to the University of Melbourne. As well, Doubell would catch up with Bob Giegengack, the Yale University coach, when he competed in the US in the late 1960s. Ron Clarke would become Doubell's teammate, while 57 years after he read the Olympic Oath in Melbourne, John Landy, who served as Governor of Victoria from 2001 until 2006, would read a speech when a sculpture of Doubell was unveiled in the grounds of his alma mater, Melbourne High School.

The parade of people from around the world had opened Doubell's eyes to other cultures and made him wonder about international travel for the first time. Most significantly, the performance of Olympic athletics planted a seed at the back of his mind. Cricket and footy might be the main sports in Australia, but he could see there was also a place for runners like Cuthbert and Kuts.

CHAPTER 5

First Victory

It was many years before the seed planted in Doubell's mind during the Melbourne Olympic Games saw the light of day. He did not show any promise on the athletics track until his final year at Melbourne High School and even then he didn't produce anything special until the very end of Sixth Form. He was selected in the school athletics team at the beginning of 1962, his final year at Melbourne High, but he isn't mentioned in the results for either the open or under-17 440-yards or 880-yards races at the school athletics carnival that was held at the beginning of the year. A boy named Alex Daniliuc won all the races he entered: the open 100 yards, 440 yards, 880 yards and the mile. Daniliuc's time of 1:58.5 in the 880 yards broke the previous school record by 1.4 seconds. Malcolm Foster, who was in Como House with Doubell, won the under-17 880 yards and also the mile. In the year report for Como House in the *Unicorn,*

Foster is one of the athletes listed as bringing 'honour to Como' while others, 'including Dick Lee, Norm Franzi and Ralph Doubell deserve some praise'. It was hardly a portent of things to come.

Doubell's first athletics victory of any kind came at the Metropolitan High Schools' Sports Association, Central Division, meeting at Olympic Park. Melbourne High performed well at the carnival, winning the aggregate point score ahead of Box Hill High, Northcote High, Brighton High, University High and Camberwell High. The *Unicorn* notes that this was an excellent achievement 'in the absence of Alex Daniliuc'. Doubell stepped up for his school and won the 440 yards in 51.8 seconds and the 880 yards in 2:01.7. The two races were held within an hour of each other. Soon afterwards, he finished second in the 880 yards at the All High Schools Meeting. He was appropriately rewarded with School Colours in athletics.

What had happened? How did Doubell progress from being an also-ran in the inter-house C-grade Third Form hop, skip and jump to a schoolboy champion at the end of Sixth Form?

When he was in Fourth Form, the quietly held self-belief he had in his athletic ability led him to convince his mother to buy him a pair of running spikes. This would have been a luxury purchase for the Doubells at the time. It was a big deal and he remembers the shoes clearly and fondly. They were black and made of hard leather, had a stiff sole and featured long spikes for Australia's grass tracks. Soon after he began running in them, Doubell started to move out of the inter-house C-grade events.

Doubell's other secret weapon was puberty. During his final year at school, he matured physically as well as mentally. His body began to develop and catch up with his schoolmates. He grew about 15 centimetres in the months between the school athletics carnival at the beginning of the year, at which he failed to even secure a placing in an event, and his double victory at the Central Division Metropolitan High School Athletics meeting in November.

A third critical factor was that Melbourne High employed Mike Agostini as a teacher. In 1954, Agostini had become the first athlete from Trinidad to win a gold medal at the British Empire and Commonwealth Games (now known as the Commonwealth Games) when he won the 100-yards final in Vancouver, Canada. The favourite in that race was an Australian, Hector Hogan, who finished third. Agostini was also a finalist in the 100 metres and 200 metres at the Melbourne Olympics and gained some notoriety by doing his sprint start warm-ups on the Melbourne Cricket Ground's bowling greens. He went on to win a bronze medal in the 100 yards at the 1958 British Empire and Commonwealth Games in Cardiff. Soon afterwards, Agostini moved to Australia, where he married and had three children. He received Australian citizenship in 1961.

'Agostini was a sprinter and didn't know much about middle distance running, but he developed a basic program for me and helped me focus on what to do both in training and racing,' Doubell recalls. 'Importantly, he helped me believe that I had some running talent. He didn't say much more than, "I think you've got something and I'll help you if you want to." But even that was a huge boost to my confidence.'

Until now, Doubell hadn't received much positive reinforcement from his parents or teachers. British culture, and its descendant in Australia, was more stand-offish; the message was usually along the lines of 'do as you are told'. Agostini, with his Caribbean background, took a different approach and in doing so gave Doubell the confidence to succeed at athletics in his final year at school. Agostini was a valuable mentor, which was significant given that Doubell had lost his father. He was Doubell's first experience of how important a coach can be in motivating athletes to improve their performance and then challenge them to achieve their absolute best.

At the top of the first page in the school record summarising Doubell's four years at Melbourne High, there is a section next to the heading 'Temperament, etc' in which there are three words written in blue ink: 'calm, interested, interesting'. Those words are telling, and very complimentary adjectives to ascribe to a quiet 17-year-old boy who had to cope with his father's death when he was 14 and whose family was doing it very tough.

Even so, no one at Melbourne High in 1962, least of all Doubell, would have predicted that 50 years later a sculpture of him would be erected on the hill between the main school building and the sports oval. An anonymous donor wanted to highlight the fact that Melbourne High was much more than an academic school and to celebrate the performances of some old boys who had become outstanding sportsmen. The first sculptures celebrated achievements in Australian football and cricket, because these were the main sports played at the school. Neil Roberts, who played for St Kilda from 1952 until 1962 and was awarded the Brownlow Medal in 1958 for being the 'fairest and best' player in the Victorian Football League, was selected to represent the school's footy achievements. The cricketers are represented by two Australian legends, Bill Woodfull and the champion all-rounder Keith Miller. A few years later, the donor decided to recognise three great athletes who had attended the school: Merv Lincoln, Ron Clarke and Ralph

Doubell. The three sculptures, the work of Peter Schipperheyn, were unveiled on 20 May 2013. Clarke and Doubell attended the unveiling, but Lincoln was too unwell to do so and was represented by family members. John Landy was invited to speak at the event and gave an entertaining and insightful analysis of why each athlete was important.

The anonymous donor who funded the sculptures turned out to be Lindsay Fox, who had attended Melbourne High School for a couple of years in the early 1950s. Fox was asked to leave the school when he was in Fourth Form due to his lack of interest in his studies. Fox started working as a truck driver and founded his own company, Linfox, in 1956 with one truck. Linfox has become a logistics giant and Lindsay Fox's wealth was estimated at $3.56 billion by the *Australian Financial Review* in its 2018 Rich List.

At the end of Sixth Form, Doubell knew he had been fortunate to receive a quality education at Melbourne High School under the leadership and guidance of Bill Woodfull. He had spent his time there surrounded by bright boys from Melbourne's working class and together they learned the importance of striving for excellence. He had also discovered he could run a bit. Doubell knew this was just the start. The next step was University.

CHAPTER 6

Hooked on Travel

Doubell has never forgotten the day when his Science teacher described his Third Form results as the worst he had ever seen. Young Doubell resolved that Science was the subject he would focus on when he left school.

'I was determined to prove that teacher wrong, or at least get even with him for making me look like a fool,' he explains. 'I swore under my breath that I would.'

In his own way, he did. When he finished school, Doubell enrolled in a Science degree at the University of Melbourne. The truth is that he didn't have a passion for Science and he found that he didn't enjoy the course much at all. But he had proved the teacher wrong. Doubell believes his decision to study Science following his classroom humiliation highlights two traits that benefited his future athletics career: drive and obstinacy.

However, before he could even attend one lecture, there was a significant barrier to overcome if he was to achieve his goal. His mother couldn't afford to support him at university. He needed financial support, so in his final year at Melbourne High he applied for a scholarship from the Dafydd Lewis Trust. These merit-based scholarships were, and still are, available to 'young men who might not have otherwise received a university education due to the limited financial resources of their parents'. Dafydd Lewis was a Welshman who migrated to Australia in 1890, aged 24, and became a very successful and wealthy businessman and philanthropist. When he died in 1941 his will established the Dafydd Lewis Trust to fund the scholarships.

Doubell's application was successful. His first year at the University of Melbourne was 1963, a time when the world was changing dramatically. Students were at the forefront of a challenge to the status quo on a range of issues, from women's rights to the Vietnam War. There was the beginning of Beatlemania and, at the end of the year, the shocking assassination of US President John F. Kennedy. Doubell, however, did not get involved in the counterculture movement on campus. Despite the exciting times he was living in, he describes his routine at university as 'pretty dull'. He went to his chemistry, psychology and zoology lectures and became more focused on running. After study and training, there wasn't much time for revolution.

The University of Melbourne has a fine tradition in athletics, stretching back to the 19th century. A small university athletics club was formed in 1872 but it failed to gain much of a following for several years. The Melbourne University Athletics Club was formally established in 1890 as athletics began to grow in popularity in Australia. Intervarsity competition began in 1897 and MUAC won the first seven titles. In the decades that followed, the club produced many Australian champions and record holders.

When he began university, Doubell would train three nights a week after lectures and then make his way home to find on the stove a tepid dinner that had been prepared by his mother. 'It could be a stew, or liver that tasted like rubber,' he remembers. 'I would be in bed not long after dinner.' In the morning, at about 6.30am, he would run on the grass around the nearby Yarra Yarra Golf Club, because it gave his legs a kind of soft massage as the magpies swooped and the greenkeepers looked at him disapprovingly. For all the efforts of Landy, Elliott and company, running was still not a frontline sport like cricket or football and people who saw him 'jogging' through the streets and parks thought he was a bit mad. Even his mother couldn't understand why he was running so much. She always encouraged him, however, and would come to the track to watch him in every race.

At his first MUAC Championships in 1963, Doubell won the Freshers' 440 yards in 51.7 seconds. He then backed up to run in the Open 440 yards and finished in second place behind Andy Kirkham. The high jump at these championships was won with a record clearance of 6ft 10¾ inches by a dentistry student named Tony Sneazwell, who would go on to represent Australia in this event at the 1964 Tokyo and 1968 Mexico City Olympic Games. In Mexico City, Sneazwell and Doubell would be roommates.

On the basis of his strong performances at his first MUAC Championships, Doubell was selected to represent his university at the 1963 Intervarsity Championships in Adelaide in both the individual 440 yards and the 4 x 440-yards relay. He had just turned

18 and was very keen to go on the tour. Doubell had travelled outside Melbourne only once before, on a family trip to Launceston soon after his father had died. While excited about the opportunity to go to Adelaide, there was a significant problem: he didn't have the money to pay for his travel and accommodation. Education was the priority for the financially stretched Doubell family and there was simply no spare cash for Ralph to go to South Australia to compete in a couple of running races.

The solution to this problem marked another significant stage in Doubell's life and future athletics career. Alf Lazer, President of the Melbourne University Athletics Club, learned that a promising young athlete had been selected to compete in Adelaide but was unable to afford the cost. 'I was told that his father had died and that his mother was a sole carer,' Lazer recalls. 'I decided to pay for him to go.'

Lazer, who was 92 years old when interviewed for this book, says that he and Doubell still dispute — in friendly fashion — the sum involved. 'My memory tells me it was £50 while Ralph's memory tells him it was £30. I am sure it was £50.' Whatever the amount, it was a significant sum in 1963. Lazer says he was fortunate enough to be able to afford the gift. Born in 1925, he had been educated at Melbourne Grammar School. He served with the Royal Australian Air Force in World War II and afterwards studied at the University of Melbourne as part of a Federal Government program for ex-servicemen. He had been a hurdler at school and joined MUAC while he was studying, and continued to run for the club until he was in his 50s. Lazer was elected Treasurer of Melbourne University Athletics Club in 1946 and then became President in 1951. He remained President for the next 35 years.

In 1963, when Doubell was wondering how he could find the money to travel to Adelaide for the Intervarsity competition, Lazer was a successful company director with Crooks National (Holdings) Ltd and its numerous subsidiaries. He wasn't asked to fund Doubell's trip to Adelaide; he just decided that he would. Extraordinarily, Lazer had not met Doubell at this stage though he had seen him run and had heard he had potential, and he had never previously paid for an athlete to travel to a competition. The donation was anonymous and wasn't discussed with Doubell or minuted in the club records.

Doubell was blown away by this act of generosity from an unknown benefactor. He later found out that Lazer was the donor and has stayed in contact with him all his life. Lazer now jokes the payment was actually a loan that is still accruing interest. Doubell responds that, even if that were the case, he repaid it in full with his subsequent performances. He is also in no doubt as to the importance of Lazer's financial assistance to his future running career. 'I might never have become an athlete if it weren't for Alf's extraordinarily generous decision to pay for my trip to Adelaide in May 1963,' he says.

Doubell finished fourth in the individual 440 yards in Adelaide in 50.3 seconds, a good performance for a fresher. He then combined with his teammates to help the University of Melbourne secure a surprise win in the 4 x 440 yards relay. Significantly, one of his teammates in the relay was a law student named Stanley Spittle, who had recently set new University of Melbourne records for the 880 yards and the mile. Spittle would become Doubell's most valued training mate and a lifelong friend. The team photo states that University of Melbourne won the QIVA Cup, Waddy Cup, Denton-Rees Trophy, Suhan Tickner

Trophy and Booth-Solomon Trophy in Adelaide. No wonder they all have broad smiles, including the usually reserved Doubell.

While in Adelaide, Doubell learned that an Australian universities team had just travelled to New Zealand for a Trans-Tasman athletics competition. Furthermore, their expenses had been covered by the controlling body for Australian university sport. Doubell listened to the stories of this adventure with awe and envy. He found himself becoming hooked on the lure of travel. For a working-class teenager who had lived all his life in the suburbs of Melbourne, the world was becoming just a little bit larger. Lazer's support for his trip to Adelaide was not just a wonderful act of generosity, it was an epiphany for Doubell. He realised that if he took athletics seriously it would open up opportunities for him to travel, not just to other cities in Australia but even overseas to New Zealand. Furthermore, if he ran fast enough someone else would cover the sometimes considerable expense of competing in major competition.

Travel was not only exciting in itself; for Doubell it played a vital role in helping to alleviate the inevitable boredom of repetitive athletics training. He believes that if he had spent his entire athletics career training and racing in Victoria, with only a few trips to compete interstate each year, it would have been very difficult to constantly motivate himself to train at the elite level. The possibility of travelling to new and exotic locations gave him something to aim for. It made it easier for him to rise early each day for his morning jog around the golf course and to put on his running gear in the evenings for a hard session in the cold or rain. Combined with an inner drive to succeed that was simply part of his nature, the lure of travel now inspired Doubell to do something that would take his running to the next level.

CHAPTER 7

The Coach

Doubell now made what was arguably the most important decision of his young life. He went to meet with the legendary Franz Stampfl, who was employed as an athletics coach by the University of Melbourne. Doubell had met Stampfl previously at a training camp, but here he formally introduced himself and said he would like to run 440 yards in 48 seconds and that he was prepared to train three times a week. Stampfl peered at Doubell through his monocle and said, in his Austrian accent: 'Very well. But I will tell you how to train and when to train and how often to train, so let's start training.' That is how this transformational relationship started.

Stampfl's appointment as a professional coach had been a major innovation in Australian athletics. He had famously coached Roger Bannister to become the first person to break the four-minute mile, and had also coached Chris Chataway and Chris Brasher, Bannister's teammates who played essential roles in helping Bannister achieve that Everest on the track.

Some have questioned the extent of Stampfl's influence on Bannister, but Bannister had been trying to break the four-minute barrier for some time before he joined Stampfl's squad. Stampfl pushed him harder than he had been training previously and Bannister had no doubts about the role the coach played in his historic achievement. In *Twin Tracks*, his autobiography published 60 years after the four-minute mile barrier was broken, Bannister wrote: 'Between the four of us, with Franz Stampfl, my Viennese coach, carefully co-ordinating our trainings, a strategy emerged as to how this ultimate athletic challenge could be overcome.'

Bannister has also highlighted on many occasions his vital, though unscheduled, meeting with Stampfl on the morning of the famous race. Bannister had planned to travel from London to Oxford alone to give himself time to focus on the historic challenge ahead of him, but he bumped into Stampfl unexpectedly when he boarded the train at Paddington station. Bannister was in peak physical condition, but it had turned out to be a windy day and he was worried the conditions would make breaking four minutes impossible:

I had almost decided when I entered the carriage at Paddington that, unless the wind dropped soon, I would postpone the attempt. Franz understood my dilemma. He said: 'If you pass it up today, you may never forgive yourself for the rest of your life.' He stiffened my resolve as the train arrived in Oxford. I had been wrong to think that the athlete could be self-sufficient.

As Doubell would learn a decade later, Stampfl's forte as a coach was preparing his athletes not just physically, but also mentally.

Five months after Bannister broke the four-minute mile in Oxford, Chris Chataway broke the 5000-metres world record in a thrilling victory over the great Vladimir Kuts. Chataway has always credited Stampfl for his essential role in this achievement. Chris Brasher also acknowledged Stampfl's huge contribution to his success on the track. Apart from the targeted training regime and general coaching, Stampfl convinced Brasher to stop smoking, put his passion for mountain climbing on hold and even break up with his girlfriend in order to focus on the 1956 Melbourne Olympic Games. Brasher was rewarded with a gold medal in the 3000-metres steeplechase, a result that surprised everyone — except Stampfl.

In 1955, Stampfl was recruited by the University of Melbourne to introduce more modern and scientific training methods to Australia. Two of the key players in this coup were Associate Professor Bill Rawlinson, President of the University of Melbourne Sports Union, and Alf Lazer, President of the Melbourne University Athletics Club. Rawlinson was Victorian javelin champion in 1938, 1940 and 1951 and had represented England at the World University Games from 1947 to 1949 while he was studying at the University of London. He had met Stampfl when the Austrian was in Australia during World War II. Stampfl had been a javelin thrower in his youth and this established a connection between the pair. Rawlinson watched Stampfl demonstrate a javelin throw while wearing a sports coat and was amazed to see the spear soar further than the then Victorian record. Needless to say, he was impressed. Rawlinson met Stampfl again at the 1952 Helsinki Olympics and discovered that, having married an Australian in 1947, the coach was interested in returning to Australia if the right opportunity arose.

Rawlinson set out to raise the money needed to bring Stampfl to Australia, which was a salary of about £1500 a year. He tried to convince the University of Melbourne's Vice Chancellor, Professor George Paton, and various Melbourne athletics clubs to contribute to this cause, but he was unsuccessful. One day in early 1954, Rawlinson's wife Hilda, who was fully aware of her husband's campaign to attract Stampfl 'down under', was waiting to pay the family's bill in a newsagency in the suburb of Eaglemont. A copy of the *Sporting Globe* newspaper was sitting on the counter and she happened to see an article in which Sir Frank Beaurepaire expressed his belief that there should be investment made in a coaching scheme for young swimmers. In a decision that would have extraordinary consequences for generations of University of Melbourne sportsmen and women, including Doubell, Hilda went home and suggested to her husband that he contact Beaurepaire to see if he would contribute to Stampfl's salary.

FRANK BEAUREPAIRE WAS BORN in Melbourne in 1891 and began competitive swimming at an early age. He was the Victorian champion in several events at the age of 15 and two years later, at the 1908 London Olympics, he won a silver medal in the 400-metres freestyle and a bronze medal in the 1500-metres freestyle. He broke several world records in the following years but was not allowed to compete at the 1912 Stockholm Olympics because he was deemed to have lost his amateur status. His egregious action was to have taken a job as a swimming instructor with the Victorian Education Department. At both the 1920 Antwerp and 1924 Paris Olympics he won the silver medal in the 4 x 200-metres freestyle relay and the bronze in the 1500-metres freestyle. The gold medal in the 1500 metres in Paris was won by a young Australian named Andrew 'Boy' Charlton.

In 1922 Beaurepaire was awarded the Royal Shipwreck Relief and Humane Society Gold Medal and the substantial sum of £550 after he bravely rescued a swimmer, Milton Coughlan, who had been attacked by a shark off Coogee Beach in Sydney. He used this money to establish the 'Beaurepaire Tyre Service' business that specialised in tyres, wheels and batteries, and over the next few decades the company grew substantially and he became a very wealthy man. Beaurepaire was Lord Mayor of Melbourne from 1940 until 1942 and then spent 10 years as a member of Victoria's Legislative Council, the upper house of that state's Parliament. He was a key member of the delegation that successfully lobbied for Melbourne to host the 1956 Olympic Games but he died of a heart attack in the barber's chair at the Hotel Windsor just six months before the opening ceremony.

Rawlinson discussed his wife's suggestion to approach Beaurepaire with Alf Lazer and Bill Tickner, Secretary of the Sports Union, and it was decided that Rawlinson and Tickner should meet with Beaurepaire. Not wishing to push their luck too far, they asked Sir Frank whether he would be interested in funding some, not all, of Stampfl's salary. Beaurepaire replied that he would 'guarantee' the coach's salary for the first year. He added that many years previously he had offered to fund the building of a swimming pool at the university, but he had never heard back from the Vice Chancellor. Would the university like a swimming pool? Rawlinson and Tickner could not believe what they had just heard.

The next day, Rawlinson came home to be told by his wife that Beaurepaire had rung and left a message for him to call back. Rawlinson feared that Sir Frank had changed his mind. On the contrary, Beaurepaire said he was prepared to provide an endowment for a swimming pool, gymnasium and 'extensive facilities for physical education, training and research, together with a trophy hall, or meeting place, which would form a focus of interest in university life'. In the official letter detailing his bequest, Beaurepaire wrote:

> In many universities visited by me when abroad I have been impressed with their schools or centres for sport and athletics, and physical education generally — features regarded as of special importance in most overseas countries … we all know that under proper control they not only make for healthier men and women but also can play a most important role in the development of character and leadership.

On 29 April 1954, at the Annual General Meeting of the University of Melbourne Sports Union, it was announced that Sir Frank Beaurepaire had made a donation of £165,000 that was 'without parallel in the history of the University of Melbourne'. The sum donated would ultimately total around £200,000. By the end of the year, the site for the Beaurepaire Centre had been identified. The plans included a new shale running track to replace the old grass field that was appropriately named Bull Paddock. Before the 1956 Olympic Games there was no running track at the University of Melbourne. Track-and-field meetings were held on the cricket field. Rawlinson and Lazer managed to convince the Melbourne Olympic

Organising Committee to pay up to £20,000 of the cost of the new running track because athletes would be able to use it for training during the Games.

The new all-weather track was state-of-the-art for its time. The deeper foundation was made up of broken bricks, which allowed for quick drainage, and the upper layer was made from a mix of Wonthaggi shale (the town of Wonthaggi lies about 130 kilometres south-east of Melbourne, on the Bass Strait coast), clay and oil. This created an *En-Tout-Cas* style of running track that had been used for the 1948 London Olympics and also at Iffley Road, Oxford, where Roger Bannister broke the four-minute mile. The red *En-Tout-Cas* surface, derived from the French term for an all-weather umbrella, had been used for tennis courts since 1909 and by the mid-'50s was recognised as the highest quality surface for athletics. It would also be the first running track in Australia to use metric measurements. Together with the new Beaurepaire Centre, the University of Melbourne could therefore offer world-class facilities to welcome its new and internationally renowned athletics coach, Franz Stampfl.

Lazer recalls that the appointment of Stampfl was very controversial. Until that time, all athletics coaching positions at the university had been unpaid, honorary roles:

> Others were very jealous of the fact that a foreigner had been brought in and was being paid to do the job. But we believed that athletes are attracted to a coach, not a club, and we knew many athletes were looking for a good coach at the time. A big splash was made when Stampfl started. The Vice Chancellor held a reception for Stampfl in his office, which was very unusual

at the time — and it wouldn't happen today. Stampfl was, of course, dressed elegantly as always and wearing handmade shoes. I remember him asking our number one sprinter at the time, John Clarke, what he did in training. Clarke told him. Stampfl replied in his Austrian accent: 'Tomorrow, you do ten 100-metre run-throughs.'

That was enormously more than any of the sprinters had been doing. No one could believe it. And that was day one. He brought a completely new and different concept — that by working hard you made yourself strong. Before then there was a ridiculous idea that if you trained too much you got stale or 'muscle-bound'. We didn't even know what 'muscle-bound' really meant, but that was the expression that was used.

CHAPTER 8

Franz

Franz Ferdinand Leopold Stampfl was born in Vienna in 1913, one of seven children raised in a working-class suburb where French was spoken at home. He was a competitive skier and athlete in his youth, his best event being the javelin. In an interview with ABC radio, he explained how the rise of Adolf Hitler led to him leaving Austria and becoming an athletics coach. In particular, the 1936 Olympic Games in Berlin had made him terribly worried about the future: 'I saw the militarism and the brutality of it all at the time. And I made up my mind I will not stay in Austria, but leave and go over to England.'

Stampfl studied art at the Chelsea School of Arts but after Germany annexed Austria in 1938 he was in danger of being deported:

I wanted, of course, to stay in England and I made an application to the Home Office. And the Home Office said to me: 'I'm afraid you can't stay here unless you do a job which no other Englishman can do.' Well, I thought, I would now put into action my ideas. And so I went to the Amateur Athletic Association and asked for an interview and asked them to give me a chance. Oddly enough, the person who interviewed me was Harold Abrahams, who at one time won the 100 metres in the Olympic Games [in Paris in 1924, as made famous in the movie *Chariots of Fire*]. He spoke to me for some time and said that he will give me a chance. And that's when I started coaching.

Stampfl secured a coaching job at Queen Elizabeth's Grammar School in Northern Ireland. But then World War II broke out and all Europeans in Great Britain, particularly those who spoke German, were viewed with increasing suspicion. *How could anyone be sure they weren't Nazi spies?* This xenophobia took hold even though many of these Europeans were refugees fleeing Nazi persecution, including thousands of Jews. British suspicions intensified following the fall of France and the evacuation of Dunkirk, and the government responded to the growing public concern over 'the enemy within' by sending thousands of Europeans to internment camps.

Stampfl was sent to several camps and then, on 10 July 1940, he was one of 2542 male 'enemy aliens' who were loaded on to the former troop ship HMT *Dunera* in Liverpool without knowing its destination. Documents held in Australia's National Archives state, 'Although the group included some 250 German Nazis and 200

Italian Fascists, the vast majority of the deportees were strongly anti-Fascist and two-thirds of them were Jews.'

As they boarded the *Dunera*, many thought they were going to Canada or America. Some were told their wives and children would follow close behind them. None of this was true. While some internees would be sent to Canada, the *Dunera* was bound for Australia. In an article titled *On the Subject of Hell-Ships*, which was published in the *Jewish Standard* in August 1947, Abraham Abrahams detailed the treatment experienced by Stampfl and his fellow passengers as they boarded:

They were told they could each carry eight pounds of luggage, would be given satisfactory accommodation, and would be treated like ordinary passengers aboard ship. But within a few hours they were to find that they were in the hands of a savage, murderous and villainous band of [British] soldiers ... [They] had to proceed through a narrow doorway on to a landing stage. Behind this door soldiers were posted who subjected everybody to an exceedingly rough search. Everything carried in the hands or loose in the pockets was taken off the internees [and] thrown disorderly on the ground. Valuables were stuck into sacks ... appeals to officers were fruitless ... attempts of protest were roughly suppressed.

When the ship left, the refugees were forced below decks and crowded together with insufficient sleeping accommodation ... Buckets for urine were provided. The buckets were soon overflowing and sewage flooded the decks as the ship moved. In the midst of it, men were lying on the floor to sleep, for in the early part of the journey there were neither hammocks nor blankets.

The eight-week voyage to Australia was truly terrible for the 'Dunera Boys', as they became known. They were rarely allowed on deck:

> For weeks the hatches were kept down. Neither daylight nor natural air ever reached the decks ... The hatches were opened later periodically [but] the portholes remained closed the whole time ... the upper parts of the ship, where one would have been in the fresh air, were absolutely out of bounds, being barred by barbed wire and sentries with bayonets.

The conditions below deck were extremely cramped and the hygiene was appalling. Water was strictly rationed and there were only two dozen seats in the latrines for over 2000 men. Because their luggage was confiscated as they boarded, the men only had one set of clothes each and very few had managed to keep a toothbrush or hairbrush. They had no soap for the first few weeks and then one piece of soap was provided for every 20 men once a week. Towels also had to be shared, with one for every ten men. Not surprisingly, skin diseases and dysentery were common.

There were 309 guards and seven crew on board and they abused, bashed and robbed the Dunera Boys regularly:

> The internees were pushed by officers, sergeants and privates, beaten, driven along with the butts of rifles, and otherwise ill-treated. During searches and confiscations — carried out through the whole period of the journey — internees were beaten and on some occasions stabbed with bayonets.

When the *Dunera* arrived in Sydney on 6 September 1940, the Australian medical army officer, Alan Frost, was appalled by what he saw. His report led to the court martial of the officer in charge of the ship, Lieutenant-Colonel William Scott, and disciplinary action against several other officers.

'It was a miserable experience,' Stampfl told the ABC. 'I arrived in Australia, I'm quite certain, like the original prisoners and convicts.'

Stampfl and the other Dunera Boys received much better treatment once they landed in Australia and travelled 750 kilometres by train to a camp in the town of Hay in south-western New South Wales. The men immediately started to organise a range of activities and, in an interview for *The Dunera Internees*, Stampfl told how he focused on physical fitness:

I could see that a large number of the internees there were suffering as a result of boredom and loneliness as if they were rejected from anything worthwhile. The only reason I could attribute to such a state of personal feelings was because they had nothing particular to do. Like some others in the camp, I sensed the danger of the situation and decided to make a personal effort to improve it.

I introduced sporting activities and, as time progressed, the first group led to the organisation of many others which engaged themselves in many spheres of sport from athletics to boxing, wrestling, football and others … It was very hot in Hay during the day but very cold at night. I worked very hard with all the sporting groups. I made them continue with their physical exercises under all conditions, climactic and others, and gradually began to feel the satisfaction of succeeding in my efforts, if not wholly then at least partly ... At that time it was not just a job for me. It was an inner desire to survive and remain sane for myself and my friends in the camps. It was a matter of urgency to develop physical fitness without which many of us could have perished, as happened with some internees who did not even try to overcome their feelings of indifference and melancholy.

Stampfl later moved to another camp, at Tatura in country Victoria, and in December 1942 he met his future wife, Patsy, at a dance in Melbourne. They would marry in 1947 in Britain. Stampfl had returned there almost immediately after World War II ended, resuming his coaching career in Northern Ireland after again being assisted by Harold Abrahams. After a few years, he was able to move to London as his reputation spread, mainly through word of mouth. He coached athletes from a number of clubs, including Belgrave Harriers, Blackheath Harriers and South London Harriers, as well as from Oxford and Cambridge universities. He held his training sessions at the Battersea Park track and at the Duke of York's barracks near Chelsea, charging one shilling per session. It is estimated that about 100 athletes trained with Stampfl at this time, including Chris Chataway, Chris Brasher and, eventually, Roger Bannister.

As a young competitive skier in Austria, Stampfl had been used to training six to eight hours each day. When he began working with athletes, he was shocked by the relatively small amount of training they did and the unsophisticated training methods being used. The prevailing view was that good athletes didn't need to train much but that style was extremely important. He explained:

We spoke constantly in terms of styles and arm action. I remember I practised arm actions, perhaps a dozen variations of arm actions in sprinting. We experimented constantly, but mainly in a way that it looked nice and easy, rhythmical and beautiful. We looked marvellous, but our performances were not in actual fact as great. But considering that we trained so little, it was not too bad; it was more natural talent that mattered. Anybody who trained we thought had no talent at all. The one who had no talent had to work, and he would never get there. And the one with talent need not train, and in fact it would be shameful for him to train. So naturally I was highly confused, and it made me wonder whether one cannot find a more scientific level.

In 1955, the year he moved to Australia, *Franz Stampfl On Running* was published in London. This book set out in detail his views on training all runners — sprinters, middle-distance and long-distance athletes. It quickly became hugely popular among runners and coaches around the world, selling over half-a-million copies. Stampfl described training as 'principally an act of faith':

The athlete must believe in its efficacy: he must believe that through training he will become fitter and stronger; that by constant repetition of the same movements he will become more skilful and his muscles more relaxed. He must believe that through training his performance will improve and continue to improve indefinitely for as long as he continues to train to progressively stiffer standards. He must be a fanatic for hard work and enthusiastic enough to enjoy it ...

There is almost no limit to the achievements of the man who responds gladly and cheerfully to the rigorous demands of a tough training schedule, who does not look for miracle transformations, but is patiently content with the slow but well-founded progress which emerges. Constant regular training not only toughens him physically, but strengthening his muscles, developing his lungs and heart and improving his blood circulation, heightens his perception and teaches him to perform every movement with the greatest economy of effort.

As a child learning to write gradually improves in speed and legibility, until finally the act of writing becomes so automatic that it needs no conscious thought, so the athlete by constant repetition of the same movements eventually reaches a stage where all his attention can be concentrated on the single act of winning. Even that pain of bursting lungs and aching limbs is not sufficient to distract him from his purpose. From long practice he has become accustomed to this sort of pain and has slowly lengthened the period over which he is able to ignore it. His body cries for an easing of the pressure but, because to keep on running has become instinctive in him, he presses on without surcease. To the onlooker such fortitude is heroic, but the heroism does not belong to this particular few seconds in which the athlete defies pain but to the many months spent in conditioning the mind to triumph over the demands of the body.

Stampfl's scientific methods included recording the weather conditions, as well as the temperature and humidity, under which his athletes trained. He would monitor their pulse and blood pressure. He stressed that it was essential for athletes in training to be timed with a stopwatch so they could measure their improvement. This does not sound like rocket science today, but it was not accepted wisdom at the time. He was also a firm believer in the importance of regular competition because a lack of it led to 'staleness':

[An athlete] needs the stimulus of competition to give point to the hours of hard work spent in training; without it, practice runs and exercises lose their meaning and, when that happens, much of their value too.

Stampfl believed in a spectrum of increasingly severe training methods, proposing that easy cross-country running, which posed the least demand on the human frame, should occur first on a training program. This would be followed by 'Fartlek' (a Swedish word meaning 'speed play'), run over longer distances on undulating country with untimed variations of pace, and a little more demanding than the cross-country exercise but still not harsh. Next came 'interval training', which was severe, following by repetition running, harder still, and finally time trials, which provided the sternest test of all.

Stampfl was particularly renowned for his development of interval training. He described it this way:

A method of training involving continuous changes of pace over accurately measured and timed distances, a fast run being followed by a slow one. Thus, ten laps of 440-yard interval running in 60 seconds per fast lap call for twenty 440-yard laps altogether, each fast 60-second lap being followed by a slow one. The slow lap is called the recovery or interval …

Every run must be accurately timed and the athlete must endeavour to keep as closely as possible within the pre-determined time. The recovery run must always be long enough and slow enough for the athlete to recover normal breathing and to recover from fatigue. The recovery time is customarily two-and-a-half to three times as long as that of the fast lap, but with increased fitness this should decrease steadily.

It took Stampfl more than 20 years to refine his interval training methods. Athletes and coaches around the world became increasingly interested in his approach to interval training when they discovered it had been used to prepare Bannister for his attack on the four-minute mile:

And then it became a new form of training, and it is to this very day a basic form of training. Not because it is anything that would give you better performances, but because it gives you better control. It gives you an idea what you are doing, whether you do enough or whether you do too little or whether you do too much. And that to my mind also makes an enormous difference. It is a stress adaptation.

For Doubell, Stampfl's training was a very controlled and disciplined way of running. It was tough, but Stampfl's doctrine was:

Do not worry, it is only pain.

Doubell described a week of his training in the book *Athletics: The Australian Way*, published in 1971:

I might start on Monday by running 50 x 100 yards, with a 40-yard rest interval between each one. The effort in running each 100 yards is naturally not 100 per cent, while the 40-yard rest interval is not dawdling but a brisk walk.

On Tuesday I might run eight three-quarter miles, and again the same principles apply. The distance may be run in about three-and-a-half minutes or 70 seconds a lap — while the rest or recovery interval will be two laps of jogging, taking about seven minutes.

The next night might be 20 x 330 yards, while the following night may be 10 x 660 yards. In both cases, the principle is the same — run at a sustained pace and then rest.

I usually try and rest on Friday, either for competition or just a break from training. On Saturday and Sunday, the same type of training is completed doing, for example, 30 x 220 yards on Saturday and 20 x 440 yards on Sunday.

I find a very slow four to five-mile jog early in the morning works out a lot of the stiffness and breaks some of the monotony of running around a track. Preceding all these interval workouts I usually jog three miles, so in a day I often total 12 to 15 miles.

These workouts have been developed to suit me specifically. When I started running, I was doing about half this, and I would not say anyone should start this amount of work without gradually building into it. I cannot overstress the fact that all training workouts should be suited to the individual and other people's workloads should not be followed religiously. As often as not, they are suitable only for the person who developed them.

The workouts I have mentioned would be suitable for a very solid winter build-up but as the competitive season approaches, the volume of the workouts is generally halved while the speed of the distances run is increased. Speed itself should not be neglected completely during the year and even during the winter build-up time trials should be arranged over such distances as 220, 330, 440 and 660 yards.

So, if you choose to analyse what elements are involved in training for middle-distance events, you will see that both speed and strength are of equal importance. Additional efforts may be made in gaining strength by the use of weights, but these should only be supplementary to other workouts and can often be fitted in with a long run if the weather is bad and you cannot use the track. All the exercise using weights should be supervised but, generally, I use a combination of half-back squats, bench presses, alternate curls and the normal running action with your arms lifting dumbbells.

While Stampfl had an intense focus on training and the physical aspects of running, he also realised that this was only one factor in motivating an athlete to achieve his or her full potential. 'The mental aspect is so little understood and so little applied,' he told the ABC. 'Every Viennese believes he is another Freud, and I felt that, of course. Any performance, any human act, there is nothing completely physical, and nothing completely mental either.' In *Franz Stampfl On Running*, he wrote:

The coach's job is 20-per-cent technical and 80-per-cent inspirational. He may know all there is to know about tactics, technique and training, but if he cannot win the confidence and comradeship of his pupils he will never be a good coach ...

[A] successful coach must be a practising psychologist, adjusting his approach to each pupil so that it makes its most forceful impact. He must know how to talk to each in the terms which the pupil best understands, realising that some require gentle encouragement, some coercion and some downright bullying in order to produce the desired response. To do this he must get under the skin of the personality of each man in his care, noting where the strength and weakness lie and forming an honest and accurate assessment of the man's limitations and capabilities.

Doubell describes Stampfl as a driven man, perhaps even more so because of his difficult experiences during World War II:

I believe that all successful coaches and all successful athletes are absolutely driven from within. Stampfl had a confidence which is critical in any success, whether you are an athlete or a coach. He had complete faith in himself and he was never wrong. I occasionally pointed out that he could have been wrong, but he always corrected me quickly. I was wrong! Stampfl had only one standard, and that was the world standard. He was dictatorial and adamant in his views but, critically, he had the ability to inspire. He could motivate me, and others, to do the extra training and to come back the next day and do it again.

To Stampfl, running was an art and every runner had to be thought of as an artist, as an individual with a complex personality, full of personal likes, dislikes and idiosyncrasies, as an athlete whose nerves were so highly tuned on occasions that he or she could be as temperamental as any *prima donna*. He continued:

> By meeting the athlete, by talking to him on all manner of subjects, by learning something of his background and ambitions, [the coach] can form a very accurate understanding of the man and what makes him tick. Armed with this knowledge, he can prescribe the form of training most likely to produce the best results.

He would normally ignore any complaints of soreness or injury from his athletes. 'We just toughed it out and kept running,' Doubell says. Stampfl was always focused on the ultimate goal. He wasn't particularly interested in diet, leaving each athlete to determine whether he or she was eating too much or putting on too much weight.

Stampfl had the magical gift of bringing out the best in people. He managed to get very close to many athletes, including Doubell. 'He worked hard to understand what made his athletes tick,' Doubell says. 'He then wound them up so that they would not only tick, but hum and achieve more than they ever thought they could.'

Quite often during the season, Stampfl and several members of his squad would have lunch on Lygon Street in Carlton on a Friday. 'We would be first there at lunch and the last to leave,' Doubell recalls. 'Then we'd go to Jimmy Watson's wine bar. Between midday and 4pm we would have an earful of Franz and by the end of it I believed I could beat anybody in the world.'

Chris Chataway had similar memories of Stampfl on the other side of the world:

> We'd have these sessions with Franz, once or twice a week, at the track on the Kings Road in Chelsea. Then afterwards we'd go and have supper and a bottle of wine in a restaurant nearby. And Franz would talk. He was amazing. I would sometimes think, and I suspect the others would too, that I'd had enough of all this running. But say anything like that to Franz and there was a torrent of words. By the time he finished you would believe that if you could get a world record it would be as good as painting the Mona Lisa, that your place in history would be secured. He was tremendous. He really had an ability to persuade such as I've never come across in anyone else.

When Stampfl moved to Australia in 1955, Chris Brasher was so keen to maintain contact with him that he convinced Stampfl to record detailed coaching sessions on to spools of tape that the coach shipped back to England and Brasher played on a tape recorder.

Stampfl believed strongly that athletes could not make running their entire life. In his book, he expressed his views in typically forthright terms:

> The athlete who believes that all normal social life and entertainment must be abandoned in the interest of rigorous and continuous training is a man devoid of imagination and proper understanding of the value of recreation. A colourless, Spartan life in which all other interests are sacrificed to a single ideal is no existence for a man intent on achieving physical and

mental fitness. Indeed, the relaxation and mental stimulation that hobbies, books, music and the company of friends provide are as necessary to his well-being and athletic ambitions as the two hours of physical effort that comprise his daily programme. Nobody, unless he is a complete moron, can eat, drink and sleep athletics without the fun that ought to be there giving way to drudgery.

One of the coach's roles, however, was to keep an eye on their athletes to ensure they did not succumb to excess away from the training ground:

Any coach who is worth his salt will quickly spot the man who has been overdoing the good things of life, and by the simple expedient of slightly increasing the man's work will make the good things seem rather less attractive. He does this unobtrusively and without explanation so that the athlete is hardly conscious of it. All he is aware of is a new measure of discomfort during training which he attributes to his recent excesses and as a consequence settles down to more restrained living.

Despite the extraordinary success of his athletes over many decades, Stampfl's unconventional approach and idiosyncratic personality meant he was never embraced by the athletics establishment in England or Australia. He was never asked to coach a national team. He became a quadriplegic in 1980 after a young driver crashed into the back of his stationary Triumph TR3 sports car while he was sitting in traffic on the Punt Road Bridge in Melbourne. One year later, he was awarded an MBE and Stampfl said at the time that he had to break his neck, literally, to gain that recognition. He continued to coach for many more years from his wheelchair because, as he had written a quarter of a century earlier, coaching was his vocation:

> Guide, philosopher and friend, counsellor and confessor, a prop at times of mental tension, a coach's job is big enough for any man. Indeed, it is more than a job, it is a vocation which one follows from the same sort of compulsion that drives some to write, some to paint and some to build bridges. And when all the shouting is over, when the senior partner in the firm has broken the record, made the headlines and joined the immortals, the junior partner's reward comes from the satisfaction of a good job well done. Who could ask for more?

Doubell's feelings for Stampfl were evident when he spoke at his coach's funeral in 1995:

> It may be difficult for people outside the sporting arena to understand the bond between athlete and coach, but there is something there that transcends even family relationships. My father had died when I was a young boy of only 14. At university, Franz became not only my coach but my mentor, guardian and guide. At times the relationship was almost psychic. In a race, I could feel his thinking about what I should do next, when to make my move. I knew even before he spoke when he would be critical of me and when he would be pleased — and he was, just once or twice.

Franz was always controversial. Did he have a strong personality? Was he eccentric? He had both characteristics and he was certainly forthright. We all know he called a spade a bloody shovel. We all remember his spectacular outbursts of frustration and anger. He was fairly mean with praise. He was outrageous ... he was dictatorial. You never devised a training session, he did! And you would be foolish to question him; the training load would only be doubled ... But underneath it all, he loved us, he loved our success and he never sought to hijack the glory.

Most great coaches, like Franz, have a strong personality — or they are just plain eccentric. They polarise people's affections, and disaffections. Athletes are either inspired and have faith or seek inspiration elsewhere. Franz Stampfl was my inspiration. I could live with his personality, with his eccentricities and idiosyncrasies. We had enormous respect for each other ...

Franz was right. He was always right. He was the inspiration that got us through our training and none of his athletes would deny that. He shared our disappointments and quietly applauded our wins. At the end of the day he knew us better than we knew ourselves — better than our families knew us, in many cases.

The other high-profile, and unconventional, athletics coach in Australia in the 1950s and '60s was Percy Cerutty, who had established a training base at Portsea in Victoria soon after World War II. There, his athletes, most famously Herb Elliott, exhausted themselves on the surrounding sandhills, beaches and bush tracks. He and Franz Stampfl became huge rivals. Cerutty had suffered a series of nervous breakdowns from the age of 43 and his eventual recovery involved a huge change in his diet and a lot of exercise, including running. Based on his experience and studies, he developed his 'Stotan' philosophy, a mixture of Stoic and Spartan principles. Elliott said that Cerutty was capable of producing 'two contrasting reactions in the people he meets: some think he's a genius, the others a ratbag'. Elliott, of course, fell into the first category. Here is one example of Cerutty describing Stotanism:

Stotans will, by virtue of their philosophy, be nature lovers with a respect and appreciation of all evolved or created things. They will appreciate the sanctity of creative effort both in themselves and in others. They will strive to understand the significance implied by reality, will be able to discern the real from the spurious, and see no anomaly in nudity, either in body or mind. But neither will they cast pearls before swine. Stotans — for all the reasons that their philosophy stands for hardness, toughness, unswerving devotion to an ideal, and many more — will look upon the sea as their pristine element and endeavour to associate themselves with their primeval source of life by going into the sea at least once per month in all seasons of the year. No practice is more disposed to toughen both the body and the morale than this. Stotans believe that neither the body nor mind can be maintained at a high pitch of efficiency unless sufficient regular rest is obtained, and aim at a daily average of eight hours sleep (that is for younger men, older men need only six hours). Stotans also will not be found in social places after midnight. Stotans shall regulate their lives so that at the end of a period, varying with the intensity of the effort, each shall realise that he has attained, without conscious striving, to a state of knowledge and a position of leadership in the community. It is axiomatic that only the pure can understand purity, only the cultivated appreciate beauty, and only the strong measure their strength. Therefore, only the self-disciplined can command genuine respect.

Unlike Stampfl, Cerutty was very strict with his athletes' diet. 'We are not souls, or brain, or thinking substance, we are bones and meat and blood,' he contended. 'And this is made from the food that we eat, the fluids that are drunk and the air that is inhaled. Poor materials can make only poor buildings and adulterated foods cannot be expected to produce the best results.' Cerutty prescribed a breakfast of raw oatmeal with raisins, nuts, bananas, sultanas and other fruit. It was seen as strange at the time; now we just call it 'muesli'. Lunch was salad while dinner was fish or poultry with raw or very lightly cooked vegetables. Interestingly, this could be substantiated with wholemeal bread or French fries cooked in oil.

'Cerutty was a bit extreme for me,' says Doubell. 'He was also very extroverted while I am a quiet person, and this was another reason I felt more comfortable with Stampfl.'

Cerutty was also a very combative character, exemplified by his clash with Mike Agostini while the pair were commentating together on television during the 1962 British Empire and Commonwealth Games. Cerutty exploded when Agostini referred to John Landy as a 'self-made champion'. While many wouldn't have understood the reference, Agostini was alluding to the well-known fact that Landy had stopped training with Cerutty after the Helsinki Olympics and had then run all his best times, when he essentially trained on his own. Cerutty snapped. 'Who are you,

Agostini? You're only a visitor to this country. Behave yourself or I will walk off this show. I'm not going to take this from you, you visitor.' The argument continued and their session together had to be stopped by the program director.

Cerutty was very envious when Stampfl secured the job of athletics coach at the University of Melbourne in 1955. He was openly critical of Stampfl's methods, particularly the timing of every training session and the use of detailed daily programs. 'Such concepts as the rigid schedule, the worked-out and laid-down day-by-day training routines, find no sympathy with me or my ideas,' he wrote. 'Despite the efforts of the industrialist, we are still humans, not machines.'

Elliott made a similar criticism of Stampfl in *The Golden Mile*. 'Stampfl's methods are ideal for mass coaching of classes but not, in my opinion, individual athletes,' he wrote. 'He believes in scientific training schedules, gradually building up the amount and intensity of an athlete's work until, in theory, he systematically reduces his times. Under this kind of unimaginative drudgery, an athlete becomes a machine governed by a chart. He doesn't run as he feels; he runs as his coach tells him. In time, he loses his initiative, his originality and any brilliance he might possess.'

After the retirement of John Landy, the mantle of Australian mile champion was decided on 30 January 1958 at Olympic Park, Melbourne, in a race featuring the Cerutty-trained Herb Elliott and the Stampfl-trained Merv Lincoln. Bruce Welch of *The Age* newspaper previewed the affair:

Supporters of the different training methods of rival coaches Franz Stampfl and Percy Cerutty see the big mile clash between

Merv Lincoln and Herb Elliott as a 'battle of the coaches' too. No race since the war has created so much intense argument on coaching methods ... It is no secret that Stampfl and Cerutty do not see eye to eye on a lot of things. The extent to which their training methods differ is not clear to anyone except Lincoln and Elliott. Stampfl does use a large amount of repetition work in training and Cerutty says he does not believe in this. But because Cerutty prepares his runners at Portsea, and away from tracks, the nature of his routines is hidden.

Elliott won the race in 3:58.7 with Merv Lincoln also breaking four minutes, the first time two runners had beaten that barrier in the same race in Australia. A photo of the finish was given to Cerutty by Elliott with the inscription: 'A victory for Cerutty-Elliott against Stampfl-Lincoln. We've proved to the public what we've always known — Herb.'

Over the next two-and-a-half years Elliott maintained his dominance over Lincoln — and the rest of the world. He was unbeaten over 1500 metres and the mile during his career, which climaxed with his gold-medal run in world record time at the 1960 Rome Olympic Games. He then retired from competitive athletics, at age 22. Elliott always had a respectful rivalry with Lincoln and, although he was renowned for being extremely competitive, he thought Cerutty sometimes took things too far in his battle with Stampfl. 'There's no doubt that Percy felt hate towards Franz, which alarmed me a little and made me feel uncomfortable,' he wrote. 'I wanted no part of that.'

Cerutty not only doubted Stampfl's methods, he questioned Stampfl's past, including his claimed attendance at the Berlin

Olympics. More offensively, he alluded to Stampfl's Austrian origins, telling the media: 'His sort of training is for Nazis. It's for people who like to be dominated.'

Doubell believes that while Stampfl and Cerutty competed intensely against each other for many years, and disagreed on many issues, at the end of the day they actually had a very strong respect for each other. Importantly, they epitomise the critical role that a coach can play in an athlete's success at the highest level.

CHAPTER 9

Growing in Confidence

After a few months of training with Stampfl, Doubell ran an 880-yards time trial in 1:54.8. He was still only 18 and, while the time was already a big improvement on his previous efforts, he knew he could go faster. Soon afterwards, on 21 January 1964, he competed in the Victorian 800-metres championship that was held separately from the Victorian Amateur Athletics Championships, which were run over imperial distances. The race favourite at Oakleigh Football Club Oval was Stanley Spittle, who was three years ahead of Doubell at the University of Melbourne and one of the best half-milers in the country. Doubell was undaunted by his older and more experienced competitors and crossed the line in first place in 1:52.8, ahead of Spittle and Noel Clough, who both recorded 1:53.0.

Doubell's substantial improvement after just six months of serious training was noticed by a number of people in Victoria's athletics community, and for the first time he attracted some media attention. Graeme Kelly reported in *The Age*:

> Victoria appears to have uncovered one of Australia's top middle-distance prospects in 18-year-old University science student Ralph Doubell. He scored a shock win in the Victorian championships last Wednesday night and returned a 1 min 53.3 sec. half mile at University on Saturday.
>
> Doubell, a first-year runner, has already beaten Victoria's best half-milers and might have been unlucky not to be included in the state team to oppose New South Wales next weekend. However, he should force his way into the team for the Australian championships in March.
>
> Although he shows outstanding promise, Doubell has no aspirations about making this year's Tokyo Olympic Games team. 'I am still a long way outside the qualifying standard for Tokyo and I have decided to set the 1966 Commonwealth Games in Jamaica as my target,' Doubell commented. 'By then I will probably be concentrating on miles.'

Doubell enjoyed being a club runner who competed over a range of distances each weekend during the athletics season. He could run 10.3 seconds for 100 yards and 22.4 seconds for 220 yards. One week, he might compete in the 100 yards, the 440 yards and a relay and the next he might race in the 220 yards, the 880 yards and a relay. Later, he would add the mile to his repertoire. He would do this season after season and it was a critical part of his development, not just for the physical fitness but also to toughen him up mentally. He learned to race and win over different distances and in varying situations and conditions. Doubell was never overly concerned with the time he ran. The key was to do what he needed to do to win his particular race. One thing he was learning quickly was that he had a special gift for a middle-distance runner: rare acceleration over five to ten metres. He could gain a metre or two over his competitors in that short distance. This was his real competitive advantage. He needed to build his strength and race knowledge so he could use this gift to its greatest strategic effect.

Doubell won the 1964 Melbourne University Athletics Club 880-yards championship and then, on 11 April 1964 at Sandringham Athletic Ground, he equalled the Victorian residential record of 1:49.8 for 800 metres. Australia's major races were still being held over the imperial distance of 880 yards at this time, but officials often organised for runners to be timed at the 800-metres mark. The distance of 800 metres is equal to 874 yards and is 4.67 metres shorter than 880 yards. If there were no official timekeepers at the 800-metres mark, runners would estimate the difference as 0.7 seconds.

On 30 May 1964, Doubell won the 880-yards race at the Australia v New Zealand Universities meeting held in Melbourne in a time of 1:50.9. He was starting to get noticed more widely. The following article was published in *The Age* on 18 November 1964, under the headline 'Student, 19, could be heir to Snell':

A slightly built student at Melbourne University could be the successor to New Zealand's Peter Snell as the world's top middle-distance athlete. Ralph Doubell, 19, is the runner who could return to Australia the crown once worn by Herb Elliott and John Landy.

Doubell, who weighs about 10st. 4lb. and is almost 6ft, is a second year Science student. He entered the university from Melbourne High School at the beginning of last year. At that time, he could not break two minutes for 800 metres, but after six months of expert coaching was able to run it in 1.49.8.

This summer should tell whether Doubell is likely to reach the top in athletics. He has set himself a hard campaign and has also added the mile to his program. His university teammates expect that he will run a sub four-minute mile by the end of this season.

Doubell's greatest asset, apart from his natural ability, is his appetite for hard work, both on the training track and in the gymnasium. He has managed to reduce his pulse rate to about 46 beats a minute in the past year through hard training. The pulse rate of a normal man not in training is about 76 beats a minute.

Doubell has placed considerable emphasis on weight training, realising that he needs to develop his slight frame to generate the speed which is essential to the modern middle-distance runner.

The young runner is described by his friends as being serious and intense and as talented academically as he is at athletics. Doubell believes intensive training for running helps his study. He finds that, when in peak condition, he can concentrate longer and more intensely. Because of this, there is no chance that the young runner will ever have to make a choice between academics and athletics.

The author of this story might not have been aware that Doubell had suffered his first serious injury during the winter of 1964. He fractured the fibula just above his right ankle during a road training run. He had to lay off training for five weeks and, when he resumed, he developed shin soreness that kept him away for training for another four weeks. By this time, university examinations were imminent so he barely trained at all for another month. Stampfl was concerned about the impact this would have on his 1964–65 season, because the winter training was a vital build-up for the athletics competition the next summer. It was particularly important if Doubell was going to start focusing on the mile as well as the half-mile.

At the end of his second year at university, Doubell was proud to be one of only five students awarded a Full Blue for Athletics. A Full Blue is awarded by universities to recognise the highest level of athletic achievement. Half Blues can also be awarded. The Blue awards originated at Oxford and Cambridge and were later adopted by universities in a number of countries, including Australia and New Zealand.

A few weeks later, on 21 December 1964, Doubell competed in his first mile race at an interclub meeting held at University Oval. The mile still had a magical appeal in athletics and Australia had a great tradition over the distance, particularly through John Landy and Herb Elliott. There was quite a lot of interest in how close Doubell would go to the four-minute mark, even though he made it clear before the race that he hadn't been able to prepare properly for the distance because of his injuries during the winter. Derek Clayton, who three years later would break the marathon world record in Fukuoka, Japan, while becoming the first person to break 2 hours 10 minutes for that event, took the field through the first lap in 61 seconds. Gordon Noble, an experienced miler who had competed for Australia at the 1962 British Empire and

Commonwealth Games, was leading as the bell went at 3 minutes 7 seconds. Doubell was still in contact at the bell, but Noble moved away and won in 4:06.5 with Doubell crossing the line in 4:11.0.

'I was very happy with the time, but I really went to pieces over the last 350 yards,' Doubell told Ron Carter of *The Age*. 'I've learnt a lot from this first race. Before today I had no idea what to expect.'

Stampfl was typically effusive when he spoke to the media. 'I believe Doubell is world-record mile material,' he said. 'It may take a few years, but he has the build, natural speed and determination to become the world's top miler. That is the fastest first-up mile I have ever seen. The performance was even more amazing when you realise Doubell's training program over the past three months has been interrupted by injuries and university examinations. His preparation was very light for 880 yards running, let alone taking on miles.'

These words from Stampfl highlight a largely forgotten aspect of Doubell's training. While Doubell is known for his excellence over half a mile, Stampfl's main plan was for him to be a miler. Stampfl had, after all, achieved global fame through his training of Roger Bannister and now he had found someone in Australia who he believed had the potential to be one of the world's finest runners over 1760 yards.

Doubell would respect Stampfl's ambitions and continue to train for the mile — including gruelling three-quarter mile time trials — for a few more years. However, he never really felt comfortable racing over a mile. In contrast, he was far more confident that he could control a race over 800 metres or 880 yards. 'I always felt that I was a possible placegetter in a mile race, but I expected to win over half a mile,' he says.

On 2 January 1965, Stampfl used Doubell as a case study in his newspaper column on pulse rates:

Doubell has a resting pulse rate of 42 a minute. He came down to this level from normal pulse rate of 68 within a year.

After a typical workout of five miles of interval training — which includes 10 alternate quarter runs of 60 seconds each, interspersed with 10 recovery quarter mile runs of two minutes each — his pulse rate is generally up to 176 a minute. He follows up with an easy mile run, after which his pulse usually drops to 150 a minute. After two minutes' rest, it comes down to 116 and the next morning it is back to a normal 42.

Doubell's highest pulse rate, recorded after a very hard run, was more than 240 but, at this level, he felt no distress.

The English MP and former 5000-metres world record holder, Chris Chataway, had a resting pulse of 38, the same as the Australian, Merv Lincoln, when in top form.

To be of value, pulse counts must be taken regularly and over a long period. Pulse rates must be correlated to, and compared with, everything the athlete does during the day. All his training runs must be carefully timed, the distances carefully measured and the rate of recovery at any stage of training measured and timed. A great many variations in the pulse rate can take place which may not have anything to do with training. During last year's examination period, Doubell's resting pulse rate rose from 42 to 68 while his haemoglobin level, and the number of oxygen carrying red cells in the blood, dropped almost to the anaemic stage.

Later in January, Doubell won the 880 yards at the Victorian Amateur Athletics Championships held at Olympic Park in 1:51.3, after running 52.5 seconds for the first lap. He also competed in the mile, but he failed to follow Stampfl's advice. Doubell made his finishing move too early, instead of waiting until the last 200 metres, and faded to finish fourth. It was another lesson learned on the track.

A few weeks later, Doubell again competed in the mile, this time against Australian champion and record holder Albie Thomas as well as Ron Clarke, who had recently set new world records for three miles and 5000 metres, to add to the world records he also held for six miles and 10,000 metres. Clarke surprised Thomas to win in 4:04.4, with Doubell just one second behind in third place. His time of 4:05.4 was a personal best by three seconds.

In late February, Doubell was selected to represent Victoria in the 880 yards at the Australian Amateur Athletics Championships. The competition was held on a grass track at North Hobart Oval in Tasmania and the conditions on the day were blustery, so fast times weren't expected. The first lap was extremely slow by any standard, about 57 seconds, so Doubell decided to start his finishing burst much earlier than usual, approximately 300 metres from the finish line. He ran 53 seconds for the second lap to finish in 1:50.6, almost 10 metres ahead of his Victorian teammate Bob Smith and Chris Woods of South Australia.

Doubell had just turned 20. He was the Australian 880-yards champion. Of course, he was excited at his achievement, but there was no excessive show of celebration as he crossed the finish line. 'In those days,' he says, 'the attitude was that you were selected to finish first and, if you did, your teammates would say, "Well done."

You would then return to training and work with your coach to run faster.' Doubell knew he had broken a significant barrier, but he knew he was not yet at world-class standard and that he would have to continue to improve if he was to compete at the Commonwealth Games, let alone at the Olympics.

Doubell's coach from Melbourne High School, Mike Agostini, was writing a column for the *Sunday Telegraph*. A week after the 1965 Australian Championships, Agostini wrote that 'Australia appears on the brink of a very bright track-and-field athletics period'. He highlighted the sensational recent performances of Ron Clarke and also noted that Doubell was performing as well as Herb Elliott over 880 yards or 800 metres at the same age. His former student, he wrote, had much potential:

> Doubell has been running for only two years. From a 1 min 59 sec half-miler two seasons ago, he improved enough to win this year's championship in 1 min 50.6 sec. This is an even greater improvement in times than Elliott achieved over a similar period.
>
> Doubell is only 19 [in fact, he had just turned 20] and Elliott set his national junior record at 1 min. 50.9 sec. only a few weeks before his 19th birthday. Doubell is speedy, intelligent, likes to run and can tolerate much hard work. The future for him could be bright and there is little doubt that he will eventually hold all Australian records for the half mile and should also become a four-minute miler.

While Doubell was too focused on his training and his studies to get involved in the big political issues of the time, it didn't mean he was immune from what was happening in the world around him.

In particular, there was a real risk that conscription could have ended his nascent running career.

The National Service Scheme was introduced in Australia by the Menzies Government in November 1964. All 20-year-old men had to register with the Department of Labour and National Service and their fate was determined by 'The Birthday Ballot'. Marbles with numbers corresponding to birthdates were drawn out of a barrel and if your birthdate was selected you would have to serve full-time for two years in the regular army and then spend three years part-time in the Army Reserve. Australia's involvement in the Vietnam War began with 30 military advisers in July 1962. By 1965, there were more than 7000 Australian troops in Vietnam.

Doubell turned 20 on 11 February 1965. He did not know what he would do if his birthdate was drawn. There wasn't much opposition in the general public to the war at this stage and it was still more than a year before Sir Robert Menzies' successor as Prime Minister, Harold Holt, would tell the US that Australia was 'a staunch friend that will be all the way with LBJ'. In early 1965, most young men felt that if their number was drawn in The Birthday Ballot they would just accept it and do their duty. Doubell was extremely relieved when his marble remained in the barrel. If it had been drawn, his life would have been completely different.

Stampfl again used Doubell as a case study for a newspaper article on 4 March 1965, this time in *The Australian*. Opinionated and controversial as always, Stampfl articulated clearly why he thought Doubell had so much potential over 800 metres or 880 yards. It may not have received much attention at the time, but it is remarkable how prescient Stampfl's story, headlined 'Speed and more speed is today's cry', was:

The half mile is no longer a middle-distance race — it has turned into a sprint in which natural and inborn speed is the runner's essential basic quality for success. We have reached a stage in world athletics generally where speed is of fundamental importance.

This applies not only in sprinting but in all of the 22 Olympic track-and-field events, including distance running up to the marathon. One day soon a marathon champion will emerge who can also run 100 yards in 10 seconds ...

To make a success of running, an even-time sprinter [10 seconds for 100 yards] now must move up into the longer distances — the half mile and, preferably, the mile ... What is new in this event is not so much the idea of speed itself but the entire conception of the degree of speed necessary for world-class performances combined with an entirely new outlook on the limits of endurance to sustain such a speed ...

Speed, which is very much an inborn quality, cannot be developed by training as much, or as easily, as endurance. I doubt very much whether a youth of 18 who runs 100 yards in 10 seconds could ever develop into a 9.1 sec sprinter, no matter how hard he trained. By sheer hard work, however, it is possible to increase his powers of endurance to such an extent he may be able to sustain a high degree of speed over longer distances. This fact is still not fully recognised and appreciated by Australian athletes. If some of our 9.8 or 10 secs sprinters were to leave the short sprints to concentrate entirely on the longer distances, we would soon have many half-milers in world class ...

Since, by training, endurance can be developed to an incredibly high degree, it is perfectly possible for a comparatively slow runner to become a world beater in distance events. Ron Clarke is a typical example of such a runner who has little sprinting ability but who has, by sheer training, developed phenomenal powers of endurance. But such runners, although they can produce world records, rarely if ever win Olympic titles or important races. The reason for this is that whenever they come up against runners of equal stamina, plus greater natural speed, they cannot match their rush for the tape ...

The New Zealander Peter Snell, twice 800-metres Olympic champion, winner of the 1500 metres in Tokyo and holder of the 800-metres, 880-yards and mile world records, has set the pattern for the future. He is a reasonable sprinter — among the six best in New Zealand — who can run any distance well right up to the marathon.

At this stage of his development, to compare Ralph Doubell, the Australian half-mile champion, with Snell or Herb Elliott may appear over-optimistic. But, at the same time, to maintain that this 20-year-old Melbourne University science student will never produce world-class middle-distance performances would be extremely short-sighted and unjustified.

Of course, nobody can tell accurately beforehand whether he will match or become better than Snell. There are, however, remarkable similarities between the two, and all the indications are that, within the next few years, Doubell will be among the world's best.

Doubell doesn't remember this article. If he did read it when it was first published, he would not have believed that Stampfl's instincts were accurate and that three-and-a-half years later he would equal Snell's world-record time for 800 metres.

Doubell won the Melbourne University 880-yards Championship again in May 1965, finishing 0.4 seconds outside Tony Blue's Australian residential record of 1:48.6. He ran a fast first lap of 51.8 seconds and paid for it in the final straight. Doubell was disappointed not to break the record but encouraged by the fact he had now taken more than 10 seconds off his 880-yards time over just 18 months.

The media was taking an increasing interest in Doubell and began to speculate about his chances in the British Empire and Commonwealth Games, which were to be held in Kingston, Jamaica, in August 1966. In addition, athletics authorities and the media were starting to focus on the next Olympic Games, even though the opening ceremony was more than three years away. The reason was that Mexico City had been selected as the host city and serious concerns were being raised about the dangers of distance running in venues located well above sea level.

Onni Niskanen was the Scandinavian coach of Ethiopia's Abebe Bikila, who won the marathon at both the 1960 Rome and 1964 Tokyo Olympic Games. In an interview with Chris Brasher, who was now a journalist, in October 1964, Niskanen said that while North Africans were used to running at altitude, those who weren't had no idea how the lack of oxygen would affect them as they pushed themselves to the limit. 'Suddenly, blackout,' Niskanen told Brasher. 'There will be those who will die.'

Brasher was an outspoken and early critic of the Mexico City Games, exemplified by these words he wrote for *The Observer*:

My opinion on such a matter may not carry much weight, but Dr Roger Bannister has said that he does not consider it justified to hold the endurance events in Mexico City. He does not go nearly as far as Niskanen. Bannister does not say there will be 'those who will die', but he does believe that there is the possibility that someone may be permanently affected. Surely the International Olympic Committee cannot take such a risk.

A man who has lived all his life at over 7000 feet will be far better acclimatised than someone who has only spent a month at this altitude. It is on this question of the time taken to acclimatise that I base the weight of my argument. To hold the endurance events in Mexico City is to commit what I will call an offence against the spirit of the Olympic Games.

The debate over this issue would continue through and beyond the 1968 Olympic Games.

With the growing concern about distance running at Mexico City, the Australian Sports Medicine Federation joined with the University of Melbourne's Physiology School in late 1965 to conduct research into the effects of altitude on athletes. The project was funded by the Australian Olympic Committee and Doubell was one of nine athletes who volunteered to be guinea pigs. They spent five weeks in a ski lodge at Falls Creek in north-east Victoria, which has an altitude at its highest point of 1780 metres. The athletes did sprints, cross-country runs and 20-minute sessions on a bicycle ergometer while cardiographs and blood tests were conducted regularly. There were also special tests for the long jumpers and high jumpers. The athletes' performances at Falls Creek were then compared with their performances at sea level.

The Australian researchers concluded that sprinters would not be much affected by the altitude and would be able to compete at their highest level if they arrived in Mexico City three weeks before their event. Those competing in events that took longer than two minutes to complete, however, could be significantly affected and would require one week to adjust and then four weeks of training to acclimatise before competing. All athletes were expected to lose their appetite in the first week, show increased fatigue after training and take longer to recover. The experts advised that athletes should aim for 12 hours' sleep each night.

The research concluded that Doubell's principal event, the 800 metres, would not be affected much by the altitude because it was completed in less than two minutes. This was very much in line with the views of experts from other countries who had examined the issue. Furthermore, physiological tests concluded that Doubell himself seemed less likely to be affected by altitude than most other athletes.

Back on the race track after Falls Creek, Doubell ran his first mile of the season on 18 December 1965 and won in 4:08.9 from Gordon Noble. Nine days later, he beat Ron Clarke in a mile for the first time at a meeting at Frankston. Doubell made a move at the end of the third lap and ran the last lap in a fast 56 seconds, beating Clarke by about seven metres. Clarke said after the race that Doubell had caught him napping. Doubell's time of 4:04.0 was a new personal best by 1.4 seconds.

Melbourne newspapers, including *The Age* and *The Herald*, began predicting that Doubell would be the next Australian to break the four-minute mile ... and that he would do it soon.

CHAPTER 10

Promise and Disappointment

In January 1966, Doubell was one of a small group of Australian athletes invited to New Zealand to compete in a series of meetings. Once again, athletics opened the aircraft doors to travel opportunities. He ran 1:52.9 in the 800 metres on a heavy track in Nelson and then a new personal best of 4:02.7 for the mile at Queen Elizabeth Park in Masterton. The first two laps were too slow to give him a chance to break the four-minute barrier, even though he ran 56 seconds for the last lap. Two days later, on Australia Day, at the Basin Reserve in Wellington, Doubell sprinted away from Soviet champion Oleg Rayko to win the 800 metres by three seconds in an impressive time of 1:48.7. On 3 February, he won a mile race in Dunedin in 4:07.3 and then finished the tour with victory in the North Otago 880-yards championship, crossing the line in 1:49.0.

Doubell had again undertaken a heavy schedule of racing, but he and Franz Stampfl believed it provided a strong foundation for the Australian season and, in particular, for Doubell's attempt to qualify for the British Empire and Commonwealth Games in Kingston later that year.

On 12 February 1966, the day after he celebrated his 21st birthday, Doubell retained his 880-yards title at the Victorian Amateur Athletics Championships at Olympic Park. He won by 20 yards and his time of 1:48.5 broke Tony Blue's six-year-old Australian national resident 880-yards record by one-tenth of a second. Furthermore, the officials organised for Doubell to be timed at the 800-metres mark of the same race, and his time of 1:47.7 broke Blue's Australian national resident record, also set six years earlier, by two-tenths of a second. It also equalled the open Victorian 800-metres record, which had been set by American Tom Courtney at the 1956 Melbourne Olympic Games. Doubell's time was just one-tenth of a second outside the open Australian 800-metres record, held by Peter Snell of New Zealand.

The Sun reported that Doubell 'looked a likely Commonwealth Games gold medal winner at Olympic Park on Saturday', which was extremely premature since the team would not be selected for many months. Doubell told the media after the race: 'I turned 21 yesterday and this was the best present I could have.' He didn't have a birthday party, however — not because he was racing or training the next day, but because neither he nor his family could afford it.

One week later, Doubell won the Victorian mile championship in 4:02.0, beating Ron Clarke by five metres with Trevor Vincent one-tenth of a second behind in third place. Clarke was leading at the bell, but Doubell ran his race to plan and took the lead in the back straight and held on to the finish line. It was a new personal best, seven-tenths of a second faster than his time in New Zealand a few weeks earlier.

The race received quite a bit of press coverage, with *The Herald* reporting that 'Doubell's chance of running the first four-minute mile in Australia this season was ruled out by a blustery wind' and *The Sun* criticising the race organisers:

> Victorian Amateur Athletics Association officials must ensure that top distance runners do not get another raw deal like they did in the mile championships at Olympic Park on Saturday. Putting 15 athletes into the mile — the glamour event of Saturday's titles — went close to turning a brilliant race into a farce.
>
> Ralph Doubell ran the fastest mile in Australia this season by clocking 4 min 2 sec, defeating international star Ron Clarke (4:02.6) and Trevor Vincent (4:02.7). Yet Doubell, Clarke and Vincent — as well as a couple of other runners — could have been knocked off their feet in severe jostling in the third and final laps.
>
> Clarke said: 'The field was too big. It was ridiculous having 15 in the field.'
>
> With the first four runners clocking under 4 min 4 sec the mile was one of the best attractions at Olympic Park in recent years ...

The Age also criticised the size of the field and debated whether Clarke and three of his teammates from Glenhuntly Athletic Club (as it was known at the time) — Trevor Vincent, Tony Cook and John Coyle — had tried to work together to box Doubell in during the race. Ron Carter reported that a leading official, Reg Clemson, thought there had been collusion but the chief referee, George Beslee, and chief umpire Bill Leach decided not to take any action. The fact that Doubell won must have made their decision easier. The Glenhuntly runners all denied implementing team tactics against Doubell, asserting that they were all out to win individually. Doubell told Carter: 'I thought the Glenhuntly runners might run as a team but I was never conscious of this during the race.'

Doubell was again selected to represent Victoria at the Australian Amateur Athletics Championships, which were held in mid-March at Perry Lakes Stadium in Perth. The 1966 Championships were the first where races were held over the metric distances, such as 800 metres and 1500 metres, rather than the old imperial distances, such as 880 yards and a mile. Even more significantly, the Championships were effectively selection trials for the British Empire and Commonwealth Games. Australia's Commonwealth and Empire Games Association had decided to significantly reduce the number of track-and-field athletes who would represent Australia in Kingston, compared with the large team selected for the 1962 Games in Perth, which meant running a qualifying time at the Championships would not necessarily mean selection in the Games team.

There was therefore huge pressure on all athletes not just to win, but to win with a strong qualifying time. Doubell ran poorly in the 1500 metres on Saturday, finishing fourth in 3:46.1. This put even more pressure on him to perform in the 800 metres; he knew he had to improve substantially to convince the selectors. He had recovered well from the 1500 metres and felt confident that he would be able to do something special. This confidence proved to be well placed. The race went to plan and he sprinted away from the field over the last 200 metres to win in 1:47.3 — a convincing victory that was sweetened by the fact that he broke Peter Snell's open Australian record by three-tenths of a second. Doubell's Victorian teammate Noel Clough came second, with Chris Woods of South Australia third and Keith Wheeler of Western Australia fourth. Doubell and Clough were duly selected to run in the 880 yards in Jamaica. Wheeler was picked to run in the mile.

Doubell was also chosen to be an Australian representative in an athletics team that had been invited to compete in a two-day USA v British Commonwealth competition at the end of July, only a few weeks before the Kingston Games. The event was called 'The Los Angeles Times International Games' and was held at the Los Angeles Memorial Coliseum, venue for the 1932 and 1984 Olympic Games. It had been originally planned as a USA v USSR competition, but the Cold War was particularly frosty at this time and the Soviets pulled out at the last minute. The American organisers, who had already invested in the meeting, realised that a lot of Commonwealth teams travelling to Kingston had to go via Los Angeles, so they revamped the competition at short notice. The Australians left Sydney for Los Angeles on 19 July in a chartered jet.

The flight to the US was not an easy one for Doubell. He wrote a postcard to his mother when he arrived, telling her that he was staying at the University of Southern California, just up the road from the track where they would be competing. After the race, he would fly to Mexico and then Jamaica. 'I hope that this plane journey is better than that from Sydney, on which I was sick until we reached Honolulu,' he wrote. 'I picked up some wog in Sydney but have completely recovered now.'

Doubell was selected to run in the 880 yards against Jim Ryun, a 19-year-old from the University of Kansas who had recently set new world records for the 800 metres and the mile. The field also included Tom Farrell, the reigning American 880-yards champion, and the highly rated John Boulter from England. Doubell was very excited by the opportunity to race Ryun, because the young American was now the fastest middle-distance runner in the world. This was another reason Doubell loved to travel — not just to see and experience other countries, but to test himself against the best. The world-class quality of the field in the 880 yards, as well as many of the other events, drew a crowd of more than 34,000.

Doubell was feeling so good before the race he decided he would not just have a training run for Kingston. He would try to beat Ryun on his home turf. Boulter led early, but Ryun was in front at the 660-yards mark, with Farrell and a third American, Ted Nelson, close behind. Doubell was fourth and, as they came into the final straight, he accelerated in an effort to pass Ryun. He didn't succeed, however, and faded to finish fourth behind the three Americans, with Boulter fifth. Ryun crossed the line in 1:46.2. Doubell was exactly one second behind, having run a new personal best.

For Doubell, this race in Los Angeles was extremely significant. It had a huge and positive impact on him. He explains:

I couldn't believe that none of the Americans tried to beat Ryun. They were content to just run a minor place behind him. My approach was to try to win and if I 'blew up' in the straight I would hopefully finish with a minor place. I ultimately finished fourth, but in my mind I knew that I had challenged the world record holder and was close to matching it with him.

Doubell didn't realise that Tom Farrell wasn't quite at his best on the night, as the American recalls, half a century after the race:

> Jim Ryun won the race and though I was closing on him I finished second. Ryun was *the* runner at that time and I actually should have beaten him in that race. I had been in great shape but I got married a few weeks before the meet and went to Barbados on my honeymoon. So I didn't really train like I should have and I came up a bit short in the end. But I didn't tell my wife that if we hadn't got married I would have beaten Jim Ryun!

While he was focused on his own efforts to beat Ryun, Farrell clearly remembers Doubell's performance that night:

> He finished fourth and I remember talking to him after the race. He had run his personal best and he was real excited. He had come from nowhere. I had never heard of him before then.

Not many people talk about Doubell being excited — he is usually described as quiet and calm — so Farrell's recollection is telling. It confirms how significant this run was to Doubell. The fact that he had run his fastest time in Los Angeles was not the most important result from this race. Doubell never focused on time alone. It was that he knew he had been able to mix it with Ryun, and this convinced him that he had 'something'. Doubell has always credited this race with giving him the confidence to compete against the world's best athletes and the motivation to keep training hard over the next few years so that he could win at the highest level. It also taught him that too many athletes are intimidated by reputations.

AFTER PERFORMING SO WELL in Los Angeles, Doubell was feeling excited and positive about his prospects at the Kingston Games, which were now only a fortnight away. Some in the Australian media had been impressed by Doubell's run against Ryun and thought he was a real chance of a gold medal in a race that would feature a high-quality field. He sent another postcard home to his mother, telling her he had run his best ever time in Los Angeles and the fourth fastest time in the world that season. He added: 'I've got a tremendous headache from the race and the heat. I have yet to catch up on some lost sleep. We leave for Jamaica this afternoon and arrive at 4am!'

The headache turned out to be the first signs of tonsillitis, which Doubell contracted from the Los Angeles smog. He didn't talk about it at the time, except to the team doctor, but it would significantly affect his performance in Kingston.

The Commonwealth Games, or British Empire and Commonwealth Games as it was known in 1966, do not begin with young maidens in flowing robes lighting a flame with the sun's rays in front of temple ruins in Olympia, Greece. Since the 1958 edition in Cardiff, it has begun with Queen Elizabeth II handing a baton containing a message to the first of a series of relay runners. At the opening ceremony, the final relay runner hands the Queen's Baton to the Queen, or her representative, who reads the message aloud to officially open the Games.

On 26 July 1966, Queen Elizabeth II handed the Queen's Baton to Bruce Kidd from Canada, who had won gold in the six miles race four years earlier at the Games in Perth, Western Australia. Kidd carried it across Hyde Park and gave it to Sir Alexander Downer, the Australian High Commissioner, to acknowledge the link with the previous Games. The baton was then taken to Heathrow Airport, where it was handed to Laurence Lindo, the Jamaican High Commissioner. Lindo then passed it to Keith Gardner, a Jamaican athlete who won a gold medal in the 120-yards hurdles at the 1954 Games in Vancouver, two gold medals (120-yards hurdles and 100-yards sprint), a silver medal (220 yards) and a bronze medal (4 x 440-yards relay) at Cardiff in 1958, and a bronze medal in the 4 x 400-metres relay at the 1960 Rome Olympics. Gardner boarded the plane, taking the baton as carry-on luggage for his flight to Kingston via New York.

Five hundred youth club boys and girls carried the Queen's Baton through the streets of Jamaica over the next week before Gardner and a selection of other Jamaican medallists, as well as six boys and girls representing the youth of the island nation, carried it around the track in the National Stadium and presented it to Prince Philip, who was again representing his wife at an opening ceremony, which took place on 4 August. A few days earlier, their son, Prince Charles, had left the Timbertop Annex of Geelong Grammar School in Victoria, where he had been boarding, to make his way, via Mexico, to Kingston, where he joined his father.

The Kingston Games, as Melbourne had in 1956, faced many doubters. At the ballot to determine the 1966 host, held during the Perth Games in 1962, Kingston won by just one vote (17 to 16) over Edinburgh, Scotland. It was the first time the British Empire and Commonwealth Games would be held outside Britain, Canada,

Australia or New Zealand, and the first time a 'third world' nation was given the honour. Herbert Macdonald, Chairman and President of Jamaica's Organising Committee, said: 'This narrowest of victories was a great challenge to us and we never lost sight of the fact that some countries, particularly the larger ones, were in some doubt as to our ability to stage the Games, believing perhaps that only the larger countries could cope.'

It was true that many critics, including members of the media, did wonder aloud whether Jamaica would be able to organise the event successfully. The country's population at the time was only 1.5 million and at the last British Empire and Commonwealth Games its athletes had competed as part of the West Indies Federation. These fears seemed to have some foundation when the Jamaican national track championships held earlier in 1966 had to be delayed because someone forgot to bring the starter's pistol.

Once the Games started, many athletes complained about the timing of events, the standard of the venues, the security of the city and the quality of the food. There was no hot water for showers in the Games Village, but that wasn't such a problem given the heat. Doubell remembers the competition as being run 'on Jamaica time', and that some athletes enjoyed a little too much rum, but that did not concern him: he thought he was a chance to win the 880 yards and he was very focused on achieving this goal. The athletes were warned that Kingston could be dangerous, so they mostly kept to the Games Village except for escorted visits to the beach and official functions. Doubell followed his usual routine, which was to keep a low profile and spend time quietly with his teammates, some of whom he had known for years through the University of Melbourne and the Stampfl squad.

The athletics events were held at night to avoid the heat of the Jamaican sun. The temperature approached 40 degrees Celsius on most days. Doubell made his way comfortably through his 880-yards heat and won his semi-final in 1:48.3, but he knew he wasn't 100 per cent. The tonsillitis was taking its toll. Furthermore, the field that qualified for the final was exceptional. At that time, Commonwealth runners were the best in the world over 880 yards and 800 metres. The legendary Peter Snell, who had won the 880 yards in Perth four years earlier and the 800 metres at the 1960 and 1964 Olympic Games, had retired. But the runners who finished second, third and fourth behind the great New Zealander in Tokyo — Bill Crothers of Canada, Wilson Kiprugut of Kenya and George Kerr of Jamaica — were all on the starting line in Kingston. Kerr was favourite, only because it was thought he might have a home-ground advantage.

It was the wonderfully named Lennox Yearwood of Trinidad who set a very fast early pace in the 880-yards final, running the first lap in just under 50 seconds. The rest of the field was one second behind and Doubell was sitting in fourth place. Kiprugut took the lead at the 660-yards mark and then the crowd roared as Kerr, the local favourite, joined him as they entered the final straight. Kerr managed to edge in front and then, to the surprise of everyone, Australia's Noel Clough dashed past them both to break the tape and win gold in 1:46.9. Kiprugut was second in 1:47.2 and Kerr third with the same time. Crothers finished one tenth of a second behind in fourth place, meaning the first four finishers all broke Snell's Commonwealth record set in Perth four years earlier. Doubell, debilitated by his illness, couldn't find his finishing kick and crossed the line in sixth place in 1:48.3. This was regarded as a disappointing run at the time, but the facts are that he was not the favourite, he had been fighting tonsillitis and the field for the final was undoubtedly world class.

There had been no sign of Clough's winning form when he ran 1:53.8 behind Ryun and Doubell in Los Angeles a few weeks earlier. Before arriving in Kingston, Clough's fastest time was 1:48.3, a substantial 1.4 seconds slower than his gold medal-winning time. He was 29 years old when he raced in Kingston and a journeyman of Victorian athletics. He had been a good all-round sportsman at Coburg High School and then ran with Coburg Harriers Athletic Club. Clough competed over 440 yards, 440-yards hurdles and 880 yards, but he didn't ever win a Victorian or Australian title, although he finished in the top three on a number of occasions, and he was unsuccessful in his attempts to make the Australian Olympic team in 1960 and 1964. Kingston was the only time he travelled outside Australia for an athletics competition before he enjoyed success overseas as a Masters athlete. Today, from his home in Geelong, he recalls what was undoubtedly the highlight of his running career:

I had a feeling I could do reasonably well, even though my times weren't up there with Kiprugut, Kerr and Crothers. I ran economically in my heat, which wasn't terribly difficult, and though the semi-final was tougher I finished second and felt good. In the final, there was a false start. I think it was Yearwood. For whatever reason, I blacked out for a moment. I was still standing but everything went black and then white. I held it together and walked back to the start.

Yearwood went out very fast and then folded at the end of the first lap. This concertinaed the field as he slowed down. I got spat out the side like a wet pip going up the back straight on the second lap, but with 200 yards to go I thought I had a chance. I went out wide as we came into the final straight and finished over the top of them.

Asked why he thought he performed so well in Kingston, much better than he ever did before or afterwards, Clough points out that he trained very well in the lead-up to the competition:

I did a lot of speed work with Peter Norman and Gary Holdsworth, as well as my longer sessions, and I had a good taper. This included a hot bath about five days before my first race to help us relax, as recommended by my coach Neville Sillitoe. There was no hot water in the Village, so we asked Ron Carter, a journalist with *The Age*, if we could have a bath in his hotel room.

Clough's roommate, Lawrie Peckham, won the gold medal in the high jump the same night that Clough won the 880 yards, but Clough didn't have the energy to celebrate with him. Soon after winning the 880-yards final, he had to back up to run a heat of the 440 yards. Extraordinarily, the semi-final and final of the 440 yards were run on the same night. A tired Clough finished eighth in the final.

The toughness gained from training through illness and injury with Stampfl meant Doubell decided to compete in the mile a few days after the 880-yards final. He qualified for the final of the mile with a good heat time of 4:04.0 but, while he was up with the leaders at the halfway mark, he did not finish due to his weakened condition. It was the only 'DNF' of his career. The final was won by a huge distance in 3:55.3 by Kip Keino of Kenya, a rising superstar who was approaching the peak of his powers. Keino had broken the world 3000-metres record and Ron Clarke's 5000-metres record in late 1965 and now he was the Commonwealth mile champion. The first six finishers all broke four minutes, including Australia's Keith Wheeler, who ran 3:59.8 to break the barrier for the first time.

Australia finished second behind England on the medal table in Kingston, with 23 gold medals, 28 silver and 22 bronze. Australia won 10 of the 13 men's swimming events and Australian women won seven gold medals in track and field while their male teammates won four. Ron Clarke had to settle for championship 'minor' medals yet again. He was beaten by Keino in the three miles and by another Kenyan, Naftali Temu, in the six miles. Temu was unheralded before Kingston, but he would go on to win gold in the 10,000 metres and bronze in the 5000 at the 1968 Mexico City Olympic Games.

A week after the Kingston closing ceremony, Doubell was in London to race against Keino over a mile in the British Games at White City. Keino won comfortably and Doubell ran 4:00.4, his fastest ever mile. He did this, he reveals, 'despite the lingering effects of tonsillitis, jet lag and a week of partying in Kingston'.

Two days later, Doubell combined with three of his teammates from Kingston — Noel Clough, Keith Wheeler and Ken Roche — in a rare 4 x 880-yards relay race at a two-day international meeting at the Morton Stadium, more commonly known as the Santry track, in Dublin. Ken Roche was a 440-yards hurdler who had never competed over 880 yards and the Irish team, led by European record holder Noel Carroll, was expected to win. Carroll was about to get married, and the organisers were so confident of an Irish victory that they organised for four sewing machines to be the prizes for the winning team. At the time, sewing machines were expensive and a highly valued wedding present. The Australian team surprised everyone by winning the relay in 7:19.7, an Irish all-comers record and still the Australian record for this rarely run event. Roche performed above expectations while Doubell ran 1:48.0, the fastest leg by anyone in the race.

The next day, Doubell won the 880 yards, comfortably beating Carroll even though it was a relatively slow time of 1:50. Carroll, who was preparing to compete in the European Championships, was given a hard time by the local press, while the organisers had to determine what to do with the four sewing machines. They were large and heavy and only Keith Wheeler, who was about to get married, wanted to transport his back to Australia, so three of the machines were given good Irish homes. To avoid being charged a large sum to check in the fourth sewing machine with their already heavy luggage, the returning athletes said it was crockery that had to be handled very carefully. They checked it in as hand luggage and guided it successfully past suspicious flight attendants and through various airports until it took pride of place in the Wheeler home in Western Australia.

The trip to the United Kingdom was a boost for Doubell after the disappointment of Kingston. He knew that tonsillitis had cruelled his chances in Jamaica and the fact he had pushed Jim Ryun in Los Angeles motivated him to step up his training when he returned to Australia. Stampfl remained calm, saying in typically direct fashion:

'You have to work harder.'

CHAPTER 11

The Importance of Training Mates

Many of those who trained with Doubell, or watched him train, believed that he drove himself harder than most other athletes. There were times, of course, when Doubell found training monotonous. This is why it was so important for him to be part of the Stampfl squad. It makes a huge difference to athletes if they can work with others who are going through similar challenges and are prepared to help each other get through the exhausting workouts and the tough times.

One of the biggest benefits of training with Stampfl was the team environment. Stampfl attracted the full gamut of male and female athletes, including sprinters, middle-distance and long-distance runners, jumpers and throwers. No other coach had the same ability, or enjoyed such success, across such a variety of fields in athletics. This is one of Stampfl's achievements that is often overlooked. Importantly, he built a wonderful team spirit among all those striving to achieve their best under his tutelage.

One member of the Stampfl squad was high jumper Tony Sneazwell, who Doubell had first got to know well in Adelaide in 1963 and who represented Australia at the 1964 Tokyo and 1968 Mexico City Olympic Games. Sneazwell had cleared 6ft 5in (195cm) in his final year at Parade College in Melbourne and decided to try Stampfl as a coach when he began studying at the University of Melbourne in 1961. He was particularly impressed by the improvements made by one of his rivals, Graeme Morrish.

'In the 1960s, Victorian athletics was very strong,' Sneazwell recalls from his home in Edmonton, Canada. After working as a dentist in Melbourne in the late 1960s and early 1970s, he studied at the University of Southern California in 1974 and then graduated from the University of Washington with a Masters in Prosthodontics, a specialty in dental prosthetics such as crowns and bridges. In 1977, Sneazwell moved to Edmonton, where he practised dentistry until 2011. He still lectures at the University of Alberta. He says Stampfl in the '60s had 'a great group':

If you look at the athletes that were training with Stampfl at the time, and also the other athletes in Victoria, it was just a wonderful place to be. There were runners, throwers and jumpers. On Sunday mornings, people would come to training from all different directions, dressed in all kinds of clothes depending on where they had been on Saturday night. Ralph was just part of the group.

Bill Hooker, who was four years younger than Doubell, joined
the Stampfl squad in late 1966 when he was in his final year
at Northcote High School. Hooker would go on to represent
Australia in the 400 metres and the 400-metres hurdles at the
1969 Pacific Conference Games in Tokyo, finish third in the 400
metres and second in the 800 at the 1973 Pacific Conference
Games in Toronto and compete in the 400 metres, 800 metres
and 4 x 400-metres relay at the 1974 Commonwealth Games
in Christchurch. He finished sixth in the 800-metres final in
Christchurch, with John Kipkurgat of Kenya winning in 1:43.91,
just two-tenths of a second outside the world record at the time.
Kipkurgat's compatriot Mike Boit was second with local Kiwi
legend John Walker taking bronze. Hooker's son Steve won the
pole vault at the 2008 Beijing Olympics, the first Australian man
to win a gold medal in Olympic track and field since 1968. Bill
Hooker recalls:

> I was a young guy coming up through the group when Ralph
> was at his peak and it was just a great environment to train in.
> It is always better to have someone to help you get through the
> long and hard sessions, to keep your concentration levels up —
> and Ralph was the best in the world! Every training session
> with Ralph was a good one. There was never any slacking off.
> But everyone pushed hard and no one was treated differently to
> anyone else. As long as you wanted to put in the work, you were
> treated the same. And at the same time, Ralph didn't behave as
> if he was the elite athlete of the group. He would just do what
> the rest of us were doing.

Ralph Doubell — Olympic 800-metres champion and Australian 800-metres record holder for five decades — on his home track at the University of Melbourne.

The Melbourne University Athletics Club team that competed in the 1963 Intervarsity competition in Adelaide. Doubell is second from left in the middle row, with Stanley Spittle, who would become one of his closest friends, seated second from left, and future Olympic high jumper Tony Sneazwell seated third from left.

Doubell with Franz Stampfl, a remarkable man he proudly remembers as 'my coach, mentor, guide and inspiration'.

Left: Doubell's first national title, Hobart, 1965. *Below left*: A year later, he defeated Ron Clarke in the Victorian mile championship. *Below right*: A competitive fourth behind the highly rated Americans Jim Ryun and Tom Farrell in LA in early August 1966 gave Doubell a major psychological boost.

Above: The Australian athletics team for the 1966 British Empire and Commonwealth Games in Kingston, Jamaica. Doubell is in the second back row, fifth from left. Among his colleagues are Tony Sneazwell (back row, second from left), Noel Clough (back row, centre), Ken Roche (back row, far right), Ron Clarke (second back row, third from right), Allen Crawley (second back row, second from right), and Keith Wheeler (front, second from right).

Below: Doubell hands the baton to Wheeler, as an Australian 4 x 880-yards team also featuring Clough and Roche stun the Irish in Dublin in late August '66.

As Doubell's regular training partner, Stanley Spittle — at right winning the mile at the intervarsity competition in Adelaide in 1963 — had a close-up view of his mate's style and imposing stride (below). 'He could accelerate so hard that no one in the world could keep with him for five yards,' Spittle recalls. 'His sprint finish was explosive and it would hit you physically, bang, as he went past.'

Above: After graduating with a science degree, Doubell joined Shell in 1967.

Left: Doubell qualifies for the Mexico City Olympics at Olympic Park in Melbourne on 28 March 1968, producing the then fastest 800-metres time ever run by an Australian on home soil in the process.

Ray Weinberg, Australia's athletics coach at the Mexico City Olympics, with track stars Dianne Burge, Raelene Boyle, Pam Kilborn and Jenny Lamy.

Doubell cruises up to Poland's Henryk Szordykowski in his heat of the 800 metres on the opening day of competition at the '68 Games.

The three Australian men who have won Olympic gold on the track: Edwin Flack (top left), Herb Elliott (top right) and Ralph Doubell.

Hooker highlights the benefits of the diversity of the Stampfl squad:

> Athletics is a very personal sport and you have to be a bit of
> an egotist, because once you get out there it is very individual.
> In a lot of touring teams, the sprinters talk sprinting until
> the cows come home, the middle-distance runners hang out
> with themselves, the throwers are a bit crazy and the jumpers
> are somewhere in the middle. But because we were part of
> the Stampfl group, we were lucky because we had learned to
> appreciate what the other athletes were doing. We knew what
> a good discus distance was, for example. It broadened our
> knowledge and we enjoyed the competitions and tours a lot
> more because of it.

While they trained extremely hard, Hooker says it was a very
different era:

> I don't think we ever talked about diet or hydration. Looking
> back now, I'm sure I ran dehydrated on many occasions.
> Furthermore, after our usual Saturday morning session, more
> often than not we would go to Jimmy Watson's Wine Bar
> afterwards and solve some of the world's problems. If Stampfl
> came with us, it tended to be a longer session.

Critically, Hooker says that being part of the Stampfl group meant
that everyone 'raised their sights':

> The national championships were just the first step and
> then you were eyeing off international success, because that's

what the people around you did. It was just great to be a part of it.

'There were, of course, days when I dreaded going to training,' Doubell told the audience at Melbourne University Athletics Club's 125th anniversary celebrations in 2015. 'But it was the great friendships that carried us through.' He continued:

There was a spark amongst all of us at the club and we all tried to help each other. No one received preferential treatment. No one ever got an easier program. Everyone was told in no uncertain terms to pull their finger out and train harder. And we did. And we each enjoyed each other's successes.

Stampfl knew it was important to release the pressure at times. He loved champagne and Doubell remembers fondly how everyone would be told to attend training on New Year's Day at the normal time of 10am with at least one bottle of champagne and a roast chicken. Stampfl always insisted that the champagne had to be French. After a normal training session followed by a glass or two of bubbly, there would be a special race that required hurdling empty champagne bottles over 400 metres. 'I don't remember how frequently we had to hurdle a bottle,' Doubell recalls, 'but at the end of 400 metres it seemed like it was at least every two metres and each bottle seemed about a metre high. We were then allowed to have something to eat … and enjoy the champagne that was left in the Esky.'

DOUBELL SAYS THAT HIS most important training mate was Stanley Spittle, a Law student who was three years ahead of him at the University of Melbourne. Spittle was born on 12 April 1941, when his father was the manager of the Queerah meatworks at the wonderfully named Skeleton Creek, near Cairns in Far North Queensland. In 1954 the Spittle family moved south and soon after settled at Wagga Wagga, in the Riverina region of New South Wales. Stanley attended Wagga Wagga High School and, as the year progressed, 'Nana', his paternal grandmother, put her foot down and insisted he be educated at a good school. In 1955, when he was 14 years old, Stanley began boarding at Ballarat Church of England Grammar School in north-west Victoria. He remembers going to the 'book room' on his first day and being issued with a school diary that listed all the school's athletic records. In particular, his attention was captured by the 880-yards record of 2 minutes and 3 seconds.

Spittle was at Ballarat Grammar from 1955 until 1959, and from his first year there he loved the cross-country training. He would run with the juniors on Monday, the middle seniors on Tuesday, and the seniors on Wednesday. Whenever there was a cross-country training session Stanley would turn up. He ran well in the school cross-country races. 'Not because I was that good, but because I was that much fitter than the others, because of the extra training I had been doing,' he recalls.

Spittle was tall, 'six foot and half an inch' (184cm), and lean, with a long stride. As he started to show form on the athletics track in 1957, two of the school's top middle-distance runners, Gus Hannaford and John 'Len' McRae, befriended him and invited him to join them on their training runs. This included a lot of interval work and the occasional long run. Spittle struggled to stay with them at times, but he completed all the sessions and became even fitter.

In 1958, Spittle was selected by Ballarat Grammar as their second-string runner in the 880 yards for the Combined Schools sports competition. Very early on the morning of the competition, a House Master and teacher, Geoff Tunbridge, walked into the senior dormitory. Tunbridge had been a student at Ballarat Grammar and was now at the beginning of a 30-year career at the school. From 1957 until 1962, while he was teaching at Ballarat Grammar, Tunbridge played 117 games for Melbourne in the Victorian Football League. During that time, Melbourne won the premiership in 1957, 1959 and 1960.

Spittle was still in bed when Tunbridge leant over and informed him that the school needed him to run in the 440 yards as well as the 880 yards. This was a complete surprise, as the school's leading sprinter was expected to do very well in the 100 yards, 220 yards and 440 yards. However, he had disappeared overnight — his girlfriend was pregnant and the pair had eloped on the eve of the competition. 'Well, the spaghetti really hit the fan,' Spittle says with a smile. It meant Spittle had to step up to be the second-string runner in the 440 yards and other boys were called upon to compete in the shorter sprints.

Spittle finished second to the Ballarat Grammar champion, Len McRae, in the 880 yards and then went on to surprise himself and everyone else by taking third place in the 440 yards. As a result, he qualified for his School Athletics Colours, which gave him 'a hell of a lift'. Inspired by his athletics progress, during the summer holidays he borrowed two books from the Wagga Wagga City Library that would have a significant impact on him. One was *The First Four Minutes*, the 1955 autobiography of Roger Bannister. On a nearby shelf was a small green book, *How to Run a Sub Four-Minute Mile*, by Franz

Stampfl. Spittle believed he could do Stampfl's training programs, even though they were meant for older, more experienced athletes.

On his return to Ballarat Grammar in 1959, his final year of school, Spittle stroked the school's Fourth Crew to victory at the Head of the Lake regatta, a performance that further boosted his confidence. Importantly, the rowing also helped to strengthen his lean physique. During the winter months he did not play any football. Instead he began, as best he could, to follow Stampfl's training program for the mile. After a couple of months, however, he found the schedule too demanding. 'I fell in a heap,' he recalls.

A fellow runner in Ballarat suggested he contact Neil Robbins in Melbourne. Robbins had finished seventh in the final of 3000-metres steeplechase at the 1956 Melbourne Olympic Games and was now coaching some athletes. Spittle had kept a training diary, which he showed to Robbins, who quickly concluded that Spittle needed to slow down. He designed a more appropriate training schedule and Spittle did what he was told: 'I soon found I was full of energy and bursting out of my skin,' he says.

The Ballarat Grammar athletics championship in 1959 was held in mid-October. Spittle was up against Len McRae in the 880 yards. The first lap was a slow 64 seconds and when Spittle heard the time, 'I took off a few yards after the bell.' He ran the second lap in 57.1 seconds and won in a new school record time of 2:01.2. Unfortunately, later that day he injured his left foot in the 440 yards. This affected him in the 880 yards at the Combined Schools competition two weeks later and he finished second to McRae, although he again broke the school record. Soon after these races, Spittle was referred to an orthopaedic specialist and X-rays indicated he had suffered a stress fracture. He was placed in a plaster cast for six weeks. He focused on his final examinations, matriculated and was admitted as a student in the Law faculty at the University of Melbourne.

In his first year at university, 1960, Spittle shared a house in Berry Street, near the Melbourne Cricket Ground, with another student. Money was always in short supply because Spittle's father took the view that it was a waste of time for Stanley to go to university. He would only reimburse his student son for what he considered to be genuine expenses, and not a penny more, and only after he received a letter setting out all the expenditure details. Receipts, including all tram tickets purchased, were enclosed in Stanley's weekly missive home.

In his first term, Spittle won the University of Melbourne 880 yards and this meant he was selected for his first intervarsity competition, which was held in Hobart. He was keen to see how far he could go with his athletics career and to train with the best, so when he learned that Merv Lincoln was training in the dark at Olympic Park on Tuesday and Thursday nights, he decided to see if he could join him. Lincoln had run in the final of the 1500 metres at the 1956 Melbourne Olympics, earned a silver medal behind Herb Elliott in the mile at the 1958 British Empire and Commonwealth Games in Cardiff, and been selected to represent Australia in the 1500 metres at the Rome Olympics, to be held from August 25 to September 11. Whenever possible, 19-year-old Spittle would make his way to Olympic Park to train with the 27-year-old Lincoln and stick with the Olympian during training as best he could.

One night, just before they started training, a thunderstorm drenched the track. Spittle was still running in the old pair of spikes he had worn at Ballarat Grammar, which he had bought second hand years before, and soon after they started their 440 yards interval session his spikes became saturated and one of the heels came off. He was unable to continue running and had no choice but to pull out of the training session. The next morning, Spittle received a phone call from Lincoln telling him to go to the Melbourne Sports Depot, a sporting goods store in Elizabeth Street and 'ask for Judy Patching'.

At the time, Julius 'Judy' Patching was the manager of the Melbourne Sports Depot and a well-known figure in Australian athletics. He had been a hurdler and pentathlete in his youth, was chief starter at the 1956 Melbourne Olympic Games, and would go on to be Athletics Manager for the Australian team at the 1960 Olympics, Assistant General Manager at the 1964 Olympics, and Australia's Chef de Mission at the 1968 and 1972 Olympics. Patching was also a delegate to the International Amateur Athletic Federation from 1960 to 1970 and Secretary-General of the Australian Olympic Committee from 1973 to 1985.

Patching took Spittle to the back of the shop and gave him a pair of Dreske spikes. Dreske was a Western Australian company that had earned a reputation for making excellent lightweight running shoes for athletes such as Herb Elliott. As a student with no money, the free spikes were 'a gift from the gods' to Spittle.

Spittle surprised his father by not only passing his first-year Law examinations but winning a Commonwealth Scholarship. This included a living away from home allowance and a travel allowance. For the first time in his life, Stanley Spittle had pocket money. Furthermore, he was accepted into the prestigious Trinity College, the ivy-clad institution that had been founded in 1872 and was the first residential college of the University of Melbourne.

For Spittle, one of the college's greatest assets was that it was situated right on the perimeter of the university athletics track, a quality facility that had been built as a training centre in the lead up to the 1956 Olympics. Spittle loved to run around that circuit, which was nestled between Trinity and the other colleges. It was maintained fastidiously by a Scotsman known as 'Mac', after whom the grandstand is now named. Mac would work out of a small shed near the Beaurepaire Pool and Stampfl would sit above it, sunbathing in his 'budgie smugglers' while he kept an eye on his athletes. In 2014, the university revealed plans to replace the athletics track with an indoor sports centre featuring courts for basketball and badminton. Spittle and Doubell led the objections to the development, arguing that the track's sporting history should be respected and retained. The submission was accepted and the track has so far survived.

Spittle retained his University of Melbourne 880-yards title in 1961 and also won the intercollegiate 880 yards and mile. His room at Trinity College became a changing room of sorts for many top Victorian athletes, which sparked the fascination of other students. This interest was particularly high when Ron Clarke, who had made some headlines after enjoying success overseas, would turn up at Spittle's room for a training run. A group of eager students would wait at the bottom of the stairs, excited by the opportunity to join the celebrity for a 10-mile run around nearby Princes Park. Clarke was always extremely polite and would say hello to everyone before they headed off. The initial pace would also be 'polite', so that most could keep up for the first mile or so, but then Clarke would slowly increase it to six-minute mile pace and soon only the better and fitter athletes could hang on. Spittle says that many of those student runners still talk today about how they trained with Ron Clarke in the early 1960s.

Spittle continued to improve in 1962 and then, as a 21st birthday present, his Nana paid for him to go to the British Empire and Commonwealth Games in Perth at the end of the year. He saw Peter Snell win the 880 yards and the mile and another New Zealander, Murray Halberg, beat Ron Clarke in the three miles. Halberg had won the gold medal in the 5000 metres at the 1960 Rome Olympics. The Perth Games made a huge impression on Spittle and must have been a factor in his significantly improved performances in 1963. On 23 March, he finished seventh in the mile at the Australian Amateur Athletics Championships in Adelaide, with Albie Thomas winning in 4:05.0.

Thomas was one of the best-known athletes in Australia. He competed for Australia at the 1956, 1960 and 1964 Olympics as well as at the 1958 and 1962 British Empire and Commonwealth Games, and most notably enjoyed an extraordinary few months of success during 1958. On 9 July of that year, he set a new world record of 13:10.8 for three miles at the Santry track in Dublin. Later that month, he competed at the British Empire and Commonwealth Games in Cardiff and took home a bronze medal in the mile, behind Herb Elliott and Merv Lincoln, and a silver medal in the three miles, behind Murray Halberg. Thomas returned to the Santry track on 6 August to be the pace maker as Elliott set a new world record for the mile of 3:54.5. Lincoln was second in 3:55.9 and Thomas finished fifth in 3:58.6. The following night, Thomas set a new world record for two miles of 8:32.0.

Two days after running in the final of the mile at the 1963 Australian Amateur Athletics Championships in Adelaide, Spittle finished fifth in his heat of the 880 yards with a time of 1:53.3. He was very disappointed with this performance, but in April of that year he won both the 880 yards and the mile at the University of Melbourne Championships, breaking two University of Melbourne records in four days. He ran 4:11.0 for the mile to beat John Landy's previous mark by four seconds and three days later ran 1:52.1 to break Russell Oakley's 880-yards record by four tenths of a second.

In May 1963, Spittle was back in Adelaide as a member of the University of Melbourne's intervarsity athletics team and won the mile in 4:14.2, though he remembers feeling 'crook and dizzy' after the race. However, he was able to recover in time to compete in the 4 x 440 yards relay a few hours later and was pleased with his performance in the circumstances, especially as he helped the University of Melbourne team to cross the line in first place. Two days later, fully recovered, he won the 880 yards in 1:55.6.

Ralph Doubell was also a member of the University of Melbourne's winning 4 x 440 yards relay team. This was the first time that Doubell and Spittle spent any time together — the start of a long and strong relationship that played an extremely important role in Doubell's future success on the track.

SPITTLE FINISHED THE 1963 season holding the University of Melbourne and intercollegiate records for both the 880 yards and the mile, and he received a treasured Full Blue from the University in recognition of his performances. He started to think seriously about representing Australia at the 1964 Tokyo Olympics. But the qualifying time for 800 metres was 1:49.4 and Spittle was very unsure he could run that fast. His detailed running diaries reflect a marked lack of the self-confidence that is vital to pulling out a top-class performance when it is required. Spittle says this was a big difference between him and Doubell. His training mate 'could not only do the hard preparatory work, but he also had an innate ability, a gifted self-confidence to perform under pressure at the highest level when it really mattered'.

Spittle's confidence was further shaken when he raced against Doubell for the first time in the Victorian 800-metres championship at Oakleigh Football Club Oval on 21 January 1964. The more experienced and in-form Spittle was favourite for the event, but Doubell won in 1:52.8 while Spittle crossed the line in second place in 1:53.0, the same time as Noel Clough. This was a confidence-boosting run for the young Doubell, but it was a real disappointment for Spittle.

On 2 February, Spittle was selected to represent Victoria at a meeting held in Sydney. Tony Blue won in 1:49.4, the qualifying time for Tokyo, while Spittle was disheartened with his time of 1:52.7.

There was no improvement into March, so Spittle invited Franz Stampfl to lunch at Trinity College to seek his advice. He showed Stampfl his general training plans for 1964, which included the tough 17-mile course in the Dandenong Ranges that Ron Clarke, Trevor Vincent and other top middle-distance athletes would run on weekends.

Vincent had won the gold medal in the 3000-metres steeplechase at the 1962 British Empire and Commonwealth Games. Stampfl told Spittle he was doing too much mileage.

'Don't look on the four-minute mile as such a difficult thing,' he said. 'It doesn't require all this work.'

In Stampfl's view, Spittle was overtraining. A short time later, a doctor recommended that Spittle start a course of vitamin B injections to help his body recover. Spittle then decided to train with Stampfl and found he 'got on great guns' with the coach and his program. Stampfl stressed the importance of speed work and Spittle remembers 'standing on the edge of the track in April 1964, watching Doubell roll out a session of 10 x 400 metres at an average of 62 seconds':

> The last two laps were run in 58 seconds and 54.9 seconds and Doubell's pulse rate was measured at 240 after the last 400-metres effort. Even at this early stage, Stampfl was speaking openly to me about Doubell's outstanding success.

During 1964, Spittle and Doubell would often train together, over long and short distances. The longer runs would be at six-minute mile pace, with the course going around Princes Park or over to the Royal Botanic Gardens. The shorter sessions might include 12 x 150 yards with 150 yards recovery between each sprint. Spittle recalls:

> When we would do the 150s, we would not be running flat out but we would be close to it. Every now and then I was disappointed, I suppose you could say 'cheesed off', by the fact that Doubell was always on top and impossible to hold on the short sprint work. I would frequently try to jump him and I would put in a super effort 30 or 40 metres from the finish, but he would always come home and beat me. At that time, Doubell could accelerate so hard that no one in the world could keep with him for five yards. His sprint finish was explosive and it would hit you physically, bang, as he went past. It gave him a huge psychological edge.

During the winter of 1964, Spittle had a serious setback with an injury to his left calf and foot. In late July he was diagnosed with plantar fasciitis, a common running injury caused by inflammation of the ligament-like structure that runs along the sole of the foot. It results in pain in the heel and arch, and Spittle took time out to recover.

Having finished his Law degree at the end of that year, in 1965 Spittle successfully obtained his Articles of Clerkship with the firm of Ellison Hewison & Whitehead. That firm would merge with Minter Simpson & Co. in 1986 and is now known as Minter Ellison. Articles paid very little, approximately £5 per week, and Spittle's father was still very tight with the purse strings, so to make ends meet Spittle found a position as a House Master at Caulfield Grammar School. His foot injury persisted through 1965, which meant that when he visited the Rawlinson Track at the University of Melbourne it was purely as an observer.

'Watching Doubell churning out all his work gave me the "irrits", because I couldn't run,' he says.

Spittle could not resume training with any continuity until 1966. In that year, he also started working as a solicitor with Baird & McGregor in Ballarat, a law firm that was established in 1898 and still exists today, and on 17 May he married Rosemary Jackson, whom he had met at the University of Melbourne when she was a student at Women's College. She was one of the few women studying Commerce at the time, and she would tell Spittle how the male students would wolf whistle and whoop when she walked into the lecture theatre with its banked seating. 'The boys gave the girls hell in those days,' he remembers. He trained in Ballarat and also travelled to Melbourne every week to train with Stampfl and

Doubell, a two-hour drive each way. So what motivated him to make this effort? 'I had unfinished business, and was still determined to improve and to do something with my athletics career.'

While Spittle focused on his own dreams, his weekly travel to Melbourne was critical for Doubell's training. This is because he was the only member of Stampfl's squad at this time who could do the same volume of training as Doubell, even though he couldn't quite keep up with him during the intense speed work sessions. 'When he turned it on I would be lost in the dust,' Spittle recalls ruefully. 'No one would be within cooee of him. The speed at which he did those sessions was extraordinary.' He says the two of them 'sponged off each other'. While Doubell was better at the shorter speed work, Spittle had the upper hand over the longer distances. Most importantly, they formed a bond that helped them get through Stampfl's repetitive and rigorous training program.

For Doubell, Spittle also possessed another invaluable attribute — an ability to tell stories and to do so with a sense of humour. During the course of a training session, whether it be during the warm-up or the recovery phases, as well as on long runs, Spittle would tell stories gleaned from his days in court. In those days, Spittle often had 'crash and bash' insurance claims and Family Law maintenance cases. He was a born raconteur and Doubell loved the levity that Spittle added to their training sessions because it made the hard, repetitive work just that bit more palatable.

Doubell and Spittle became close friends, as well as training mates until the day Doubell retired. Spittle was the best man at Doubell's wedding and they remain extremely close to this day. Asked why he thinks this relationship developed, Spittle says they were both reserved young men who shared a love of running. Significantly,

Spittle says that neither of them had much money to pursue any interests outside their studies and daily training. 'When you've got no money, you don't venture out much,' he explains. Indeed, they didn't have many close friends outside athletics. They just got on extremely well and didn't try too much to analyse why. Doubell has no doubt having Spittle as a training mate was extremely important to his accomplishments on the track.

Emboldened by the success he was having in the Ballarat courts, Spittle left Baird & McGregor in late 1968 and in 1969 he was admitted to the Bar as a Barrister-at-Law in Melbourne. All new barristers are required to train with a Master, and Spittle's Master was FX Costigan. Frank Costigan was a barrister who 'took silk' in 1973 and, as Queen's Counsel, was appointed by the Federal Government to chair the 1980 Royal Commission into the activities of the Federated Ship Painters and Dockers Union. This inquiry made headlines with its revelations of tax evasion and organised crime. From the outset, Spittle was successful at the Victorian Bar. Even in his first year he found that he was earning twice as much money as he had been when he was a solicitor.

When he moved back to Melbourne in late 1968, Spittle resumed training with Doubell. During the week, they would train together at 5.30pm each evening after work. In addition to the interval work on the track, they often ran a 10-mile course, starting at the Beaurepaire Centre at the University. They would run across to the Royal Exhibition Building then through the Treasury Gardens, past the Melbourne Cricket Ground, across the Yarra River and around the Tan Track at the bottom of the Anderson Street hill. The Tan Track, which goes around King's Domain and the Royal Botanic Gardens, was originally used for horse riding, and many believe it takes its name from the tan bark used to build it. They would run two laps of The Tan before returning to the university.

So what does Spittle think are the main reasons for his friend's success on the athletics track? He emphasises again that Doubell was 'a gifted athlete with great natural ability and extraordinary acceleration over five to ten yards when he kicked'. Then he adds: 'Critically, he was driven to work harder than anyone else and was intensely competitive, even in training sessions.' Spittle believes that this competitive spirit can be traced back to the death of Doubell's father when he was 14 years old:

> His father died when he was very young. His mother was working, putting her heart and soul into each day's effort to keep the family going. Ralph found something he was good at and he didn't want to fold up like a flower in the desert. He really blossomed under Stampfl. Here was a new father figure, here was inspiration and from here on he gained supreme confidence in his own ability.

Spittle retired after a successful 46-year career at the Victorian Bar. While at university, he also competed in rowing, and since 2010 has been heavily involved in World Rowing Masters Championships. Since 2013 he has been a member of crews that have won medals in races held in Italy, Japan and Germany.

Spittle still looks back at his athletics career with some regret. He wonders what he might have achieved if not for the injury in 1964 that upset his plans and dreams. He never represented Australia, but Spittle epitomises the very good athlete who trains hard and consistently week after week over many years. Looking back, he realises that he 'lacked that "divine spark", the self-confidence, ability or luck that is so essential to make it at the elite level'. Spittle talks down his role in Doubell's success, but Doubell has no doubts about how important Spittle was. He made a vital contribution, not just by helping Doubell get through his tough and monotonous workouts, but also by ensuring that Doubell pushed himself that little bit harder. In the speed sessions, Spittle was always haunting his friend and ready to jump at any opportunity to cross the line first. This competitiveness was also evident on their longer endurance runs.

Athletics is often regarded as an individual sport, but Doubell clearly valued being part of a team — whether it be the Stampfl squad, the University of Melbourne Athletics Club, Victoria or Australia. Stanley Spittle was his most valued teammate and to this day Doubell remains grateful for his mateship both on and off the track.

CHAPTER 12

Dreaming of Mexico

While Stampfl continued to experiment with the volume and intensity of Doubell's training, it was still always timed, controlled and exhausting. The injuries came and went, and Doubell had to study for and pass his university examinations. He kept training hard.

In late 1966, Doubell was one of four Australian athletes invited to compete in a series of races in America in the January of the following year. His love of travel and competition meant he was keen to go but Stampfl was against it. This was mainly because Doubell had missed a lot of training due to a tonsillectomy at the end of November, and then he had to successfully complete his end-of-year examinations. Stampfl was concerned Doubell would be a long way from his best and therefore it wouldn't be right for him to go.

On 20 December 1966, just three weeks after having his tonsils removed, Doubell defeated Wilson Kiprugut over 1000 metres in a meeting held at Olympic Park. He sprinted past the Olympic 800-metres bronze medallist from Tokyo with about 200 metres to go and held on for the win. Stanley Spittle finished third. Kiprugut, who was touring Australia with two other top Kenyan athletes, Naftali Temu and Benjamin Kogo, told *The Sun*: 'That is the first time I have ever been beaten over that distance. I misjudged the opposition.'

Despite this win over Kiprugut, Doubell decided not to tour America. It was extremely satisfying to have beaten the Kenyan and the lure of travel remained compelling, but he knew his time wasn't that fast and he recognised that he didn't have enough training behind him for a month of tough racing in the USA.

In early February 1967, Doubell beat Noel Clough, the reigning Commonwealth champion, to win the Victorian Amateur Athletics 880-yards Championship in 1:52.1. The first lap was pedestrian and, while he sprinted away from Clough to win by 10 metres, it was a slow time. The first three laps of the mile, held a few days later, were also slow and Doubell finished second behind Tony Benson.

The 1967 Australian Amateur Athletics Championships were held in Adelaide at the end of February. Doubell's first event was the 1500 metres, which evolved into a pretty rough race with lots of chopping and changing. Doubell was well positioned coming into the final bend but then he was spiked. He stumbled and almost fell. Some newspaper reports suggest that Doubell tried to take the inside running when there wasn't enough room, and Doubell admitted privately that they might have been right. Nevertheless, he recovered to finish third behind Laurie Toogood of New South

Wales and Peter Watson of Western Australia. Ron Clarke, who was also spiked during the race, was fourth.

Doubell didn't make any tactical mistakes in the 800-metres final a few days later, winning the race in 1:49.8 and beating Clough by 10 metres.

A fortnight after the Australian Championships, Doubell competed in the 880 yards at the Highland Games held at Adelaide Oval. He attended a dinner party the night before the final, stayed out late and only had about five hours' sleep. Remarkably, he won the race in 1:48.0, cutting half a second off his national record. Clough finished second, almost three seconds behind him. The key to Doubell's fast time was that a South Australian athlete named Peter Woon ran the first lap in 53 seconds. Doubell sat behind Woon and South Australian champion Chris Woods, before moving away from them with about 250 metres to go and holding his form to the finish.

Despite Doubell's consistent victories over Clough, both before and after Kingston, the selectors chose Clough to run the 800 metres at a British Commonwealth versus USA meeting in Los Angeles in early July, a decision that a number of journalists thought was in error because it was not based on form. Steve Hayward of *The Herald* was particularly hot under the collar:

> The omission of Victorian middle-distance runner Ralph Doubell from the British Commonwealth athletics team to meet the United States at Los Angeles on July 8 and 9 is nothing short of a sporting 'crime'.
>
> Doubell should have walked into the team ahead of Victorian Noel Clough who has been preferred. Obviously, Clough has

been chosen for the 800 metres on his win in the 880 yards at the Jamaica Commonwealth Games last August in the Games record time of 1:46.9.

Clough was set back by appendicitis last November but he had plenty of time to recover last season when he was repeatedly overshadowed by Doubell. Last season, Doubell was clearly Australia's most consistently brilliant performer over 800 metres, 880 yards, 1500 metres and the mile.

Doubell was certainly disappointed, not least because he would have enjoyed an all-expenses-paid trip to Los Angeles, however a new opportunity soon emerged. He was selected to represent Australia in the 800 metres and the 4 x 400-metres relay at the World University Games, or Universiade, in Tokyo in early September. Unlike the Los Angeles event, however, each of the 30 or so members of the team had to pay $250 to go to Tokyo.

Doubell wrote a postcard to his mother from Tokyo, telling her that they had been held up in Hong Kong due to a storm. He went on:

The facilities here are tremendous. When we arrived, we were given two bags full of 'goodies' eg. batteries, toiletries, etc. We are staying 5 in a room, so you can imagine the mess it is in. It's extremely hot every day — it has been about 90 degrees [Fahrenheit]. It is a bit of a change from Melbourne. Somehow, I've been elected captain. I have not got that much to do. So far I have not spent much but no doubt that will be changed.

The 800-metres field in Tokyo was a strong one, by international not just university standards. It included Wade Bell of the USA, who had run 1:45.0 to win the Commonwealth v USA 800 metres the previous month, Bodo Tümmler of West Germany, who had won gold in the 1500 metres and bronze in the 800 metres at the 1966 European Championships, and Tümmler's compatriot Franz-Josef Kemper, who was the European record holder over 800 metres and the co-holder of the world record for 1000 metres. In the final, Tümmler led out the field with a slow first lap of 54 seconds. Kemper joined him as they came around the final bend with Doubell in third place and Bell fourth. Kemper burst into the lead as they entered the final straight, but then Doubell accelerated past Tummler and closed in on Kemper. The German moved out from the inside of the track to about lane two, clashing elbows with Doubell, who describes what happened next as 'using my Aussie rules football training to help guide us back into lane one'.

Doubell and Kemper ran side by side for the last 80 metres, but Doubell defeated Kemper in a photo finish. It was his first major international win over 800 metres and his time of 1:46.7 was not just a personal best but a new Universiade record by a full second. It was also the fastest time ever run by an Australian. Doubell was now ranked equal eighth in the world over 800 metres.

Kemper told the Japanese media after the race that he thought he would win with 150 metres to go until Doubell came at him. Initially, he thought it had been Wade Bell threatening, but he had been wrong. It was Doubell. After a pause, Kemper added: 'I didn't know him.' This was a very significant run for Doubell. The snub from the British Commonwealth selectors had turned out to be a blessing in disguise.

Doubell's increasingly strong performances led to another invitation to compete in a series of indoor races in America in early 1968. Doubell was worried that the organisers might have blacklisted him after he withdrew from the series the previous year, but they clearly accepted he had a valid reason for not competing. The tour consisted of six races: two in Boston, two in New York, one in Philadelphia and one in Los Angeles. Doubell was looking forward to the tour immensely. One reason, of course, was that he would get to enjoy overseas travel with all his expenses paid. Doubell explained how this system worked in the amateur age in a column he wrote for *The Age* in January 1970. With Australia having converted to decimal currency in February 1966, he was now writing of dollars rather than pounds:

Who does pay for these trips? The answer is quite simple in that the meet promoters share the cost amongst themselves.

A single trip to America like the one I'm on now costs about $1800. The air fares cost about $1400 and living expenses about $400. Living expenses are given on the basis for $20 per day and cover all accommodation, meals, extra travelling expenses, etc. This, of course, is not an exorbitant amount when you consider the cost of living in America. Usually a fair bit has to come out of your own pocket unless you can persuade a number of people to take you out to dinner.

All of these expenses are controlled by the AAU [Amateur Athletic Union] of America, who coordinate the various meets. In about the middle of each year the meet directors ask who they would like to invite from overseas and the invitation is issued by the American AAU to the local AAU. Individual athletes are then notified and asked whether they are available to go and when they are available. The meet directors are then notified how many athletes are available and how much money they must contribute towards the personal cost.

While Doubell was looking forward to his tour of the US because of his love of travel, another significant factor was that he realised he would gain invaluable experience by testing himself against strong international competition in different conditions from those he was used to. The American indoor athletics season is run during the northern hemisphere's winter months, December to March, and is extremely popular with sports fans who sit very close to the athletes and the action. Today, the tracks are synthetic and each lap is 200 metres. In the 1960s, the tracks were timber, made of Canadian spruce or pine, and there were usually 11 laps to the mile. This obviously meant the straights were very short and so the ability to accelerate faster over a short distance than everyone else, which was Doubell's greatest asset, was critical. The wooden surface also provided a lot more bounce than the outdoor grass and cinder tracks of the time, a feature that Doubell enjoyed immensely. Most indoor tracks also had banked turns which could be used to an athlete's advantage during a race.

Doubell revelled in both the travel to and across the US, and the indoor format, winning all six of his races on this tour. He began on 14 January with a victory in the 1000 yards at the Knights of Columbus Games in Boston and his time of 2:07.7 was a meeting record. On 25 January, he won the 880 yards at the Millrose Indoor Games at New York's Madison Square Garden in 1:53.2, beating Canadian champion Bill Crothers. who had won the silver medal in the 800 metres at the 1964 Olympic Games. Two days later, Doubell was back in Boston, where he won the

Boston Amateur Athletics Union 1000 yards in 2:08.0 in front of a crowd estimated at 10,000. On 3 February, he won the 880 yards in New York in 1:51.5, just four-tenths of a second outside the meeting record. The next day he beat Noel Carroll of Ireland to win the 880 yards in 1:53.3 at the Philadelphia Track Classic in front of more than 7000 spectators. He then flew to Los Angeles and on 10 February won the 1000 yards at the Los Angeles Times Indoor Games in 2:08.2.

American Olympian Tom Farrell had last seen Doubell when he ran against him in Los Angeles in 1966 and he couldn't help but be impressed by his performances on the US indoor circuit:

He was coming off the Australian summer season, so he had good training behind him, and he won everything. He had a quick start, he was very fast and he had quick acceleration during the race. He was tanned, he was fast and he was good — he beat everyone that he raced against. He was a real hot shot. He was also a personable guy, a well-liked guy, and the press liked him. He really made a big hit in that indoor season.

Farrell was in the army at the time and his athletics training was focused entirely on the upcoming US Olympic trials 'because if you don't finish in the first three, you watch it on TV'. He was happy to spend as much time away from the army as possible as he competed on the indoor circuit:

We trained at Yale University, where they had an indoor facility, between meets on the East Coast. I remember hanging out with Ralph for a few weeks during that winter in New Haven, Connecticut. We would train and go to the movies and maybe have a few beers. Ralph was a happy-go-lucky guy and you could see that he had some brains as well as being loaded with talent. He was a fierce competitor, even in training.

A *New York Post* report provides an insight into the friendships formed between Doubell and some of the American athletes, including Farrell, while he competed on the US indoor circuit:

> It was all very friendly up in New Haven, where some of the class athletes in tonight's K of C [Knights of Columbus] meet were working out all week.
>
> Tom Farrell and Jim Kemp and Preston Davis and Australia's Ralph Doubell held the stopwatches for each other and paced each other through their laps. In another corner of Yale's huge field house, the Czechoslovakian contingent put its miler, Josef Odložil, through his paces ...
>
> The other day a reporter put through a phone call to Doubell, who's been sprinting away from everyone so far in his indoor races in this country.
>
> 'How do you feel about the K of C 880?' he was asked.
>
> 'What's the field?'
>
> 'Well, there's you and Noel Carroll from Ireland and Preston Davis ...'
>
> 'Preston Davis? You hear that, Preston?' (A howl in the background.) 'I don't think,' Doubell said after a pause, 'that Preston wants to run the 880 very much. I think he's in the 1000.'

A day later the K of C had the following announcement: 'Preston Davis says he's feeling sick and will run in the 1000 instead of the 880.'

Tom Farrell's observation that the US press liked Doubell was extremely accurate. Peter Tonge, sports writer at *The Christian Science Monitor*, wrote that Doubell was 'another track star in the making' after his first three indoor races in the USA:

When Australia's Ralph Doubell left his native Melbourne a few weeks ago it was a hot 90 degrees. But when he touched down in Boston not many hours later, the mercury was struggling to make zero.

In between, the slender Doubell had lost a lot of warm air, so he compromised by setting a hot pace in his track events — too hot for any of his opponents.

At this writing, the young Australian has competed three times since his arrival in the United States and won on each occasion ...

For a newcomer to a board track, Doubell adjusted remarkably quickly. 'I like it indoors,' he said. 'You've got to lean over a little more sharply around the bends, but that's not so difficult. I like the feeling of being close to the crowd. The atmosphere is great.'

The renowned Frank Litsky, who had been writing track and field and other sport for *The New York Times* for a decade and would do so for another four, was also impressed by Doubell's success in an unfamiliar environment:

Foreigners running on an American indoor track for the first time often finish their races — if they finish — with battle fatigue. They are elbowed, kicked, pushed, bumped and bruised. In short, they are treated like any other runners in a sport in which self-preservation is as important as speed and endurance.

So it was surprising when Ralph Doubell of Australia, in his first race on boards, won a 1000-yards run in Boston 10 days ago in 2 minutes 7.7 seconds. Only four men have ever run that event faster, and all had considerable experience on boards.

Litsky noted that when Doubell was asked, at a Track Writers Association lunch at Mamma Leone's in Manhattan, what he thought of indoor running, his answer was 'atypical'. He told them he liked it: 'I had heard stories about races getting pretty crowded and I did run into a few people,' Doubell said, 'but it wasn't all that bad.'

There is no doubt that Doubell's club running experience, during which he raced regularly over distances from 100 yards to the mile, helped him to be prepared for the rough and tumble of the US indoor circuit.

But Doubell had his eyes on a bigger prize than these American indoor victories. The last paragraph of one media report notes that he had arranged to return to Australia via Mexico City after his indoor races. 'I want to see for myself what the altitude and other conditions are in Mexico,' Doubell told the reporter.

However, there was still a lot of work for him to do before he would get the chance to compete at the 1968 Olympics. Despite his success at the 1967 Universiade in Tokyo and on the US indoor circuit, Doubell still had to run faster than the qualifying standard of 1:48.0 in the right time-period to qualify for the 800 metres in

Mexico City. His time of 1:46.7 in Tokyo was recorded more than a year before the Games, so it could not be relied upon.

DOUBELL HAD GRADUATED FROM the University of Melbourne with a Science degree at the end of 1967 and started work as soon as he returned from the US indoor tour. He was employed as a graduate by Shell, a company that had a tremendous record at the time of supporting young athletes. Herb Elliott and Kevan Gosper, who won a silver medal in the 4 x 400-metres relay at the 1956 Olympics, were just two of the many athletes who had been employed as graduates by Shell. Gosper later became Chairman and CEO of Shell in Australia.

Shell's interest in supporting athletes stemmed from its chairman, Lewis Luxton, who was born in Melbourne in 1910 and was a champion rower at Melbourne Grammar School before he went to Pembroke College at the University of Cambridge. In 1932, Luxton stroked the Cambridge VIII that defeated the Oxford VIII in the famous Boat Race and, as a result, he was selected to row for Great Britain in the 1932 Los Angeles Olympic Games.

Lewis Luxton's father, Sir Harold Luxton, was a long-serving member of the International Olympic Committee. When Sir Harold resigned from this role in May 1951, the IOC immediately announced that his son would be his successor. Lewis Luxton had played a key role in Melbourne winning the right to host the 1956 Olympics and he was an important figure in resolving the domestic political disputes that worried Avery Brundage and the IOC in the lead-up to the Games.

Lewis Luxton had joined Shell's Adelaide office in 1933 and he worked there until serving in the army during World War II. After the war, he rose through Shell's ranks to become managing director. In 1961, he became the first local chairman of Shell Australia.

Doubell's first job at Shell was an administrative role, and it was far from exciting. This hardly mattered to him, however, because now that his scholarship had finished he needed employment and his main focus was on qualifying for the Mexico City Olympics. Shell's offices were at the corner of Bourke and William Streets in the city centre and he would head to the University of Melbourne for training straight after work each evening, starting at about 5.30pm.

Shell was a very understanding employer, but starting full-time work was a big change from Doubell's university routine. Time was running out for him to qualify for Mexico City, but he didn't blame his new job. He just wasn't running well. He had shown enormous promise in Los Angeles in the race against Jim Ryun, but Kingston was a huge disappointment. The Universiade in Tokyo and the US indoor circuit were very positive, but running the Olympic qualifying time was proving more elusive than it should have been. Doubell didn't talk about it much at the time, but a key reason was the lack of strong competition in Australia. Doubell was not a front runner and he needed someone to push him over the first three-quarters of the race. There was no doubt Doubell could feel the pressure building, but Franz Stampfl remained composed and supportive. 'You'll get there,' he told Doubell. They knew it would probably happen, they just needed the right environment.

In late February 1968, Doubell was beaten by a young athlete named Graeme Gledhill in a close finish to the 880 yards at the Victorian Amateur Athletics Championships. Three weeks later, Gledhill ran a personal best of 1:49.4 to beat Doubell narrowly at a meeting at Olympic Park. The media were starting to seriously doubt whether Doubell would regain the form needed to qualify for the Olympic Games. At the Australian Amateur Athletics Championships in Sydney on 24 March, Doubell was the first Australian home in 1:49.3, but he was beaten by visiting American Preston Davis and his time was still well outside the Olympic qualifying standard.

Four days after the Australian Championships, Doubell had one last chance to qualify for Mexico City. The St Stephens Harriers had organised a special challenge meeting at Olympic Park in Melbourne on 28 March. Australia's Olympic selectors would make their final decisions after this meeting. There would be no more opportunities to qualify for Mexico City. It was literally now or never.

Doubell had rested well after the Australian Championships and the conditions were good. He knew he had to do something special and he felt confident. A runner he didn't know took the race out reasonably quickly with a first lap of 54 seconds. Gledhill then made his move early, with about a lap to go, and this maintained the good pace. Knowing he needed a fast time, Doubell made his move earlier than he usually would and he passed Gledhill well before the top of the final straight. From there, he raced away to win by a big margin, with Gledhill finishing second and Noel Clough third. *The Age* reported that the winning margin was '20 yards'. Critically, Doubell's time of 1:47.2 was not only one-tenth of a second better than his record for the best time run by an Australian on home soil, it was 0.8 seconds under the Olympic qualifying standard.

It had all come together at the right time. The relief was enormous. Running the qualifying time did not guarantee selection for the Olympic team, but he had done everything he could. When the team was officially approved and announced on 10 May, Doubell's name was on the list.

Many years later, Doubell discovered that the athlete who ran the fast first lap had done so deliberately to help him qualify. His name was Mark Hines. Doubell had never met him before the race and he hasn't met him since. Hines was a 22-year-old who had won the Associated Catholic Colleges mile four years earlier when he was a schoolboy and was now competing for Sandringham Athletics Club. He was a solid club competitor who had made the final of the Victorian 880-yards and mile championships several times. He recalls:

> I was getting changed before the race when some officials came up to me and said that one of the main objectives of the meeting was to get Ralph Doubell across the line to qualify for the Olympic Games. They said they thought it would help if someone ran a fast first lap and they asked me if I would be a 'rabbit' to help Ralph. I was happy to do it because I was a fringe competitor in that race, I was never going to challenge for a place. I ran about as fast as I could for the first lap and then my second lap was terrible! A New Zealander fell over in front of me and he was still able to get up and beat me.

Hines didn't know Doubell at the time, because they competed in different interclub competitions, and it was decades later that Doubell learned about Hines' role in his qualification for Mexico City. Doubell was looking to invest in property and he met with a real estate agent who recognised his name. The agent, Andrew Hines, revealed how his father had quietly told him one day how he had played a small part in Doubell's Olympic career by running a fast first lap at a night meeting at Olympic Park. Mark Hines ran for a few more years after that race before his athletics career ended when he injured his knee playing Australian rules football.

Would Doubell have run the qualifying time even if Hines hadn't agreed to be a 'rabbit'? Gledhill and Clough were also very keen to make the Olympic team and could have led out quickly, setting up Doubell for the time he needed. Doubell will never know for sure, but to this day he gives thanks to Mark Hines for agreeing anonymously to be a rabbit and run a selfless fast first lap at the St Stephens Harriers meeting.

Doubell's time at the World University Games in Tokyo had him ranked in the top 10 in the world and his success on the US indoor circuit in early 1968 showed he was a strong racer with superb acceleration. Nevertheless, many in Australia thought he was lucky to be picked for Australia's team for Mexico City. Even his friends doubted he would get beyond the heats.

Stampfl and Doubell were confident he had a chance to win.

CHAPTER 13

Altitude, Apartheid, an Invasion and a Massacre

On 18 October 1963, at the 60th meeting of the International Olympic Committee in Baden-Baden in Germany, Mexico City earned the right to host the Games of the XIX Olympiad by securing more votes than Detroit, Lyon and Buenos Aires. Detroit had been favoured to win the contest and so take the Olympic Games to the USA once again, but when IOC Chancellor Otto Mayer announced the results of the first ballot vote it appeared a decisive victory: Mexico City 30, Detroit 14, Lyon 12, Buenos Aires 2. In fact, it was close; if there had not been a winner in the first round of voting, the top two cities would have had a run-off and in that situation, and if Detroit had run second, it is believed that most if not all of the backers of Lyon and Buenos Aires would have supported the Americans.

The victory for Mexico City was significant for many reasons. It would be the first Olympic Games held in a 'developing country', the first in Latin America and the first in a Spanish-speaking country. For Mexico, it was the culmination of years of planning to convince the world, and the International Olympic Committee in particular, that Mexico was sufficiently stable and organised to successfully deliver an event of this magnitude. Winning the right to host the Games meant Mexico had the opportunity to prove that it belonged alongside the advanced nations of North America and Europe.

There were many sceptics in 1963, those who thought Mexico was a 'third world' country with a culture of *mañana* (tomorrow) that meant major problems were inevitable. But no one predicted that the 1968 Games would be one of the most controversial and politically charged in Olympic history.

Inspired by comments from concerned individuals such as Chris Brasher and Onni Niskanen, the first significant controversy to emerge was about how Mexico City's altitude might impinge on athletes' performances. The city is located on a plateau that is 2250 metres (7380 feet) above sea level, and many worried the thin air would at least disadvantage athletes from 'low lying' nations, and quite possibly be a significant threat to the health of competitors in endurance events. Mexico City had hosted the 1955 Pan-American Games and critics remembered how a number of athletes had collapsed during or after their events while others complained of feeling abnormally exhausted. The Mexican authorities did their best to calm concerns in the lead-up to the vote at Baden Baden and in the years that followed. They then arranged for an exhibition competition, which became known as the 'Little Olympics', to be held in Mexico City in 1965, almost exactly three years before the real thing. Sixteen nations accepted the invitation to compete, their officials and medical experts keen to observe performances and conduct tests in the Olympic city. Most came away believing that altitude would definitely be an issue, at the very least in the distance races, at the Mexico City Games.

Ron Clarke competed in the 5000 metres at the Little Olympics and finished one second behind Mohamed Gammoudi of Tunisia, who had won the silver medal in the 10,000 metres at the 1964 Tokyo Olympics, with Clarke taking home the bronze. In his autobiography, *The Unforgiving Minute*, Clarke says his time of 14:41.6 was 'the slowest I had run since my youth'. He recalls what happened after the pair crossed the finish line:

Immediately the race was over 'Zim' [Dr I. Zimmerman, Clarke's doctor and sometime manager] and the French doctors descended on us. Both Mohamed and I were suffering from pain in the ears and behind the eyes and we both had palpitations. My face was an ashen grey. We both recovered and there was no evidence that the run had any lasting harmful effect, except for one disturbing feature. Back in Melbourne it was discovered that there was a sixteen per cent drop in my haemoglobin, the pigment in the red corpuscles of the blood carrying oxygen. Whether the deficiency was directly related to my experience in Mexico City wasn't clear. But there was no weakening of my form. Two days after my return home, I ran a time trial over 5000 metres at the University Oval, expecting that, without the spur of competition, the time would be slow. I ran 13:40.3, the second fastest time ever run in Australia, which proved that my

Mexico race was a peak performance. A few weeks later, I also broke the world records for the one-hour run and 20,000 metres at Geelong. The conclusion was inescapable. Mexico City was going to present a sizeable problem for distance athletes in 1968 and those who shrugged it off as inconsequential were being remarkably foolish.

Billy Mills, the American who had sprinted past Gammoudi and Clarke to win the gold medal in the 10,000 metres at Tokyo, said after he had run in the Little Olympics:

There is this awful sensation of breathing deeply and not being able to pull enough air into your lungs. When you run, you feel like you've never run before. I'm cruising along on the practice track and I get ready to give it the final kick and I turn on that last big burst — and that last big burst isn't there. I don't know where it went, but it isn't there.

The British Olympic Association sent a research team to the Little Olympics and their testing focused on 5000 metre runners. The report concluded:

1. Performances in endurance events would be reduced, since maximum oxygen intake is lessened;
2. Four weeks would seem to be the minimum acceptable period that should be allowed for suitable acclimatisation;
3. There was some evidence that athletes other than those in endurance events would benefit by preliminary acclimatisation; and

4. There was no evidence from these tests that there is any risk of permanent injury, provided competitors acclimatise.

However, many people with experience in athletics refused to accept the assurances of the Mexican authorities or the findings of organisations such as the British Olympic Association. In April 1966, an open letter signed by 26 British Olympic medallists, including Chris Brasher, was published in *The Times*. It read in part: 'Mexico chose deliberately to ignore the problems of altitude when putting forward its candidature ... The fundamental principle of the Olympic movement, which is that all participants should compete on equal terms, has been completely subverted.' The letter argued that athletes who lived at high altitude, or who had been training for long periods at high-altitude camps, would enjoy an enormous advantage and therefore endurance events should be held at a 'low level' venue.

The IOC met in Rome at the end of April and confirmed that those who 'run long distances will be at a disadvantage because of the rarefied air'. The IOC ruled that competitors would not be permitted to train at altitudes higher than those to which they were accustomed for more than four weeks during the three months preceding the Mexico City opening ceremony. The IOC noted that 'to break this rule would be a gross breach of good sportsmanship, and it is sure that no one connected with the Olympic movement would wish to be guilty in any way of taking an unfair advantage over the other competitors'.

It would be impossible to police this rule, of course. A year earlier, France had built an altitude acclimatisation training centre in the village of Font Romeu in the Pyrenees at an estimated cost of

£8 million. It featured two tracks, dormitories, research laboratories and permanent medical staff and was used by athletes from across Europe. Ron Clarke was so concerned about the conditions in Mexico City that he sold his business and moved to Font Romeu with his wife and three children. The Russians established training sites at Alma-Ata (now Almaty) in Kazakhstan and at Yerevan, the capital of Armenia, both situated more than 3000 metres (10,000 feet) above sea level. Japan had a training centre at Mount Norikura and American athletes headed to the Rocky Mountains. In the lead-up to the Games, the USA used its proximity to Mexico and its variety of high-altitude training camps as an opportunity to build relationships with other countries. The US State Department issued a memorandum to all diplomatic posts on 3 July 1968 that encouraged nations to send their athletes to train at centres in Arizona, Utah and Wyoming. West Germany, Norway, Sweden, Austria and India were some of the nations that accepted this invitation. It was an interesting example of Cold War diplomacy – and it also allowed the American athletes to check out some of their competitors.

The Mexico City organising committee did make one concession in relation to altitude. The equestrian competition was moved to Oaxtepec, which is 1300 metres above sea level, or nearly 1000 metres lower than Mexico City. One member of the International Equestrian Federation explained that 'horses are inclined to go on well beyond the prudent limit of effort' while another said, 'They do not have the common sense that humans do.' Whether this observation was correct or not, humans would compete in endurance events at Mexico City despite the protests of Brasher and those who agreed with him.

The political atmosphere in Mexico and in other parts of the world also provided a series of major headaches for the organising committee.

In early 1968, almost 50 nations threatened to withdraw from the Games if South Africa was reinstated to the Olympic family and allowed to compete. South Africa had been excluded from the 1964 Winter Olympics in Innsbruck, the 1964 Summer Olympics in Tokyo and the 1968 Winter Olympics in Grenoble. The IOC had been reluctant to suspend South Africa because, in its view, banning South Africa because of its apartheid system of government would acknowledge that sport and politics were intertwined. South Africa's exclusion from the Tokyo Games was based on its contravention of the Olympic Code and particularly the principle that there be no discrimination against a country or person on the grounds of race, religion or political affiliation. South Africa clearly violated this principle because black and white athletes could not compete against each other. The South African team could therefore not be selected fairly. It was a legalistic but important distinction, because it meant the IOC could say South Africa was excluded because of a fault of the country's sports regime, not the government.

The South African Government and its Olympic Committee were extremely keen for South African athletes to be allowed to compete in Mexico City and they lobbied hard to achieve this goal. They promised they would send one team comprised of both black and white athletes who would wear the same uniform and march under the same flag. The team would stay in the same quarters and eat at the same table. Laws that existed in South Africa that prevented blacks and whites playing on the same field would be waived for all international sporting events, including the Olympic Games.

In September 1967, the IOC sent three representatives — Lord Killanin of Ireland, a white Kenyan named Reginald Alexander and Sir Ade Ademola of Nigeria — to examine what was actually happening in South Africa. The trio found that interracial competition was prohibited within the country, which meant the South African Olympic team would be selected after separate trials were held — one for white athletes and one for black athletes. The selection committee was made up of four white representatives and four black representatives. The IOC delegates also observed that sporting infrastructure for black athletes was far inferior to that enjoyed by members of the white community. Nevertheless, their report found that while there was limited progress on the ground in South Africa, there was 'an acceptable basis for a multi-racial team to [be sent to] the Mexico Olympic Games'.

The IOC voted on the South Africa issue at a meeting during the Winter Olympics in Grenoble, France in February 1968. The committee members voted 41–30 in favour of allowing South Africa to compete in Mexico City, because it had been encouraged by the changes in the South African system and the progress made towards selecting a multi-racial team based on merit. Following the vote, IOC President Avery Brundage said:

There has been a lot of talk about underprivileged non-whites in South Africa. Now, for the first time something has been done for them and they have been given an opportunity to appear in the Olympic Games on the same basis as everyone else. Who would have thought it possible a few years ago? It is a great step forward that could only be accomplished by the International Olympic Committee.

The decision to re-admit South Africa was met with a range of emotions, from joy among some South African athletes to disbelief and anger in many countries around the world. Within days, several African countries, and then the Supreme Council for Sport in Africa, which represented 32 nations, threatened an African boycott if South Africa took part. A number of other countries, including the USSR, strongly criticised the decision to allow South Africa to compete in Mexico City. The Soviets stopped short of explicitly supporting a boycott, however the door was left open to do so. The IOC knew that the USSR's position would inevitably be followed by Eastern European countries within its sphere of influence. The Scandinavian countries were also considering their position. The media reported the story prominently and enthusiastically. There was intense pressure on Brundage and the IOC.

Brundage initially refused to budge but ultimately, as the potential support for an African boycott grew even larger, he had to find a way to retreat. On 21 April the Executive Board of the IOC met in Lausanne and sent a telegram to all its members. The telegram said that the Executive Board was 'unanimously of the opinion that it would be most unwise for a South African team to participate in the Games of the XIX Olympiad'. It continued: 'Therefore, the Executive Board strongly recommends that you endorse this unanimous proposal to withdraw the invitation to these Games.' Forty-seven members voted to withdraw the invitation while 16 were against doing so and eight abstained. Three days later, Brundage announced the news at a press conference, emphasising that the IOC was 'not bowing to threats or pressures of any kind'. Less than six months before the Opening Ceremony, a debilitating boycott had been averted.

The controversy around South Africa's involvement in the Olympic Games resonated strongly with many African American athletes. From the mid-1950s, the civil rights movement in the US had gained momentum as it sought to end racial segregation and discrimination against African Americans. Sport played an important role in the drive for African American rights, because a number of black athletes enjoyed success and popularity. By the mid-'60s, however, sport began to be seen as just another example of inequality in America. Most black athletes found they were treated badly by various systems dominated by white men. Those who won scholarships to university were often made to feel unwelcome in the fraternity system or were discriminated against when they sought housing. They were excluded from social events. The universities often assumed black athletes did not want to obtain an education and they were placed in easy courses that did not benefit their future, or they were not expected to graduate at all.

Against this background, the Olympic Project for Human Rights (OPHR) was established in October 1967 by Harry Edwards, a sociology instructor and athletics coach at San José State University who was then in his mid-20s. Edwards had been an outstanding athlete in his youth and knew from personal experience that this did not help when it came to gaining entry to a white fraternity house, off-campus housing and even restaurants. OPHR consisted of mostly African American community leaders and athletes and its aim was to protest effectively against racial segregation in the USA and in other countries, such as South Africa, and against racism in sport in general. OPHR's founding statement included the words:

We must no longer allow this country to use ... a few 'Negroes' to point out to the world how much progress she has made in solving her racial problems when the oppression of Afro-Americans is greater than it ever was. We must no longer allow the Sports World to pat itself on the back as a citadel of racial justice when the racial injustices of the sports industry are infamously legendary ...

Any black person who allows himself to be used in the above matter ... is a traitor to his country because he allows racist whites the luxury of resting assured that those black people in the ghettos are there because that is where they want to be ...

So we ask why should we run in Mexico only to crawl home?

The IOC's readmission of South Africa in early 1968 had, unsurprisingly, angered the OPHR and its supporters and Edwards advocated a boycott of the Mexico City Olympic Games unless four conditions were met:

1. South Africa and Rhodesia were to be 'uninvited' from the Games;
2. Muhammad Ali's world heavyweight boxing title, which had been taken from him because he refused to fight in Vietnam, must be restored;
3. Avery Brundage, whom OPHR regarded as a white supremacist because he had done nothing to stop Hitler using the 1936 Olympic Games to promote Nazi Germany, must step down as President of the IOC; and
4. More African American coaches should be hired by the USA team.

Their position was supported by many African American leaders, including Dr Martin Luther King, but not all black athletes agreed. The great Jesse Owens, who had embarrassed Hitler at the 1936 Berlin Olympic Games by winning four gold medals, opposed the boycott:

> We shattered this so-called Aryan supremacy then by our own supremacy and by standing and saluting the American flag. I feel that the deeds of an individual are far more potent than a boycott ... I believe you contribute more by entering than staying out.

Rafer Johnson, who had won silver in the decathlon at the 1956 Melbourne Olympics and gold in the same event four years later in Rome, wrote in his autobiography *The Best That I Can Be*:

> What you have to ask yourself is, 'What good is it going to do? Is it going to help housing? Is it going to help education? Is it going to help job opportunities?' I don't see how a boycott of the Olympics is relevant at all to these problems.

The Governor of California at the time, Ronald Reagan, said: 'I disapprove greatly of what Edwards is trying to accomplish. Edwards is contributing nothing toward harmony between the races.' Avery Brundage was also critical:

> There is no discrimination whatsoever because of race, religion, colour or political affiliations ... A boycott would only disadvantage the athletes themselves. I don't think any of these

boys would be foolish enough to demonstrate at the Olympic Games. If they do, they'll be promptly sent home.

The assassination of Dr King on 4 April 1968 led to increased support for the OPHR, but ultimately even athletes aligned with the organisation decided not to boycott the Games. One reason was that there was not a unanimous view among the OPHR members that the proposed boycott should go ahead. If only half the African American athletes in the Olympic team took that action, it would be ineffectual if not meaningless. There were plenty of others who were fit and ready to take the place of any boycotters. The fact that they had all trained hard for years to get the invaluable opportunity to compete at an Olympics was also a factor. The athletes ultimately realised that the globally televised event would be watched by millions of people around the world and that this would provide an opportunity to express their views through some sort of protest.

Meanwhile, a new international crisis was threatening the Games. On 21 August 1968, less than two months before the opening ceremony, the USSR led an invasion of Czechoslovakia that was supported by its Warsaw Pact partners East Germany, Poland, Hungary and Bulgaria. The motivation for this aggression can be traced to January 1968, when Alexander Dubček was elected First Secretary of the Communist Party of Czechoslovakia. The USSR had dominated Czechoslovakia since the end of World War II and Moscow did not approve of reforms introduced by Dubček during what became known as the 'Prague Spring'. These reforms included some decentralisation of the economy and increased freedom of speech, freedom of the press and freedom of movement. After some attempts at negotiation, the Soviets lost patience and a force of more than 200,000 Soviet and Warsaw Pact troops and 2000 tanks marched into Czechoslovakia.

The invasion of Czechoslovakia led to calls for the Soviet Union and its Warsaw Pact allies to be excluded from the Olympic Games. One of the loudest voices making these calls was Emil Zátopek, the Czech Locomotive who won the 10,000 metres and came second in the 5000 metres at the 1948 London Olympics and won the superhuman treble of the 5000 metres, 10,000 metres and marathon at Helsinki in 1952. Zátopek was well known internationally and highly regarded, and he convinced the Czechoslovak Olympic Committee to address a telegram to the IOC calling for the Soviet Union to be excluded. No official action was taken, however, because the IOC said no official request was ever received.

Another major political issue that threatened the Games came from within Mexico itself. The opening ceremony was scheduled for 12 October. Only 10 days before, about 10,000 people gathered in the Plaza de las Tres Culturas (Square of the Three Cultures) in the Tlatelolco section of Mexico City. There had been nationwide strikes and increasing social unrest during 1968 and in late August as many as 200,000 people attended student-led protests. The Mexican Government did not want anything like that to occur during the upcoming Olympic Games — and to be reported by the world's media.

On the evening of 2 October, the crowd in the Plaza de las Tres Culturas gathered to protest against the government and the army, listen to speeches and shout slogans such as 'We don't want Olympics, we want revolution!' The Mexican economy was struggling, and unions, farmers and students thought the huge cost of hosting the Olympic Games was wrong in these circumstances. They also called for reforms that included the abolition of the *granaderos*, or riot police, and an end to laws that enabled authorities to imprison anyone attending gatherings of three or more people.

As night fell, two helicopters flew overhead as an estimated 5000 soldiers and 200 tankettes surrounded the plaza. A couple of flares appeared above the helicopters and then a gun was fired from somewhere. This caused panic and chaos — and more gunfire. Soldiers continued searching apartments around the plaza for protesters well into the night. Details of what became known as the Tlatelolco Massacre remain controversially unconfirmed, but it is estimated between 30 (the government's estimate) and more than 300 students and civilians were killed. More than 1000 people were arrested.

A large number of international athletes and officials were already in Mexico City at this time, because they were acclimatising before competing. They were aware of the heavy security presence on the streets, but few heard details about the massacre. The government line was that the protesters had fired first and the army had reacted appropriately. The government-controlled media toed this line. Meanwhile, Jean-Paul Sartre and Bertrand Russell, internationally renowned philosophers, writers and political activists, issued a joint statement following the Tlatelolco Massacre:

> The Mexican government has behaved with a barbarity comparable only to the massacres carried out by the occupying Nazi troops in Europe or by napalming American planes in Vietnam. Throughout the world people have been aroused to passionate anger and alarm. We express our profound solidarity with the heroic Mexican students. We ask people,

organisations and nations to boycott the Olympic Games ... Almost immediately after this ambush-massacre occurred, the Mexican Government met with the Olympic Committee and said: 'The intervention of the forces of order have assured calm and there will be no trouble to prevent the Olympics from taking place.' The same day, the United States State Department declared: 'The disturbances in Mexico City affected only a small part of the population and order is now restored.' There is a clear complicity between the United States and Mexican Governments to meet popular resistance with massacre. If the Olympic Committee agrees to hold the Games in Mexico, it stands guilty of complicity in this crime.

The IOC said it had every confidence in the Mexican Government and the Games would go on as planned.

The dangers of competing in endurance events at altitude, the apartheid policies of the South African Government, the civil rights movement in the USA, the Soviet invasion of Czechoslovakia, and a massacre on the streets of Mexico City had all threatened the Games of the XIX Olympiad. The criticisms continued, but threats of boycotts were all averted. The opening ceremony would take place as planned on 12 October.

CHAPTER 14

Go Out and Win the Next Three Races

After he qualified for the Olympic Games, Doubell's training went to another level. He was still working full-time at Shell and he would make his way to the University of Melbourne at the end of a day in the office. He would do his Franz Stampfl-prescribed workout, running about 30 to 40 times around the track, at varying speeds, night after night. The heavy workload took its toll and for about three months leading up to the Games Doubell battled an ongoing Achilles tendon injury. He sought treatment from a young physiotherapist named David Zuker, whom he knew from the days when Zuker used to run with the Stampfl squad just to keep fit.

Zuker started practising physiotherapy in 1962 and 56 years later he is still treating patients daily in his rooms on Collins Street in

Melbourne. He would become a pioneer of Australian physiotherapy and in 1987 be awarded a Medal of the Order of Australia (OAM) for services to sports medicine and physiotherapy. Soon after he started practising, Zuker was working with an orthopaedic surgeon who specialised in spinal fusion. He couldn't find much that had been written on the subject of 'bad backs', so Zuker decided to produce a paper himself. He thought he should study some good backs before he could write about bad backs and he believed he would find plenty of excellent examples in the ballet world.

Zuker approached the Australian Ballet School. 'At that stage,' he says, 'it was in a converted brothel in Brunswick Street and I found that no one had ever looked after the ballet dancers. So I offered them my services.' He began working for the Australian Ballet School, and soon also the Australian Ballet Company, and 'this gave me insights into what the human body could do'. He also offered his services to the Fitzroy Football Club. It wasn't long before footballers from other clubs, as well as a range of other sportsmen and sportswomen, came to seek his advice. His reputation was growing by word of mouth.

'Physiotherapy used to be heat, massage and exercise,' Zuker says. 'I looked at different ways of doing things.'

Zuker found a valuable mentor in Howard Toyne, who worked as a doctor with the Australian Olympic teams in 1956 and 1964 and was Australia's Chief Medical Officer at the 1968 Games. Toyne was central to obtaining the funding and organising the testing of Australian athletes at Falls Creek in 1965, as they sought to prepare for the altitude of Mexico City. Toyne was a founding member of the Australian Sports Medicine Federation and served on the executive of the Fédération Internationale de Médecine Sportive

(International Federation of Sports Medicine, or FIMS) from 1972 to 1982. Zuker says he learned a huge amount from Toyne and his dedication was rewarded when he was appointed the first Head Physiotherapist of an Australian Olympic team, for the Montreal Games in 1976. 'I looked after the whole team on my own,' Zuker says matter-of-factly. Zuker was also the Australian Olympic team's Head Physiotherapist in 1980, 1984 and 1988 and he has worked closely with several Oceania Olympic Committees.

When Doubell came to him for treatment of his Achilles injury only a few months before the Mexico City Games, Zuker knew it was a difficult injury to treat and that they didn't have much time:

We considered hyperbaric treatment, because we knew the Russians were using it, but it was unproven at that time and we didn't go ahead with it. He had intensive ultrasound treatment with me, at least twice a day, and we did a lot of icing. He also did non-weight bearing running in the Beaurepaire Pool at the University.

Doubell only rested from running for two weeks and during that time he would do his pool sessions and lie on the bed, hoping for the best, while Zuker gave him ultrasound treatment. When he did resume running, he ran in flat shoes instead of spikes. About one month before leaving for Mexico, Doubell put his spikes back on for speed sessions and recorded some fast times. He did many time trials but didn't compete in any races. He ran a 440-yards time trial in 49.9 and it felt easy. He also ran a three-quarter mile time trial in 3:01.8. Doubell and Stampfl had been concerned that he hadn't had time to do enough speed work in this critical preparation period, but his Achilles wasn't flaring up and this, combined with his good time trials, increased his confidence.

Bill Hooker, who did a lot of interval training with Doubell in the lead-up to Mexico City, recalls Doubell's approach clearly:

> I remember going down to the track only a week or two before they were due to leave and he was out there running this frenetic session. He said: 'I'm either going to burst this Achilles or I'm going to get on the plane ready to go.' That was pretty typical of him. He was very focused on his training and how to go about things.

In the official Olympic film of the Mexico City 800-metres final, made by the legendary Bud Greenspan, Stampfl paints a vivid picture of Doubell's injury. 'On the plane, his foot puffed up to *enormous* proportions,' Stampfl tells the filmmaker dramatically in his thick Austrian accent, expanding his hands as if holding an inflating balloon. 'And he thought, well this is it. I've had it. He came into Mexico City and within a day the whole lot disappeared! The swelling, the pain, everything has gone!'

Doubell, wearing a suit and tie, spoke much more quietly and matter-of-factly when he was interviewed by Greenspan:

> I tried on spikes about three weeks before I left and ran a number of good time trials. I was as fit as I thought I could be. And once I got to Mexico, my training there was excellent and I felt good.

The spikes Doubell wore in Mexico City were Adidas Azteca Gold, the latest running shoe developed by the famous German company for the 1968 Olympic Games. As the name implies, the shoes were bright gold in colour with the three black Adidas stripes on the sides. One of the features of the Azteca Gold promoted by Adidas was that the upper and most of the outsole were made of kangaroo leather.

The rivalry between Adidas and Puma was extraordinary at that time. The companies were owned by two intensely competitive brothers, Adolf and Rudolf Dassler, who were originally partners in a family sports shoe company called, as you would expect, 'Dassler Brothers' (or, to be precise, 'Dassler Brothers Sports Shoe Factory'). The brothers worked together until the mid 1940s in the small German town of Herzogenaurach, but their feuds escalated and they decided to go their separate ways in 1948. Adolf combined the letters of his nick name 'Adi' with the first three letters of his surname and called his new business 'Adidas'. His brother originally took a slightly more abbreviated approach and called his new business Ruda, before changing it to the more evocative Puma. They built factories on opposite sides of the river Aurach and the town of Herzogenaurach became split along fraternal lines — you worked for either Adidas or Puma.

At the time of the Mexico City Games, Adidas and Puma were the two leading sports shoe companies in the world and they battled fiercely to convince the best athletes to wear their brand. It was invaluable advertising if the company's shoes were worn by an Olympic champion and both had reputedly been making secret payments to Olympic athletes for years. Adidas took its tactics to a new level by building a factory in Mexico before the Games. This meant they received special dispensation to import shoes in the lead-up to, and during, the Games. Puma, on the other hand, found difficulty getting their shoes through Mexican customs.

It was widely believed that Adidas played a role in Puma's problems. The lid was finally taken off the worst-kept secret in athletics when *Sports Illustrated* ran a remarkable story by their investigative reporter John Underwood that alleged that athletes in Mexico City were receiving brown envelopes stuffed with cash, or simply cash stuffed in the shoes they received, to wear either Puma or Adidas shoes. Underwood wrote of 'cash payoffs totalling an estimated $US100,000, in addition to approximately $US350,000 worth of equipment [that was] given away in the Olympic year'. Doubell had heard the stories, but he was too low profile to be a target, other than to be one of the many athletes who received their shoes for free.

Most of the members of the Australian team, Doubell among them, arrived in Mexico City 26 days before the Games to adapt and acclimatise to the altitude, just as had been recommended three years earlier by the Australian Sports Medicine Federation following the research conducted in conjunction with the University of Melbourne's Physiology School. Doubell, who had been one of the human guinea pigs who volunteered to participate in the research at Falls Creek in 1965, remained unconcerned about the effect of the conditions on his performance. Almost everyone agreed that athletes competing in races up to 800 metres would not be impacted. 'I believed the issue would have two types of effect on athletes, physiological and psychological, and that a lot of athletes would be defeated by the psychological effect,' Doubell says. 'That is, they would be too worried about the threat that the altitude *might* have an impact on them.'

Ray Weinberg was the coach of the Australian athletics team in Mexico City. He had represented Australia in the 110-metres hurdles at the 1948 London Olympic Games and finished sixth in the final of that event at the 1952 Helsinki Olympics. He also won a silver medal in the 120-yards hurdles at the 1950 British Empire Games in Auckland. Aged 92 when interviewed for this book just weeks before he died on 30 May 2018, Weinberg remembered clearly how the coaches were concerned about the impact of the altitude:

> When we arrived at the Village, our quarters were on the third floor. I instructed the team to put their bags in the lift and to walk up the stairs. I told them to use the stairs every time they went up to their room. I wanted to use anything that would help them adjust to the altitude. On the first day, no one made it to the first floor.

Paul Jenes was 25 years old when he travelled to Mexico City for the Olympics. He had been a keen sports fan from a young age and fell in love with athletics when, just 13 years old, he was lucky enough to watch a day of athletics at the 1956 Melbourne Games. Jenes describes himself as an average athlete, competing mainly in hurdles and jumping events as a schoolboy and then for the YMCA and Ringwood athletics clubs. However, his love of athletics would see him become an official, selector and statistician. In fact, he was an Australian national selector for 17 years, including seven years as chairman. In Mexico City, he watched every session of the athletics as well as some basketball and swimming. Jenes remembers clearly the impact of the altitude on those visitors, like him, who weren't used to it:

> When I went to Mexico City I was in the armed forces and I was in a pretty fit state. I remember I had to run to catch a bus.

It was only about 100 yards but when I got on the bus I was in oxygen debt. That's when it hit me that some athletes were going to really suffer because of the altitude.

Weinberg was popular with the athletes and an important source of support and advice for those whose coaches could not afford to attend the Games. 'I travelled around Australia before the Games to meet as many athletes and their coaches as possible, to get a handle on their training schedules and find out what I could do to make it easier for them in Mexico City,' he explained. 'I sent a form to the coaches, asking them to give me details of each athlete's character and personality so I had some understanding of them.'

Weinberg had seen Doubell run many times before the 1968 Olympics, but he didn't know him very well. Unlike some other athletes, he didn't need to monitor Doubell's preparation and training after they arrived in the Olympic Village. 'Ralph was incredibly well managed by Franz Stampfl and he had a strong group from the Stampfl squad around him, so that made my job easier,' he said.

'I knew what I had to do, Stampfl made sure of that,' Doubell remembers. 'But I also knew Weinberg was there if I needed him.'

When the Australian athletics team travelled to Mexico City, it had a manager, Jim Howlin, as well as Weinberg as coach. However, tragedy struck while they were in the Olympic Village. Weinberg explained:

I was sharing a room with Jim and I woke one morning and spoke to him, but there was no response. I went immediately downstairs and got our team doctors, Dr Toyne and Dr

[Brian] Corrigan, and they came straight up. Jim was taken in an ambulance to hospital, but from what we could tell he passed away in the room before he went. It was dreadful. From that time on, I was the manager as well as the coach ...

The tightness of the Stampfl squad helped Weinberg to fulfil his expanded duties:

They all knew each other so well that if one was competing and I couldn't get there, because I couldn't be in two places at once, I could ask one of the Stampfl group to make themselves available to keep an eye on their mate and get them whatever they needed. That was done again and again and again. The camaraderie was outstanding ...

Weinberg soon began organising training sessions on the Olympic Village athletics track:

We were one of the first teams to arrive and we were fortunate because some competitions were staged on the Village track as others arrived — the Germans, the Italians and the Cubans. This was important for our athletes because we were competing out of season and they hadn't had much competition before we left. A number of our athletes started to emerge at this time, with Peter Norman, Maureen Caird and the jumpers performing well ...

Soon, however, the Village track became very crowded as more and more athletes arrived in Mexico City. Weinberg set about finding an alternative venue:

I managed to find a hidden track, near the Olympic Stadium, and we used to train there. I used to get the team together, get them on a bus and let them do their training. We had it very much to ourselves until the England team discovered it as well, but it was still much better than the crowded one in the Village.

While there has always been a lot of focus on the effects of altitude on performance at Mexico City, there hasn't been nearly as much discussion about the fact that this was the first Olympics to be run on a synthetic, all-weather 'Tartan' surface instead of the cinder tracks used previously. The name Tartan was selected by the manufacturer, 3M, which made the globally known Scotch Tape. They wanted to continue the Gaelic theme with the name of their products, even for something as different as a running track.

Few Australian athletes had any experience on Tartan tracks before they arrived in Mexico City. Doubell, and others in the team including 200-metres sprinter Peter Norman, enjoyed the bounce it gave them. They thought it was a fantastic surface. Another benefit of Tartan was that it remained in excellent condition after rain. In comparison, a cinder track would become waterlogged and much slower. This feature of the Tartan surface would be very relevant in Mexico City, which experienced a lot of rain and some severe thunderstorms during the athletics competition. For the final of the 800 metres, there would be puddles on some parts of the track.

Doubell took a few days to recover after he arrived in the Olympic Village, mainly to help get over jet lag. One of his roommates, Tony Sneazwell, remembers that they went out to find a good bar very soon after they settled in. Doubell then started track work, beginning conservatively and gradually building up to his normal intensity, although he only trained once a day. Most importantly, his Achilles injury had fully healed and he could do some speed work. He immediately felt good and his training times were impressive. He ran 21.6 for 200 metres, 46.4 for 400 metres and 1:16.5 for 600 metres.

Everything was going smoothly and Doubell didn't feel under pressure. He was out of the limelight. In the lead-up to the Games, most in the Australian media did not think he was even a medal contender. The exception was *Track and Field News*, which thought he was a possible medallist, even a gold medallist. But not many people read *Track and Field News*. Australian Chef de Mission Judy Patching was asked by the *Canberra Times* who he believed were the team's leading chances and he replied, 'Possibly Ron Clarke, Derek Clayton, [equestrian's] Bill Roycroft, yachting and hockey.' At his last intense training session, about a week before his heat, Doubell ran ten 300-metre sprints. They felt fast and a French journalist, who was not only observing but timing him, was extremely impressed with what he saw on his stopwatch. Nobody else had much interest in him.

The Olympic Village was a high-rise apartment block a long way from the stadium. It wasn't luxurious, but there was plenty of space. Doubell's roommates were both friends from the Stampfl squad: high jumper Tony Sneazwell and Allen Crawley, who had won a bronze medal in the 4 x 110 yards at the 1966 British Empire and Commonwealth Games in Kingston and was competing in the long jump in Mexico City.

Sneazwell first became friends with Doubell on the Melbourne University Athletics Club's 1963 trip to the Intervarsity competition in Adelaide, when Doubell, in Sneazwell's words, 'was just beginning to blossom as a runner and was working very hard to get better'. They were regular roommates from then until the end of their athletics careers. Asked why they were usually billeted together, Sneazwell says:

> I think it was because of our position within the Stampfl squad. We were both at the upper end of the group in terms of our standing, based on our achievements, and we just got on very well together …

Sneazwell says there was a much better team spirit within the Australian athletics team in Mexico City than there had been in Tokyo four years earlier, partly because it was a smaller team.

> It was a really tight-knit group. Four weeks is a long time to arrive in a city before a competition. We would train each day, but we would also visit the local markets, do some sightseeing and occasionally go to a restaurant. The food was good in the Village, but Ralph and I would go into town for some variety. We would order something like steak and salad. I did get Montezuma's Revenge [traveller's diarrhoea] for a day or so — I think everyone did at some stage.

The atmosphere in the city was wonderful for visiting sports fans, according to Paul Jenes. 'The Mexicans were fantastic,' he recalls fondly. 'There is a lot of poverty there but they are lovely people and they were very welcoming. The place hummed all night! There were bands on the street corners, great food and I loved it.'

The Australian team had been strongly advised by the team's Chief Medical Officer, Howard Toyne, to completely avoid drinking

Mexico City's water in case they caught Montezuma's Revenge. Weinberg remembers that the management team brought a water filtration system with them, but they insisted that all athletes be extremely careful with any water. This included closing their mouths in the shower in case they swallowed too many drops. 'It was very tempting, after a hard workout and with water from the shower running over your mouth, to take a drink,' Weinberg explained. The athletes were advised to use alternatives to the water for their oral hygiene.

'That's what I did,' Doubell recalls. 'Every day, I cleaned my teeth with either Coca-Cola or beer.'

Dr Toyne and the management team also stressed that everyone should be very selective about what they ate. Doubell remembers the food in the Village as being very good, with the dining hall divided into sections to cater for the different diets of the various countries. Australia was in the same section as the United Kingdom and the Europeans. There were plenty of options for Doubell's favoured meat-and-three-veg diet and a great supply of avocados, which were an expensive luxury in Australia at the time. Not everyone was as fortunate as Doubell, however. Peter Watson was stricken by Montezuma's Revenge the night before his 1500-metres heat and performed well below his best. 'It knocked the stuffing out of him,' said Weinberg. 'I remember finding him wandering the corridors at night trying to get some sort of movement into himself.'

Doubell spent a lot of the time in the three-and-a-half weeks leading up to his heat sitting around the Village and focusing on his plans for a three-race program. The 800 metres would involve a series of heats, two semi-finals and a final, run on consecutive days 'These are not exciting trips!' he points out. 'Different athletes handle the pressure of an Olympic Games environment very differently. Some feel the need to promote themselves while others keep quiet.' Doubell fell into the latter category, spending time with his teammates, particularly Sneazwell, and preparing himself for the biggest race of his life. He never trained more than once a day for the first few weeks and then began to taper, not training at all in the five days before his heat.

Paul Jenes says that Doubell's teammates could see that he was peaking at the right time:

> He had been injured just before the Games but the enormous training base he had behind him meant he was in great condition. I was good friends with Phil May [who would come sixth in the triple jump in Mexico City] and he told me that Ralph used to join him and [sprinters] Peter Norman and Greg Lewis doing 150-metre and 200-metre sprint sessions. Phil said that Ralph was starting to run over the top of them in these sessions. He was in superb form.

The Olympic Village was isolated, but the Australian athletes were certainly aware that there was some conflict on the streets of Mexico City. Ray Weinberg had one strong memory of the security arrangements:

> I took our marathon runners, Derek Clayton and John Farrington, to have a look at the course so they could see where it went and what it passed through. We got to a point where we couldn't go any further because this large armoured car was blocking the road. It was like an open van with seats that ran

right across from one side to the other. It would have held twenty men or more and, as they travelled, they held their shields up along the sides. We had to find a way to go around them and we joined the marathon course a lot further on. At least the boys saw the latter part of the course. Also, all of our attachés were young female students and they were either involved, or had family or friends involved, in the protest. So we certainly knew about it.

Doubell recalls that many athletes made friends with attachés and other students who then disappeared for three or four days. They discovered later that some of the students had been arrested and locked up. Doubell also remembers that the trees near the university had been painted white up to about six foot from the ground so the authorities could see people more easily.

Stampfl arrived three days before Doubell's heat and immediately asked how he was going.

'Things are shaping up well,' Doubell replied.

'In that case,' Stampfl said simply, 'go out and win the next three races.'

For Doubell, this advice was simply consistent with Stampfl's usual approach, as outlined in the first chapter of *Franz Stampfl On Running*:

In events where heats and semi-finals have to be run, especially in Olympic Games, the preliminary rounds should always be taken as seriously as the final. Some heats, and most semi-finals, are very tough and no competitor can afford to underrate them if he is to make certain of qualifying. Occasionally, for tactical reasons, a runner deliberately disguises his true form in the preliminaries, but in doing so he always takes the chance of over-playing his hand and failing to qualify. The fact is that most heats are so keenly fought that the man who tries to hold something back for the final round may well find he has saved his energy to no purpose.

Doubell is critical of Australian athletes who do not make it through their heat at an Olympic Games after running a time that is slower, often significantly slower, than the qualifying time they achieved for their event. For Doubell, expecting to run fast in your heat at a major championship is a basic lesson he learned from the moment he began training with Stampfl.

Stampfl's instruction to 'go out and win the next three races' was not a glib throw-away line. Doubell understood that it incorporated a number of important assumptions. He explains:

The first was that, like all Stampfl's athletes, I had to assume complete responsibility for my performance. I understood that Stampfl had given me all the ammunition and attitude I needed to win the race and, at the end of the day, only I could execute the plan we had been fine-tuning for years. Secondly, it assumed that I knew I had to respond to any sudden challenges from other athletes. Thirdly, I had to decide myself how the other athletes could be beaten. Finally, and most importantly, I was the only person who could decide how I was going to win the final. Stampfl had done his utmost in preparing me. It was now up to me to win it for both of us.

CHAPTER 15

Can't You Run A Bit Faster?

The opening ceremony of the Mexico City Olympic Games was held on 12 October and over 80,000 spectators filled the main stadium, the Estadio Olimpico Universitario, as representatives from the 119 competing nations marched in. The Olympic flame had left Olympia on 23 August and its journey to Mexico paid homage to Christopher Columbus' voyage to the New World. It passed through Italy and Spain before crossing the Atlantic Ocean to San Salvador, where Columbus first landed in the Americas in 1492. The flame arrived at Vera Cruz on Columbus Day and then was split among five torches, representing the five Olympic rings, and travelled to all the regions of Mexico. On the eve of the opening ceremony, the five torches were reunited at the Pyramid of the Moon at Teotihuacan, 50 kilometres north of Mexico City. The next day the Olympic torch was carried to the capital, where 20-year-old Mexican sprinter and hurdler Norma Enriqueta Basilio Sotelo became the first woman to light the Olympic cauldron at the end of the torch relay.

Doubell didn't attend the opening ceremony because his 800-metres heat was the following day. He stayed at the Olympic Village, conserving energy and focusing on his first Olympic race. His male teammates who did attend were described by the *Courier Mail* as being 'like a sober and sombre squad of Australian bowlers ... in their straw hats, green blazers, white shirts, ties, cream slacks and brown shoes, they were as outdated as Sherlock Holmes in the world of James Bond'.

The next day, Doubell made sure he left plenty of time for the long journey from the Olympic Village to the Estadio Olimpico. When he arrived, he did his usual warm-up of four or five slow laps on the track followed by some 100-metre and 150-metre sprints. There were only two warm-up tracks and they were crammed with runners. Doubell followed his usual routine of not looking at anyone else and trying to stay as composed as possible. The previous night, he had visualised today's heat. He would be well positioned at the end of the first lap, ensure he was close to the lead going around the final bend, and then use his acceleration to strike at the end of the race.

As it turned out, Doubell's heat involved a massive test of his ability to remain controlled under pressure. New rules had just been introduced, one of which stated that athletes must remain in their lane for the first 110 metres. This meant each athlete had to complete the first bend in their designated lane before merging just after they reached the back straight. This rule was designed to minimise the particularly rough stuff that used to take place at the start of an 800-metres race. Alfredo Cubias from El Salvador was in the lane next to Doubell, and it became immediately obvious that nobody had explained the new rule to him. After the gun fired, Cubias moved straight across into Doubell's lane and blocked his path. Doubell held up his arms in the air and protested but the officials didn't take any action. He realised he had to accept that he had lost a few seconds on the rest of the field and get on with the race. Stampfl had told him repeatedly over the years that he must always be prepared for unexpected actions by other runners. Years of racing at club and representative level over different distances and under various conditions helped him to settle down quickly and focus on his race plan. He moved up through the field and finished strongly over the last 200 metres to win in 1:47.2. Cubias was last in 2:08.7.

Although he had run well to win his heat, the interference from Cubias meant Doubell had been forced to work harder than he had wanted. It had been a rough run and he was now more worried about the semi-final, which was filled with high-quality competition. Once again, Stampfl had a simple message: 'Do it again tomorrow. Make sure they know you are the person to beat.' That night, after visualising his race plan for the next day, Doubell tossed and turned and didn't get to sleep until about 2am.

In the semi-final, he was racing against Wilson Kiprugut, the hot favourite from Kenya. Kiprugut had become Kenya's first Olympic medallist when he won the bronze medal in the 800 metres in Tokyo in 1964. He had started running when he was a student at Kaptebeswet Primary School, which is located in Kericho County in south-west Kenya, about 200 kilometres west of Nairobi, and continued at the nearby Sitotwet Intermediate School. His talent was obvious when he competed at the 1958 East African Athletics Championships and he was recruited into the Kenyan Army's African Rifles, where he rose to the rank of sergeant though his primary focus was athletics. He travelled to the 1962 British Empire and Commonwealth Games in Perth, where he was eliminated in the heats of the 440 yards and was a member of Kenya's 4 x 440-yards relay squad. After his historic medal-winning run at the 1964 Olympics, Kiprugut won the 400 metres and 800 metres at the inaugural All-African Games held in Brazzaville, Congo, in July 1965. He then won a silver medal, behind Australia's Noel Clough, in the 880 yards at the 1966 British Empire and Commonwealth Games in Kingston. In Mexico City, he won his heat by 15 metres and posted the best heat time of 1:46.1, a full second faster than Doubell.

Kiprugut was a classic front runner and Doubell expected him to go out fast in the semi-final. He wasn't wrong, as Kiprugut ran the first lap in just over 51 seconds, opening up a 10-metre lead on the rest of the field. Doubell was in fourth position at the bell and felt comfortable. He quickly improved to third and was surprised how easily he was able to do so. Four athletes from the semi-final would qualify for the final, so Doubell decided to move into second place. Again, it was easier than he expected. While Kiprugut was still leading, Doubell sensed he was starting to make heavy weather of it, and as they entered the final straight, he decided to test the Kenyan — and himself. He raced up alongside Kiprugut with about 60 metres to go.

'This was the start of the psychological battle,' Doubell says, stressing that it was a critical moment. 'I turned towards Kiprugut and gave him a look that suggested this seemed like an ordinary training run. *Can't you run a bit faster?* I was communicating to him.'

Doubell accelerated past the gold medal favourite and won by a metre in a personal best, and new Australian record time of 1:45.7. Kiprugut finished second in 1:45.8, Jozef Plachý of Czechoslovakia was third in 1:45.9 and Tom Farrell of the United States fourth in 1:46.1. 'This was not what Kiprugut had expected,' Doubell says with a smile. 'I had put huge doubts in his mind. And I felt terrific.' When told his time was 1:45.7 he was surprised. He thought it would be more like 1:47.

Doubell had run the fastest time in the semi-finals and he had beaten every other finalist at some stage over the previous two years. Kiprugut was still the media's top pick, but Doubell had struck an important psychological blow in the semi-final. Plachý was only 19 but he clearly had huge potential. Farrell had been 20 when he finished fifth in the 800-metres final in Tokyo four years earlier. He was now older and wiser and determined to improve on that performance.

'I hadn't competed outside of the north-east of the USA before Tokyo,' Farrell recalls. 'In 1963, I didn't even make our conference championships at University and the following year I made the Olympic final and I was standing on the starting line next to Peter Snell.' He performed strongly in the years between Tokyo and Mexico City, until a major setback occurred in February 1968:

Soon after training at Yale with Ralph, I broke my foot. It was like a stress fracture. I was on crutches for almost two months and I didn't know whether I would be able to get back. The

US trials were at Lake Tahoe and you gear everything for that race because if you don't finish in the top three you don't go. Everything clicked for me in the trials and I won in about 1:46.5, which was the fastest 800 metres ever run at altitude. I thought I was right in it for the Olympics, although I put so much emphasis into making the US team that there was somewhat of a let-down after the trials and in the month leading up to the Olympics. If I ran 50 seconds for 400 metres before the trials it was like jogging, but to run 50 seconds after the trials I had to put more effort in.

Farrell says he didn't focus on any other competitor in Mexico City, just his own performance, but then he adds:

I remember after the heats I asked one of the other American 800 metre runners, Ron Kutschinski, who had impressed him. Straight away he said: 'Doubell looks good.'

The Germans Walter Adams and Dieter Fromm, the former from West Germany and the latter from East Germany, had run first and second in the other semi-final. Thomas Saisi from Kenya, who was third in that race, was the understudy to Kiprugut, while Ben Cayenne from Trinidad and Tobago was regarded as lucky to make the final after qualifying fourth through the easier of the two semi-finals.

A thought lingered at the back of Doubell's mind. While the research conducted at Falls Creek concluded that altitude would not affect races that lasted less than two minutes, which included the 800 metres, what wasn't known was how altitude would affect an athlete's recovery. This was particularly relevant for the 800 metres in which competitors ran a heat and semi-final on consecutive days and then had to prepare for a final on day three. But Doubell knew that one of the most critical factors in the final would have nothing to do with the altitude ...

Who would be able to stay cool under pressure?

CHAPTER 16

The Finest Tactical Run I Have Ever Seen

Doubell felt confident following his semi-final victory over Kiprugut, but he was also very nervous. After his experience finding it difficult to go to sleep the previous night, he took a sleeping pill to ensure he was well rested before the final. It worked and he felt good when he awoke at about 9.30 the next morning. The final wasn't until 6pm so he spent the day trying to stay as relaxed as possible, going for a walk and watching some television. He had a light lunch around midday that consisted of avocado, a seafood cocktail and some roast beef washed down with orange juice and coffee. He wondered if any Olympic champion had enjoyed the same pre-race meal.

The semi-finals of the men's 200 metres track event were run in the early afternoon. Peter Norman finished second behind the

USA's John Carlos in the first semi, while Greg Lewis was fifth in the second semi, won by another American, Tommie Smith, and just missed the final. Doubell, watching on television, could see that it was raining. The track had a film of water on it and the thought crossed his mind that they might postpone the evening events, including the 800-metres final. This thought passed quickly when he remembered the track was Tartan. Suddenly it was 3.30pm and time to go. Judy Patching had organised a car to drive him to the Estadio Olimpico. The traffic could be terrible in Mexico City and an American athlete had missed his race because he had not allowed enough time to get to the track.

Doubell did his usual warm-up, which fortunately fit between the thunderstorms that were periodically soaking the city and the stadium, and focused on staying composed. Strangely, he wasn't as nervous as he was before his semi-final. 'I said to Ralph, "Let me know when you want to finish your warm-up and I'll give you the nod when it's time,"' Weinberg recalled. 'I gave him the nod at the agreed time and he walked over with an American runner [Tom Farrell]. I then released Ralph, if that's the right word, into the care of the officials.'

Weinberg moved to an unofficial viewing position with Howard Toyne:

At one end of the stadium, underneath one of the big scoreboards, there was a wide ramp that ran down into the stadium. It was used to get equipment in and for teams to march in. I got a spot on the ramp for myself and Howard. We weren't meant to be there, but I had managed to use kangaroo pins to negotiate a few deals with the stadium attendants since I'd been there. They knew me and my cap, with a kangaroo on it, and that's where I watched the race.

While Doubell doesn't remember doing so, Weinberg told the Australian team afterwards that Doubell quietly and politely introduced the finalists to each other as they were waiting in the tunnel before going out onto the track. This unexpected move undoubtedly unsettled some of his competitors in these nervous minutes. It was also a clear indication that he was feeling relatively cool under the pressure of an Olympic final.

The final of the 800 metres was called. As they moved from the dark of the tunnel to the light of the track, Doubell saw that David Hemery of Great Britain, who was attending Boston University and would become a US citizen before the end of the year, had just run a world record to win the 400-metres hurdles. As he made his way towards the start, Doubell heard someone barracking for Australia and that relaxed him a little. He wondered how Stampfl and Sneazwell were feeling and thought they were probably more nervous than he was. The marshal called for the finalists to take off their tracksuits and move to the start line.

Doubell's ability to maintain his composure at the highest level of competition was tested once again at the start of the final. The athlete in the lane next to him, Walter Adams from West Germany, jumped before the starter's gun. But it was Doubell who was wrongly identified as the infringing athlete:

I couldn't believe it. If I broke again I would be disqualified. I quickly realised there was no point protesting the decision, losing concentration and wasting energy. I told myself that the start rarely determines the winner of an 800-metres race and that I must stay controlled and stick to my race plan.

Doubell made sure he started after the gun so that there would be absolutely no chance of disqualification. He was therefore trailing Kiprugut by almost 20 metres when the field merged after 110 metres. The size of the gap was not only due to Doubell's cautious start; Kiprugut had begun extremely quickly.

Doubell didn't panic. He was in fourth position at the end of the first lap, which was just where he wanted to be. He knew it had been a fast first 400 metres and yet he was feeling quite comfortable. He also knew it was vital that he maintain contact with Kiprugut, who remained the clear leader. Doubell edged out a little so he wouldn't get boxed in and moved into third when Cayenne faded at about the 500-metres mark. Kiprugut made another effort as he entered the back straight and Doubell moved up on him to make sure the metaphorical rubber band between them remained taut. This was a critical part of the race. Doubell passed Fromm and moved into second place, only a few metres behind Kiprugut. The crowd, and many of Doubell's teammates, thought Kiprugut was running away with it. Doubell knew he was still in contact.

He was feeling strong, but it was essential he resisted the temptation to make his decisive move too early. He couldn't risk 'running out of gas', as he called it, before the finish line. Stampfl had hammered into him the importance of waiting until the top of the final straight before accelerating. As they entered the straight, Doubell began closing the gap. He now knew he could win it. With 80 metres to go he 'kicked', giving everything in the final sprint to the line.

Weinberg and Toyne, watching from their unofficial vantage point, were getting very excited. 'Ralph had been running so well, and of course we knew his tactics,' says Weinberg. 'We were waiting and waiting, and as he came off the top bend both Howard and I shouted 'GO!' at the same time, with absolutely no agreement between us. We were right down the other end of the track, so of course he couldn't hear us. He ran such a superb race.'

Paul Jenes had also managed to move from his officially ticketed seat to a much better vantage point:

My tickets were around the 200-metres mark and behind a pole, so I walked around to about the 70-metres mark of the front straight, about 30 metres from the finish line to see if I could find an empty seat. I couldn't get closer to the finish line because of the media area. You could do that in Mexico City because it was the last Olympic Games where there was minimal security, and nobody came around to check tickets. I was lucky enough to see some of the greatest athletics in the world from that position — and Ralph's race was the most exciting race I saw. When he came up on Kiprugut's shoulder, I was up out of my seat and I was roaring my lungs out. I'd been away from home for quite a long time, so I suppose I was a bit homesick, and here was an Australian about to win at the Olympic Games!

Soon after Weinberg, Toyne and Jenes called out from their positions in the crowd, Doubell drew ahead:

It wasn't much, but it was that magic moment when I knew physical and psychological contact had been broken and the race had been decided. I was screaming to myself to keep going and to maintain form to the finish.

And then he broke the tape. In his mind, there was an eerie silence. He had done it. There were no extravagant celebrations, just a few handshakes and pats on the back from his competitors. In Bud Greenspan's official film of the race, Doubell says he saw the time on the scoreboard and it read 1:44.3.

'I asked Tom Farrell, who came third, what the world record was, and he said, 'That's it.'

I said, 'Well, that's nice.'

Laconic and understated as ever. It was, of course, also the new Olympic record, almost a second faster than Peter Snell's previous mark of 1:45.1.

Farrell, who had outlasted Adams in a tough tussle down the straight to win the bronze medal, jogged straight over to Doubell after he crossed the finish line. 'The first thing I did was pull his hair from the back. I have that on film, because my wife filmed it on a Super 8 camera. That's when he asked me what the world record was and I said, 'That's it.''

Half a century later, Farrell says he has 'come to grips' with the fact that he was beaten by 'two better guys, Doubell and Kiprugut':

My foot injury did bother me during the competition and the false start really affected me. I just couldn't get going in the final. Also, I elected to coach myself in 1967 and 1968. Looking back, I think that was a mistake. Ralph had the benefit of having a coach, Stampfl, who he could talk to.

Once again, the importance of Stampfl as a coach is highlighted, this time by one of Doubell's competitors. Farrell recognised, as he reviewed his Olympic experience, that a coach such as Stampfl would have helped him to deal with many of the psychological challenges that face an athlete in a major competition. This included dealing mentally with his injury and the false start in the final. Doubell had met the same challenges magnificently, and he knew Stampfl was key to this. At the media conference, Doubell saw Stampfl in the room. Somehow, he had managed to talk his way in. They didn't say much to each other; they didn't need to. Robert Gray of *The Australian* wrote that Doubell went up to Stampfl and wrapped his arms around him and that this was 'a hug which all the world watched and knew reflected sincerity'.

Doubell doesn't remember much of the press conference. He was still stunned by what he had achieved. Gray reported that it was full of the usual inane questions, including an opening query in Spanish of 'What is your name?' followed by questions about his age, weight and height. Gray wrote that Doubell was 'remarkably calm' and handled himself 'like a statesman'. The report in *The Australian* noted that Roger Bannister had described Doubell's race as 'the finest tactical run I have ever seen'.

Unlike the press conference, the medal ceremony was unforgettable. It wasn't because Doubell was presented with his medal — and an olive leaf from Olympia sent by the Greek Government to all gold medallists — by Lewis Luxton, one of Australia's representative on the IOC and Chairman of Shell, his employer. It was because a sudden thunderstorm sent virtually the entire crowd running for cover. Squinting through the torrential downpour, Doubell could see there was hardly anyone sitting in the seats that surrounded the athletics track. All of those involved in the ceremony, including the Mexican girls in traditional costume, were saturated. The national anthem, *God Save The Queen*, was played but Doubell didn't sing it because he believed he had a terrible voice. As he squelched off the ground, something caught his eye. About a dozen of his teammates, including hurdlers Gary Knoke and Pam Kilborn, boxer Ray Maguire, some members of the water polo team, who had not been allowed to play in Mexico City, and Dawn Fraser, who was also a non-competitor after being controversially suspended by the Australian Swimming Union after the Tokyo Olympics but was there to provide support, had braved the rain to give him a kind of guard of honour as he left the track. Doubell shook their hands and laughed as he made his way into the stadium tunnel.

That night, Doubell celebrated with Franz Stampfl and with three of Stampfl's former athletics students: Roger Bannister, Chris Brasher and Chris Chataway. The three Englishmen, who between them had had an Olympic gold medal, three world records and the achievement of climbing Everest on the track, were respectively representing the BBC, *The Observer* and *The Times* in Mexico City. When one journalist called Doubell the next day, he replied: 'Right now, I've got a giant hangover, but I feel tremendous. I can get used to the hangover, I guess, but the gold medal is something a little different. That medal is something I will never get over.'

Doubell added that he had planned to spend the night drinking champagne, but the cost of even one bottle was much too expensive. 'So I'm afraid the toasts had to be made in cheap red wine,' he explained.

'But despite that, it was still the greatest party of my life and that wine tasted like champagne.'

The Australian media admitted that Doubell's victory came as a complete surprise to them. *The Sydney Morning Herald's* report, written by Jim Webster and Ken Knox, was headlined 'Doubell — An Unknown Ice-Cold Champion':

Ralph Doubell was nobody on Monday and somebody yesterday. He came in from the ranks of the unknown to win Australia's first gold medal of the Mexico Games in the sinking shadows of the main stadium. He triumphed in the 800-metres final and, to add to the splendour of the moment, tied the world record of 1:44.3 held by Peter Snell.

To most Australians, Doubell is a man of mystery. Few outside athletics would know much about him. Doubell is much better known in the United States where he had a highly successful stint at the indoor meetings in January and February this year, dominating 800-metre and 1000-metre races. He had six starts for six wins, so the Americans fancied his Olympic prospects much more than his countrymen ...

The Australian media's underestimation of Doubell and his achievement would not change much over the next 50 years.

THE CLOSING CEREMONY AT the Tokyo Olympic Games four years earlier was intended to be informal but, surprisingly for a Japanese event, it was disorganised and even a little chaotic. Athletes danced around haphazardly and a few of the New Zealanders stopped in front of the Japanese Emperor and bowed and blew kisses to him. The Emperor seemed unfazed but Avery Brundage and the IOC were not amused. It was decided that for the closing ceremony in Mexico City on 27 October 1968, each country would be limited to just six athletes plus a flag bearer. All the other athletes would sit respectfully in the stands.

Eric Pearce, who had just competed in his fourth consecutive Olympic Games as a member of the silver medal-winning men's hockey team, was given the honour of carrying the Australian flag. Doubell, who was not long recovered from his own bout of Montezuma's Revenge, suffered after he dropped his guard following his gold medal run, was selected as one of Australia's six representatives. He was joined by Michael Wenden (gold in the men's 100-metres and 200-metres freestyle, silver in the 4 x 200-metres freestyle relay and bronze in the 4 x 100-metres freestyle relay), Lyn McClements (gold in the women's 100-metres butterfly), Pam Kilborn (silver in the women's 80-metres hurdles) and Alf Duval (stroke of the silver medal-winning men's rowing eight). Maureen Caird, who won gold in the women's 80-metres hurdle, was also selected but she was unable to participate because of blistered feet, so 15-year-old breaststroker Judy Playfair, who won silver as a member of the women's 4 x 100-metres medley relay team, took her place.

It was a tremendous honour for Doubell to be one of seven athletes to represent his country at the closing ceremony, but the plan to limit participation failed completely. After a spectacular display of fireworks, 800 mariachi bands entered the Estadio Olimpico and circled the track playing traditional songs. It was too much for one American athlete, who could not restrain himself. He left his seat, jumped the fence and ran onto the infield to join the celebrations. A few others quickly joined him and soon hundreds of athletes and officials were streaming onto the field, many taking sombreros from their Mexican hosts as they danced with the mariachi bands. The final song was *Las Golondrinas*, which tells a story of swallows migrating south for the winter but always returning the following year. For many athletes, their focus was already on the Olympic Games to be held in Munich in four years' time. Stampfl, unsurprisingly, had clear plans for Doubell, which he revealed to Alan Trengove of *The Sun*:

> I want him to run 9.7 seconds for the 100 yards and 3 minutes 55 seconds for the mile. Then he will be ready to win the 800 metres and the 1500 metres at Munich, as Peter Snell did in Tokyo. But it is no use trying to emulate others. You must do better. I hope to see Ralph run world records.

CHAPTER 17

An Extraordinary Games

The 1968 Olympic Games featured many 'firsts'. It was the first Olympics to be held in Latin America and the first in a Spanish-speaking country. Norma Enriqueta Basilio Sotelo was the first woman to light the Olympic cauldron at the end of the torch relay and it was the first time a Tartan track was used for track-and-field events. But wait, there's more.

Mexico City was the first Olympic Games to carry out tests to determine the sex of female competitors. There was increasing suspicion around some athletes, especially from Eastern European countries, and so all female competitors were subject to a 'sex test'. This involved taking saliva from inside the mouth and examining it under a microscope. The testers looked for a chromosome known as a Barr body, which is only found in female somatic cells, and also the presence of two X chromosomes. If no Barr body was found, a sample of blood or tissue would be taken to examine the chromosomes more thoroughly. No athletes failed the test.

This was also the first Olympics to feature testing for performance-enhancing drugs. The use of amphetamines in cycling had been increasing and authorities had been testing athletes in that sport for several years. In Mexico City, the top six finishers and several others in an event could be subjected to urine tests to identify any use of banned substances. These included amphetamines, ephedrine, stimulants and painkillers such as morphine. There was increasing concern about the use of anabolic steroids, but there was no test to identify them in 1968.

Swedish modern pentathlete Hans-Gunnar Liljenwall has the distinction of becoming the first Olympic athlete to be disqualified for failing a drugs test. He tested positive for alcohol after drinking what he claimed was only 'two beers' to calm his nerves before the pistol shooting. Liljenwall had finished eighth in the individual modern pentathlon, but was disqualified, and he and his teammates had to return the bronze medals they had been awarded for finishing third in the team event.

Mexico City featured some of the greatest athletes in Olympic history. In all, there were 26 Olympic records set in 35 track and field events. Thirteen of these were world records. While the city's elevation benefited sprinters and some jumpers and throwers, the new Tartan running surface also played a key role in the fast times.

American sprinters, many of whom had experience running on Tartan at home, set new world records in the men's and women's 100 metres (Jim Hines and Wyomia Tyus), men's 200 metres (Tommie Smith) and men's 400 metres (Lee Evans). The American men and women set new world records in winning the 4 x 100-metres relays and the American men did the same in the 4 x 400-metres relay (the women's 4 x 400-metres relay would not be introduced at the Olympics until Munich in 1972). Willie Davenport equalled the Olympic record in the 110-metres hurdles.

Sprinters from other countries also set new standards. David Hemery of Great Britain broke the world record in winning the 400-metres hurdles and Polish sprinting legend Irena Szewińska won the women's 200 metres in world record time, just ahead of two Australians, 17-year-old Raelene Boyle and Jenny Lamy. Maureen Caird won the 80-metres hurdles in Olympic record time, with Pam Kilborn running second.

This was the first Olympic Games to include a significant African presence in men's distance running and they announced their arrival with strength and style. African men won at least one medal in all running events from the 800 metres to the marathon. Wilson Kiprugut won silver in the 800 metres, while his compatriot Kip Keino upset American world record holder Jim Ryun in the 1500 metres in Olympic record time. Earlier in the Games, Keino ran second to Mohamed Gammoudi of Tunisia in the 5000 metres, with another Kenyan, Naftali Temu, earning the bronze. Gammoudi finished third in the 10,000 metres on the first day of competition, with Temu claiming the gold ahead of Mamo Wolde of Ethiopia. Wolde backed up to win the marathon. Kenyans Amos Biwott and Benjamin Kogo were first and second in the 3000-metres steeplechase.

The most remarkable performance in track and field was by America's Bob Beamon, who broke the world long jump record by the massive margin of 55 centimetres. Beamon's new mark of 8.90 metres would remain the world's best for 23 years.

Romania's Viorica Viscopoleanu broke the world record in the women's long jump, while the Soviet Union's Viktor Saneyev set a new world record in the men's triple jump. Saneyev would go on to win gold in the same event at the next two Olympics and silver in 1980. American Al Oerter broke the Olympic record to win an amazing fourth consecutive men's discus gold medal, while his teammate Dick Fosbury used his new 'flop' technique to go over the bar backwards and win the high jump — and change the event forever.

In the pool, 16-year-old American Debbie Meyer became the first swimmer to win three individual gold medals at one Olympics (200-metres, 400-metres and 800-metres freestyle). The Americans dominated the meet, winning 21 of the 29 events. However, Australia's Mike Wenden broke the world record to win the 100-metres freestyle and then backed up to win the 200-metres freestyle in Olympic record time.

In the 100-metres final, an 18-year-old American named Mark Spitz finished third. Spitz claimed two relay gold medals in Mexico City, and would go on to win seven gold medals in Munich, a record that would be surpassed 36 years later by his compatriot Michael Phelps, who won eight gold medals in the pool at the 2008 Beijing Olympics. Lyn McClements, in the 100-metres butterfly, was one of only three non-American women to win a gold medal in the pool at Mexico City.

Mexicans, as well as sports fans around the world, hoped the Games would be remembered for these Olympic 'firsts' and outstanding performances. However, some of the controversies that had emerged before the Games played out through the two weeks of competition.

The men's 10,000-metres track final is traditionally held on the first day of Olympic competition. In Mexico City, what transpired immediately highlighted how the altitude would affect the distance events. Australia's Ron Clarke, the holder of the world record in this event, stayed with the leaders for as long as he could, but was unable to hold on in the closing stages. All three medallists — Naftali Temu (Kenya), Mamo Wolde (Ethiopia) and Mohamed Gammoudi (Tunisia) — were born at altitude. Temu's winning time of 29:27.4 was one minute and 48 seconds slower than Clarke's world record and a slow time by any major competition standards. Clarke finished ten seconds out of the medals in sixth place and collapsed at the end of the race. In a dramatic image seen around the world, a prostrate Clarke was given oxygen by the Australian team doctor, Brian Corrigan, who held his face in his hands while he cried in fear for Clarke's life.

'I burst into tears,' Corrigan wrote in his autobiography, *The Life of Brian*, 'I couldn't help it and I realised that courage alone would never be sufficient to overcome the problems caused by the stupidity of the IOC. Here in my arms was this great athlete who virtually had to kill himself in order to prove that these Olympics should never have been held here.'

Chris Brasher, who had been warning about the dangers of distance running at altitude for over three years, was furious. In his report of the 10,000-metres final in his *Olympic Diary* he wrote:

They call this sport. I feel bitter and angry. Altitude has now been proved to be the decisive factor. Altitude has turned one of the great races of the Olympic Games into a handicap event. The Olympic Charter talks about assembling the amateurs of all nations in a fair and equal competition. There is nothing fair or equal about these Games.

Brasher was completely disillusioned, declaring the end of his love affair with the 'spiritual beauty' of the Olympic Games. 'Now she is a raddled old tart.' Presciently, he stated that any athlete of the future who wanted to succeed at distances longer than two minutes in duration would 'have to uproot himself and take to the hills'.

The USSR's invasion of Czechoslovakia on the eve of the Olympic Games not only posed a major problem for the organisers, it significantly affected Czechoslovakia's athletes as they made their final preparations. This included champion gymnast Věra Čáslavská, who had won three gold medals and a silver medal as a 22-year-old at the 1964 Tokyo Olympics. Čáslavská was favoured to win more gold medals in Mexico City, but the invasion of her country meant her final months of training were performed with sacks of potatoes as weights and logs as beams. Despite this disruption, Čáslavská won medals in all six events she entered in Mexico City: four gold and two silver. Extraordinarily, and controversially, the judges changed the preliminary score of her Russian competitor in the floor exercise so that she tied with Čáslavská.

Čáslavská became a star in Mexico due to her phenomenal success, her good looks, her decision to use *Jarabe Tapatío* (The Mexican Hat Dance) as the music for her floor routine, and her choice of Mexico City as the venue for her wedding immediately after her final event. However, she gained even greater global fame for another reason. Čáslavská looked down and away while the Soviet national anthem was played during the medal ceremonies for the balance beam and floor exercise. It was a silent but clear protest on the world stage. Čáslavská won many fans around the world for her actions but the new regime in Czechoslovakia was not amused. When she returned home, she was forced into retirement and denied the right to travel, work and attend sporting events.

The most famous political statement in Mexico City was made by American sprinters Tommie Smith and John Carlos during the medal ceremony for the men's 200-metres track event. Smith won the gold medal in world record time of 19.83 seconds ahead of Peter Norman (20.06), with Carlos (20.10) third. Norman had been the Australian 200-metres champion for the previous three years and enjoyed a superb Olympic Games. He found the Tartan track suited his running style and set a new Olympic record in his heat, although this was quickly equalled by Smith in the quarter-finals and surpassed by Smith and Carlos in the semis. Norman was a religious man whose parents were devout members of the Salvation Army. He had been making his own statement in the Australian athletics world from 1963, when he began wearing a tracksuit with the words 'God is Love' and later 'Jesus Saves' sewn across the back.

As they walked out for the medal ceremony, Smith and Carlos wore black socks without shoes as a symbol of black poverty. Smith also wore a black scarf as a symbol of black pride and Carlos wore a string of black beads to represent lynching. Carlos, unlike Smith and Norman, had his track suit unzipped. He said this was to represent blue-collar workers and underdogs, because 'those are the people whose contributions to society are so important but they don't get recognised'.

All three medallists wore Olympic Project for Human Rights (OPHR) badges. After the race, Norman had offered to wear an OPHR badge as a sign of solidarity with Carlos and Smith. He was given one before he walked out for the medal ceremony by Paul Hoffman, the white coxswain of the American rowing VIII.

The President of the International Amateur Athletic Federation (IAAF), Lord David Burghley, the Marquess of Exeter, presented Smith, Norman and Carlos with their medals. Smith also received an olive sapling, a symbol of peace.

As the flags of the USA and Australia were raised at the end of the stadium and *The Star-Spangled Banner* began to play, Smith and Carlos lowered their heads, which is offensive to Americans while the anthem is being played, and each raised a fist encased in a black glove. It was a Black Power salute that expressed solidarity with the Black Freedom Movement. They had both planned to bring a pair of black gloves to the ceremony, but Carlos accidentally left his in the Olympic Village. Norman suggested that Carlos wear Smith's left glove, which is why Carlos raised his left hand as opposed to his right, which is the traditional Black Power salute.

The photo of this medal ceremony is one of the most recognised and poignant in Olympic history. As Lord Burghley and the three medallists made their way from the podium to the track exit, there was booing and jeering from the crowd. Smith and Carlos responded by raising their gloved fists once again.

After the medal ceremony, Smith told the media: 'People recognise me as a fast nigger but that still means I'm a nigger.' Carlos said: 'We are great American athletes for 19.8 seconds, then we are animals so far as our country is concerned.'

Avery Brundage was furious at the statements, both verbal and non-verbal, made by Smith and Carlos. In his mind, the Olympic Games were meant to be apolitical and he viewed their actions as a provocative breach of the fundamental principles of the Olympic spirit. Smith and Carlos had, he said, deliberately used the medal ceremony to 'advertise their domestic political views' despite the fact that 'one of the basic principles of the Games is that politics take no part whatsoever'.

Brundage was adamant Smith and Carlos should be kicked off the American team and banned from the Olympic Village. The United States Olympic Committee initially refused, but Brundage threatened to ban the entire American track team from the rest of the Games. The USOC then suspended Smith and Carlos from the US team and expelled them from the Village.

The USOC issued a statement expressing its 'profound regrets' to the IOC, the Games organisers and to the people of Mexico for the 'discourtesy' displayed by Smith and Carlos. It continued:

> The untypical exhibition of these athletes also violates the basic standards of sportsmanship and good manners, which are so highly regarded in the United States ... A repetition of such incidents by other members of the US team can only be considered a wilful disregard of Olympic principles that would warrant the imposition of the severest penalties at the disposal of the United States Olympic Committee.

Lee Evans, the US 400-metres champion who was a close friend of Tommie Smith, was so angered by the treatment of his teammates that he decided he would not run in the quarter-finals of his event, which were scheduled for the following day. Smith and Carlos urged him to run and Evans went on to win the final on 18 October in a world record time of 43.86. Americans Larry James and Ron Freeman finished second and third, making it a clean sweep for the USA. For the 400-metres medal ceremony, Evans, James and Freeman wore black berets, black gloves and OPHR badges. They removed their berets and stood to attention during their national anthem and so escaped censure.

Smith and Carlos received some support from white Americans, most notably the US Olympic rowing VIII, all of whom were white and from Harvard University. The crew issued the following statement:

> We, as individuals, have been concerned about the place of the black man in American society in their struggle for equal rights. As members of the US Olympic team, each of us has come to feel a moral commitment to support our black teammates in their efforts to dramatise the injustices and inequities which permeate our society.

However, the response from most white Americans, and even some African Americans, was negative. Many sections of the media in the US attacked Smith and Carlos for their actions, with the *Los Angeles Times* criticising their 'Nazi-like salute' and the *Chicago Tribune* describing it as an 'act contemptuous of the United States' and 'an insult to their countrymen'. When they returned home, Smith and Carlos received hate mail, even death threats. The public pressure on them was intense and this contributed to the breakdown of their marriages.

Norman believed he had acted moderately during the medal ceremony. He had agreed to wear the OPHR badge but then stood quietly on the podium while he accepted his medal and listened to the American national anthem. Many people congratulated him for the stand he had taken, literally and metaphorically, but he didn't think it was such a big deal. The next day he was called to a meeting with Judy Patching, Chef de Mission of the Australian team, who told Norman that a number of officials, particularly the Americans, were very unhappy with his participation in the protest. Patching told Norman that he was officially reprimanded. At the end of the discussion, he gave Norman four tickets to watch the hockey.

It is often reported that Norman became a pariah in Australia following his actions in Mexico City, but the facts do not support this. He continued to compete when he returned home and was the Australian 200-metres champion in 1969 and 1970. He was selected to represent Australia at the 1969 Pacific Conference Games in Tokyo, when he claimed a last-stride victory over teammate Greg Lewis in the 200 metres and anchored Australia's winning 4 x 100-metres relay team, and at the 1970 British Commonwealth Games in Edinburgh, when he was expected to win a medal, probably gold, but he finished fifth in the final. No one was more disappointed with this performance than Norman himself, and his life began to unravel after Edinburgh. His marriage broke down and he briefly retired from athletics in 1971.

Norman soon decided to return to the track, to try to qualify for the 1972 Munich Olympics. He recorded some fast times, including times that were below the qualifying standard, but — as is usual in an Olympic year — the Australian championships a few months before the Games was the key meeting for achieving selection. Norman finished third in the 200 metres in a slow time of 21.6. His coach later revealed that he was running with an injured knee. Norman could have been selected — on the basis of his times recorded earlier in the season that, when allied to his brilliant run in Mexico City and his record at past national championships, formed a fair argument — but, as was the case before and has been since with other athletes, the selectors did not elect to exercise this option. In fact, Australia sent no male sprinters to the 1972 Olympics.

Norman's life deteriorated from this time on and he suffered from alcoholism and depression. He died of a heart attack in 2006 and his funeral was held on 9 October 2006, almost 38 years to the day after he ran the greatest race of his life. Tommie Smith and John Carlos, with whom he had maintained contact over the decades since their famous Olympic final, flew to Australia to give eulogies and be pallbearers at his funeral.

CHAPTER 18

Ralph the Rapscallion

The Australian Olympic team exceeded expectations in Mexico City, winning five gold medals, seven silver medals and five bronze medals. The 24-member track-and-field team performed particularly well, winning six of Australia's total haul of 17 medals. They brought home two gold medals (Maureen Caird and Ralph Doubell), three silvers (Raelene Boyle, Pam Kilborn and Peter Norman) and one bronze (Jenny Lamy). Furthermore, a significant number of athletes in the team finished in the top eight of their event: Ron Clarke in the 5000 metres (fifth) and 10,000 metres (sixth); Kerry O'Brien in the 3000-metres steeplechase (fourth, just two-tenths of a second away from the bronze medal); Derek Clayton in the marathon (seventh); Lawrie Peckham in the high jump (eighth); Allen Crawley in the long jump (sixth); Phil May in the triple jump (sixth); Boyle and Dianne Burge in the 100 metres (fourth and sixth respectively); and the women's 4 x 100-metres relay team of Boyle, Burge, Lamy and Joyce Bennett (fifth).

From the day they returned to Australia on 30 October, all the medallists were the focus of media attention but the four gold medal winners — Caird, Doubell and swimmers Lyn McClements and Mike Wenden — were particularly in demand. *The Sun* newspaper, for example, came up with the idea that the quartet should sit in the back of an open-top car and be driven down the straight at Flemington on Melbourne Cup Day. The Cup, which is traditionally run on the first Tuesday in November, was run on 5 November.

On a smaller scale, the Mayor of Moorabbin, Bill Fry, organised a reception for Doubell at the Moorabbin Town Hall. The guest list included Sir Edgar Tanner, whose achievements included being Secretary of the Organising Committee for the Melbourne Olympic Games, local Members of Parliament and Councillors, as well as representatives from local sporting and community organisations. Herb Elliott, who was a Moorabbin resident at the time, was invited to say a few words. Doubell's mother Beryl attended proudly.

Notwithstanding the public and media interest immediately after he returned home, there was no rest for Doubell before he resumed his running life. He turned up late to the first Saturday morning training session with Melbourne University Athletics Club after he arrived back from Mexico City and was duly reprimanded by the squad and told he would suffer the usual punishment: extra training. Bill Hooker recalls:

We all went up to him and asked if he'd brought along his medal. He delved into the bottom of his training bag and dragged out the medal as if it was a pair of old jocks. We all got excited handling it, of course, and then we did a relatively short training session. We then headed to Jimmy Watson's Wine Bar and I think it was the first time that Jimmy's has been drunk out of champagne. And I don't think we paid for any of it. Allan Watson was there and he said, 'Your money's no good here while the medal's in the house.'

On 16 November, just one month after his Olympic triumph, Doubell returned to competition, running in an interclub 880-yards race at Melbourne University. It is common for athletes to experience a bit of a letdown after a major event like the Olympics, and Doubell was certainly feeling tired. Nevertheless, he won the race in 1:49.5, which was faster than he had expected to run, because Graeme Gledhill pushed him hard until the final stages.

Doubell continued to compete at club and interstate events through the first half of the '68–69 Australian season, winning all his races. The motivation for competing so regularly after his achievement in Mexico City was to meet his short-term aim of returning to the US for another series of indoor races. His long-term aim at this point was to train hard for another four years and defend his Olympic title in Munich. Soon, Doubell was back on an aeroplane and on 19 January 1969 he beat American Wade Bell by more than four seconds in a 1000-yards indoor race before more than 8000 spectators in Los Angeles. His time of 2:07.0 was just one second outside Peter Snell's world indoor record, but he was very happy with it given that he had only flown into the city a few days earlier after a 25-hour journey from Australia.

The following Saturday night, in front of a crowd estimated at 9000, he broke the world 880-yards indoor record at the annual

Jaycee Indoor Invitational at Tingley Coliseum in Albuquerque, New Mexico. His time of 1:47.9 was one second faster than the previous mark. 'I had rested well after Los Angeles and felt confident before the race,' he said. 'I knew there wasn't much opposition so, unusually for me, I led from the start and set out to run a fast race rather than worrying about the tactics needed to win.'

Doubell was due to travel to New York City for the 62nd annual Millrose Games, held at Madison Square Garden. The meeting was to feature more than 40 athletes who had competed at the 1968 Olympics, including eight gold medallists. The 880 yards was scheduled to include four of the first five finishers from the Olympic 800-metres final in Mexico City: Doubell, Tom Farrell, Walter Adams and Jozef Plachý . The missing runner was Wilson Kiprugut. In the end, Doubell didn't make the start because his flight into New York was re-routed to Baltimore due to fog. His next big race was back in Los Angeles on 8 February, over 1000 yards. Once again, he felt there weren't many in the field who could push him and that he needed to lead all the way. This is exactly how it turned out, and he won in 2:06.3, just three tenths of a second outside Snell's world record for this distance. Unfortunately, the first 440 yards had been too slow, about 54.5 seconds, due to his inexperience at running from the front. This ruined his chance of breaking the record.

When Doubell returned to Australia he immediately resumed racing. Although tired from the travel, he regained his Victorian 880-yards title on 16 February in 1:50.8, finishing five metres ahead of Graeme Gledhill, who had beaten him in an upset the previous year. The result was a portent for the remainder of the season: Doubell remained undefeated and on 30 March he regained his Australian

800-metres title on a very muddy track at Olympic Park. *The Canberra Times* reported that the Olympic champion won in 1:49.2 'without being extended'. It was Doubell's fifth 880-yards or 800-metres national title in six years, the only blemish on his record being the runners-up finish behind the American Preston Davis in 1968.

A few weeks later, Mike Wenden and Doubell were named among *World Sports* magazine's Olympic heroes. 'None of the great champions of athletics in the Mexico City Olympics won his title in a more classical style than Ralph Doubell of Australia,' wrote Bob Phillips, then at the start of what would be a long career in sports journalism.

In mid-1969, Doubell joined Ron Clarke and Kerry O'Brien for a six-week tour of the United States and Europe. They were given a hectic schedule, which began in southern California where, on 14 June, Doubell won the 880 yards at the Orange County Invitational at Fred Kelly Stadium in El Modena in 1:47.8. The trio then flew straight to Bergen in Norway and on 18 June Doubell won the 800 metres in 1:49.3. Two days later, he competed in Copenhagen and won the 800 metres in 1:48.9. A week later, he was in Stockholm, where he was beaten in the 800 metres by the relatively unheralded Naftali Bon of Kenya. Bon, who had won a silver medal in Mexico City as part of the Kenyan 4 x 400-metres relay team, crossed the line in the fast time of 1:46.6. Next stop was Milan in Italy, where on 3 July Doubell beat the local competition in 1:46.8. He then headed back to Scandinavia where, on 11 July, Naftali Bon beat him once again, this time in the rain in Oslo. Doubell finished the European leg of the tour on 14 July with a victory in Aarhus, Denmark.

After seven races in five countries in four weeks, Doubell had to return to Los Angeles for a two-day triangular meeting involving a Commonwealth team, the US and the Soviet Union. He didn't arrive in Los Angeles until 17 July and discovered his race had been moved a day earlier, from 48 hours' time to just a day away, so that the Belarus-born Mikhail Zhelobovsky could compete in both the 800 metres and the 1500 metres.

A crowd of 16,000 turned up at the Coliseum to watch the first night of competition, with Doubell the favourite in the 800 metres. His main opposition was expected to be Felix Johnson of the USA, but Johnson and Doubell were upstaged by 22-year-old Juris Luzins, an American who was born in Germany to Latvian parents and who had not previously won a major race. Luzins crossed the line in 1:46.7, his best time by 2.8 seconds, with Doubell second and Johnson third. Doubell was feeling the effects of an intense month of travelling and competing, but he tried not to use any of this as an excuse when he spoke to the media after the race. 'I was boxed in until the last turn but that really wasn't the reason for the loss,' the *Los Angeles Times* reported him saying. 'I just didn't have any more to give. I'm physically very tired, but this bloke who won is very, very good.'

Ford Motor Company was one of the major sponsors of athletics at the time, and many visiting athletes were given a car to drive while they were competing in the US. Doubell had been given a Ford to use and he decided to drive 40 kilometres from Los Angeles to Long Beach in search of a javelin for Ron Carlton, a friend and member of the Stampfl squad. It was hard to find good quality javelins in Australia at the time and Doubell had promised Carlton he would go shopping for him while he was in California. On the hour's drive south from downtown Los Angeles, Doubell was pulled over by the police for speeding. He had no driver's licence on him and wasn't carrying his passport, or any other form of identification. The police were unimpressed when he showed them a newspaper clipping featuring his photo and told him he would have to resolve the matter before he left the country in a few days' times. Doubell decided to go straight to court, apologise profusely and pay whatever fine he was given. He was gobsmacked when the judge sentenced him to five days in the County jail! Perhaps he had learned more than he realised from Stanley Spittle's anecdotes during their many training sessions together, because somehow Doubell convinced the judge not to lock him up and instead let him fly home. This is one story about Doubell that never made the newspapers.

Doubell had won most of his races and finished second in those he didn't win, yet he was disappointed with his results on the tour. His inner drive to succeed hadn't diminished after winning gold in Mexico City. He wanted to win every race and he had aimed to run several times in Europe under 1:46. The closest he came was 1:46.8 in Milan. 'I didn't do what I set out to do. I let myself down because my times were not fast enough,' he told Ron Carter of *The Age* on his return:

The only way to be accepted as the world's best in Europe is to run consistently fast times. That's what I must aim to do next year. Winning the Olympic Games 800 metres last year was my starting point in world athletics. This year's trip was designed to cement my place as the top half-miler in the world but I didn't do it. I ran in too many races. Travelling and a lack of sleep got me down. I'll know better next time, though. On my next trip I'll be more selective and make sure I have a break of five or six days between races. I'm confident I would have clocked faster times on this trip had I limited my races.

IT WAS AT THIS time that Doubell met Jennifer Walker at an Athletics International function in Melbourne. Jennifer remembers:

I went with David James, a platonic friend of mine. His girlfriend was sick and they had already paid for the tickets, so they didn't want to waste the money. It was a barbecue function and people were drinking beer out of pewter mugs with their name on their mug. I thought that was quite odd.

I didn't take much notice of Ralph at the barbecue but he followed me up and asked me out. I said I wasn't interested because I was madly in love with someone else. I was living at St Hilda's College at the time while I was studying social work and criminology at the University of Melbourne. My boyfriend was a medical student, and he was about to move interstate for his first job. I was terribly sad about that. He was in my room at college, telling me everything would be all right. He climbed out of my window and picked a red rose off the fence and gave it to me — and then this massive bunch of flowers arrived at the door. My boyfriend, not surprisingly, asked where they were from. I didn't know, so I read the card. I had no idea who Ralph Doubell was — but my boyfriend did! I put them on the shelf and that was fine. Except the next day another bunch came. And the next day another bunch, and then another bunch ... my room started to look like a funeral parlour and everyone at St Hilda's was cackling about it.

Ralph then called me and said: 'You said you would come out to dinner.'

I said: 'No I didn't!'

He then said we should have lunch. I told him that if he left me alone for three months and stopped sending me flowers, I would have lunch with him.

The next major competition for Doubell was the inaugural Pacific Conference Games in Tokyo in late September. Today, there are direct flights to Tokyo that take less than ten hours. In 1969, the team made its way to Japan via Papua New Guinea, where they stopped off to run against some local competition, and Hong Kong. The Pacific Conference Games was a disappointment because the USA didn't send its strongest team. Doubell labelled it a 'flop' when he spoke to the media, explaining that 'all the best American athletes were not interested in competing and consequently the fields were weak'. Australia won 15 of the 32 events, the USA won 11, Canada three, New Zealand two and Japan one. Doubell won the 800 metres easily in 1:48.0, with his Australian teammate Keith Wheeler, who was now a Church of England minister, finishing second.

Doubell was troubled by a hamstring injury when he returned from Tokyo, but he managed to win the 880 yards ahead of Reverend Wheeler at a 'Meet of Champions' held at Olympic Park, Melbourne, on 7 November. He was satisfied with his time of 1:49.0 given his physical condition and the slow track. Two days later, he set a new Queensland open record for 880 yards by crossing the line in 1:48.5 at a meeting held at Lang Park. He didn't race much over the next month due to his hamstring strain, but on 17 December 1969 he won an 800-metres race at Olympic Sports Field in Adelaide. His time of 1:46.8 was a new record for an 800-metre run in Australia, and it was almost half a second faster than his previous best on an Australian track. It was a real surprise to Doubell, because he didn't think he was fit enough.

Doubell also had other things on his mind. He had waited the agreed amount of time and contacted Jennifer Walker:

It was three months later and he rang to organise lunch — except he said he would pick me up at 6.30pm. So I did go out for dinner with him. At dinner, I was crying about my boyfriend and how he was moving away. Ralph just sat there and listened, and every now and then he would say his girlfriend was a long way away too. He had a Mexican girlfriend at the time, a sort of Miss Mexico who spoke five languages, came from a wealthy family and was very accomplished. He kept asking me out. I said I wasn't interested because of my boyfriend, but he did go to very interesting functions so I told him that if he wanted me to go with him that was fine, but I was going because I was interested in the events, not him!

Walker isn't exaggerating when she said she wasn't particularly interested in Doubell at the time. She was largely ignorant of his achievements on the athletics track. One Saturday, Doubell dropped by to visit her in Carlton after he had finished training. She recalls their conversation with a smile:

He said he'd been doing time trials and I asked what a time trial was. He said you run a certain distance as hard as you can and then you see if you can improve. I asked him how far he ran and he said 800 metres. I then asked what his fastest time was and he said 1:44.3. I didn't even know whether it was minutes or seconds, but I asked: 'Is that fast?' He said: 'Yes, it's quite fast.' My brothers explained to me later that it was the world record and they couldn't believe I had been so rude. But I don't think Ralph cared at all.

Over the following months, Walker's relationship with her interstate boyfriend began to wither and Doubell's focus and persistence, two of his key qualities, resulted in them seeing each other more regularly.

In January 1970, Doubell travelled to the USA again for a month-long series of indoor races. Before he left Australia, the Victorian Amateur Athletics Association told him that they wanted him to return in time to compete at the Victorian Championships on 14–15 February. The problem was, the American promoters wanted Doubell to run in a *Los Angeles Times* meeting on 13 February. If he did, he couldn't be home in time to run in the Victorian Championships. There were many discussions between the relevant officials and, in late January, the US promoters agreed to pay the VAAA $750 in compensation to allow Doubell to run in Los Angeles on 13 February. It was an interesting way to resolve the issue in the age of amateur athletics.

Doubell's first race on this tour was the 1000 yards at the Sunkist Invitational meeting in Los Angeles on 18 January. He ran against the two athletes who had beaten him outdoors the previous year: Juris Luzins and Naftali Bon. Doubell ran well and won the race in 2:06.5. He filed a few reports for *The Age* while he was on tour and one described his celebrations after this victory over Luzins and Bon:

I went along to a party given for the top gridiron players who had performed when the East Coast played the West Coast. Members of the winning side each got about $1500 and the losers received about $1000. About 58,000 people paid a total of some $225,000 to watch the game and a TV network paid $800,000 for the exclusive rights to televise it ...

The party was quite remarkable. Everyone tried to outdo each other with their plumage. Apparently, the footballers had already run a contest in their changing rooms to see who had the brightest and most colourful underwear, and now they were parading in their 'after six' gear.

One very big footballer had a gold and black sequined ensemble, together with a black silk shirt with splashes of red, blue and pink. An even bigger footballer had a roll of cultured pearls around his neck. I didn't comment since both were twice as big as me ... I dare not try and describe some of the female dress.

Doubell's performance in Los Angeles was excellent under any circumstances, but even more so if the report written by Pat Putnam in *Sports Illustrated*, a magazine that sold millions of copies around the world, was to be believed:

Ralph Doubell flew into Los Angeles late last Wednesday afternoon. It had taken 24 sleepless hours to transport his mammoth hangover from Australia to California, which is tough even on an Aussie, and so he forgot about his playboy image and went to bed. Sixteen hours later, the handsome Olympic 800-metres champion arose, worked his way through four bottles of German beer, one Bloody Mary, three glasses of rose and 237 pages of *Portnoy's Complaint,* and then retreated once more into feathers. By Friday, he was feeling much better. Since he was to run the following night in the Sunkist Invitational, he was tapering off with Coke.

'I feel the attitude of American runners about not drinking is very strange,' he said. Then, grinning, he added: 'Most Australians do. Just last Friday I went out with my coach and we got stoned on champagne. Of course, you can't do that all the time, just about once every fortnight.' The theory was hardly advanced before it was put to the test, over 1000 yards on Saturday night, and Doubell sped them in 2:06.5 — just five tenths in excess of Peter Snell's world record — and in the doing he blew his two toughest rivals, Kenya's Naftali Bon and America's Juris Luzins, off the bouncing boards of the Los Angeles Sports Arena.

This kind of hyperbole began to be used regularly in American press reports profiling Doubell. He was described as a 'playboy', 'party loving', 'the Champagne Kid' and even 'Ralph the Rapscallion'. Some claimed he not only enjoyed drinking port but that he had a girl in every port. Doubell was unfazed by the attention and the exaggeration, and in fact he played along willingly. Phil Pepe of New York's *Daily News* wrote a profile of Doubell a few days after the *Sports Illustrated* article was published, which read in part:

The jacket is antelope suede from London, the pants are black corduroy hip-hugging bellbottoms, the shoes are tan suede, the tie is white squares on a blue background and unstylishly narrow, the shirt is an almost-white pink. The accent is Australian, the sideburns are mod length, but trimmed, the name is Ralph Doubell, the game is track, the approach is unique. He drinks champagne, he has no interest in records, he runs when he feels like it and he delivers lines that Will Rogers would have loved, like 'the one thing I dislike about an athlete is when he's beaten me' …

Right across from the University of Melbourne, there was a place that sold champagne,' Doubell recalls. 'We used to go there after a workout and buy a bottle and drink it with our lunch. It's fun after training. It cost $1.75 a bottle … I don't think champagne hurts me. I can remember one night sitting down with my coach at dinner and finishing off three bottles between the two of us. The next morning, I got up and ran the fastest 220 of my life: 22.2.'

Doubell received a lot more media attention in America than he ever did in Australia, even after his gold medal run in Mexico City. At that time, Australia's sporting journalists were much more interested in footballers, cricketers, tennis players and the great fighter Lionel Rose, who won the world bantamweight title over Fighting Harada of Japan on 27 February 1968 and then defended it successfully three times before losing to Mexico's Ruben Olivares on 22 August 1969. The interviews and colourful profiles in the American press were all part of the fun of touring, and Doubell didn't feel any need to correct the inaccuracies in their reports.

While Doubell might not have been able to completely live up to his media reputation off the track, he continued to achieve milestones on the US indoor circuit. On 25 January 1970, Doubell was in New Mexico for the Albuquerque Invitational indoor track meet at Tingley Coliseum that was attended by about 9000 athletics fans. It was here that he finally broke Peter Snell's seven-year-old world indoor record for 1000 yards, starting his finishing burst earlier than usual to run 2:05.5 and beat Snell's old mark by half a second.

'No one seemed to want to set the pace so I decided to go after it on my own,' the *San Bernardino Sun* reported him saying after the race. One year earlier he had set the 880-yards indoor world record at the same track.

Doubell then flew to the Big Apple and, on 30 January, he won the 880 yards at the Milrose Games in Madison Square Garden in a record time of 1:49.2. The previous record had been set by Tom Farrell. Czechoslovakia's Josef Plachý, who won this event in 1969 and finished fifth behind Doubell in Mexico City, came second with Juris Luzins third.

A week later, Doubell comfortably won the 1000 yards at the Telegram-Maple Leaf Indoor Games in Toronto, Canada. He then returned to the US west coast for the final race of the tour at the Los Angeles Times Invitational at the Forum on 15 February. The organisers wanted Doubell to race over 600 yards against local champion Martin McGrady, who was the world indoor record holder for that distance, and Lee Evans, the reigning 400-metres Olympic champion. Doubell agreed and this match up helped to attract a capacity crowd of more than 16,000. He finished third, with McGrady just beating Evans to the tape in a world indoor record time of 1:08.7.

This was the first time Doubell had been beaten in 15 indoor races in North America. 'I did the best I could, but I'm just not fast enough to run the 600,' Doubell told the *San Bernardino Sun*. 'I'll never run this event again. If it had been another 100 metres I would have done all right. I would face them on the boards at the half mile.'

After another extremely successful tour of the US, Doubell returned to Australia, where he was still able to walk down the main streets and have no one recognise him. As he told journalist Jim Webster in an interview soon after he landed back on home soil, 'I never have any problem with autograph hunters ... there aren't any.'

CHAPTER 19

Slowing Down

In mid-March 1970, Doubell competed at a meeting organised by Athletics International at the new rubberised asphalt track at Olympic Park in Melbourne. Athletics International was formed in December 1967 to lift the standard of amateur athletics entertainment in Australia. The organisation was mostly made up of past and present representative athletes who wanted to put something back into the sport they loved. The meeting featured Australian Olympians such as Doubell and Ron Clarke and American track stars such as Charlie Greene, who had won gold in the 4 x 100-metres relay and bronze in the 100 metres at the 1968 Olympics, world pole vault record holder Bob Seagren and Martin McGrady, who had beaten Doubell over 600 yards in the Australian's last indoor race in the USA.

Doubell's first race at the carnival was the 1000 metres and he ran 2:20.8 to break John Murray's 13-year-old Australian record by

2.1 seconds. He had agreed, against his better judgement, to again compete against McGrady over less than 800 metres. This time it was 600 metres and it was outdoors, but the result was the same as in Los Angeles.

McGrady won in 1:14.9, with Doubell in second place four-tenths of a second behind him.

In April, Doubell was selected for the Australian team for the 1970 British Commonwealth Games, to be held from July 16 to 25 in Edinburgh, Scotland. Earlier in the year, it was feared that many African countries would withdraw from the Games because of two rugby union series: South Africa's Springboks toured the United Kingdom in the 1969–70 northern hemisphere winter and New Zealand's All Blacks were scheduled to visit South Africa from July to September 1970. The boycott did not go ahead, however, and the Edinburgh Games attracted 1383 athletes from 42 countries.

This was the first time that metric distances were used at a Commonwealth Games and the first time that electronic photo-finish technology was used. It was also the first Commonwealth Games attended by Queen Elizabeth II.

In the 10,000-metres final on the first day of track-and-field competition, most expected the winner to be either Ron Clarke, who still had not managed to win a major championship despite setting 17 world records from two miles to 20 kilometres, or the defending champion Naftali Temu of Kenya, who had won the gold medal for the 10,000 metres in Mexico City. Somehow, Clarke managed to be beaten again, this time by an unheralded Scot named Lachie Stewart. The Edinburgh crowd was ecstatic at the shock result, and it heightened local excitement for the rest of the Games. Extraordinarily, on the last day of the Games, another

Scot, Ian Stewart, who was no relation to Lachie, would beat the great Kip Keino to win the 5000 metres in another huge upset. Ron Clarke finished fifth. Peter Norman would also disappoint in Edinburgh. He was favoured to at least win a medal in the 200 metres, but he too was fifth. Kerry O'Brien, who a fortnight before the Games became the new world record holder in the 3000-metres steeplechase, fell at the final water jump when he was leading the race and was unable to finish.

Doubell won his 800-metres semi-final in pouring rain, even though John Davies of England put his hand on Doubell's shoulder as they ran down the straight to try to slow him down. Doubell finished just ahead of Davies in 1:49.1, which was not a fantastic time but he felt relatively comfortable through the race. He thought he was in very good shape.

However, like Norman, Clarke and O'Brien, Doubell disappointed himself and the Australian sporting public in his final. He was well placed during the first lap and for most of the second lap, but he could not find his usual finishing kick. For some reason, he 'ran out of gas'. Robert Uoko of Kenya won in 1:46.9, ahead of Ben Cayenne of Trinidad and William Smart of Canada. Doubell faded to finish exactly one second behind Uoko in sixth place. He was furious with himself, and certainly didn't have the excuse of tonsillitis that he had in Kingston four years earlier. When he had calmed down and could eventually face the media, he greeted them with, 'OK vultures, let's go.' But he blamed himself for the poor performance:

The only thing I can put it down to is lack of competition, and I have only myself to blame for that. I had offers to run in Europe before the Games and I turned them down. I knew after one lap that I was in trouble. I tried to get going up the finishing straight but there was nothing there. It is my own fault. I have no excuses.

On further reflection, Doubell admitted to himself that he hadn't been training as hard as he had in the years leading up to Mexico City. He was working full-time, which was a fair enough reason in itself, but he was also partying more. Not anything like the extent suggested by the American media, but certainly enough to take the edge off the heights he had reached in 1968. Subconsciously, he also didn't have as much to prove — either to himself or to anyone else. He no longer had the level of hunger that is critical to winning at the elite level of sporting competition. The result in Edinburgh was the first sign that the fire in his belly was diminishing.

DOUBELL RESUMED TRAINING WHEN he returned to Australia and he continued to win over 800 metres and 1500 metres in interclub and invitation events in late 1970 and early 1971. He flew to America in February for a three-week tour and enjoyed some success, most notably in San Diego, where he won a 1000-yards race in 2:06.3, just 0.8 seconds outside his world record. But it was a false dawn. Back home for the Australian Amateur Athletics Championships in Brisbane, he finished fourth in his heat of the 800 metres on 14 March and failed to qualify for the final. After the race, he was as stunned as the crowd. 'I can't understand it. I couldn't have gone any slower,' he told a reporter from *The Sporting Globe*.

The media pounced, epitomised by this article by Ron Carter in *The Age*, the headline of which asked, 'Is Doubell finished?':

What does the athletic future hold for reigning Olympic Games champion Ralph Doubell, who could not even run fast enough to qualify for the Australian 800-metres championship in Brisbane last weekend?

Will Doubell, 26, ever get back to his world-record pace again? Is he finished as a runner?

Doubell, the toast of Australian athletics after his win in the Olympic 800 metres two-and-a-half years ago, now does not hold either a state or national title.

His morale has really taken a beating in the past 12 months. It started with his failure at the Commonwealth Games in Edinburgh last July. His latest Brisbane debacle tops the lot.

His immediate future has already been decided — he has started what will be his longest break from athletics for eight years. As from last Sunday, Doubell is on four months holiday ...

Neither coach Franz Stampfl nor Doubell can explain the way he 'bombed out' in Brisbane. There is no clear reason for it. The only thing they can suggest is that he has had a belly full of athletics and the enthusiasm for racing is dead. Stampfl has told him, 'Get away, don't look at a pair of spikes, stay away from running tracks, don't even talk athletics, I don't want to see you again until next August.'

Doubell did as he was told and the media reported that his weight 'ballooned' to 11st 10lb (74kg). He focused on his job and the only exercise he did was to play squash, often with Stampfl. After his spell in the paddock, he gradually returned to training and continued to dream of defending his title in Munich. The qualifying time was 1:47.6, provided it was recorded after August 1971. Given the limited time to prepare, Doubell did less mileage than he had in the lead-up to Mexico City and focused more on speed work.

In mid-November 1971, Doubell began competing for the first time since the disaster at the Australian Championships in Brisbane eight months earlier. He ran some 100, 200 and 400-metres races and built up to the 800 metres. By the end of November, he was running under 1:50 for 800 metres, a satisfactory performance given the long break and his lack of racing condition. However, Doubell then suffered a hamstring injury. It wasn't severe, but it meant he had to stop racing. He and Stanley Spittle drove up to Falls Creek to do some high-altitude training in late December and early January.

On 8 January 1972, Doubell gained some confidence when he beat the reigning Australian 1500-metres champion Chris Fisher over 800 metres at a Victoria versus South Australia meeting in Adelaide. Fisher had won the national 1500 title for each of the previous two years and would compete in that event at the Munich Olympics. However, Doubell only finished second in the race, because his Victorian teammate Peter Fuller crossed the line one-tenth of a second ahead of him in 1:49.8. Ten days later, Doubell's confidence was boosted further when he won his first race for some time. He beat his old foe, Reverend Keith Wheeler, in 1:51.2 on a slow track at Sandringham.

Despite his average form while on the road to recovery, Doubell flew to America again in late January to compete in a series of races. He was driven by his love of travel and competitive racing, as usual, but he had also arranged interviews at Harvard University in Cambridge, a suburb in the Boston metropolitan area, and at Stanford University in California. Doubell was still working for Shell, and his employer continued to be extremely supportive while he competed during the athletics season. Doubell, however, was starting to think beyond sport:

> I decided I needed a 'business passport' if I was to advance my career in the way I wanted. I did my research and decided the best two courses were the Master of Business Administration degrees offered by Harvard and Stanford. I also applied to the University of Melbourne, just in case I wasn't accepted by either of the American universities.

On 29 January 1972, a crowd of 16,500 watched Doubell finish second to Juris Luzins in the 1000 yards at the Millrose Games at Madison Square Garden. Doubell actually crossed the line in third place, but the second-place getter, Tom von Ruden, a former Pan American Games gold medallist over 1500 metres, was disqualified for interfering with him on the final turn. It wasn't a difficult decision for the judges, as von Ruden nearly knocked Doubell over and onto the timber track surface. From New York, Doubell detoured to Boston, to go to Harvard, where he was interviewed for the MBA course that he believed would take his working life to the next level. He felt the interview went well, but there would be a nervous wait until he discovered whether he was successful.

The next stop on his athletics tour was Toronto, where four days after his race in New York he competed at the Telegram-Maple Leaf Indoor Games. It was just another race on the North American circuit that he now knew so well, but with about 150 metres to go Doubell felt a painful tightening in his lower leg. He jumped into the air and stopped immediately. Something was seriously wrong. He withdrew from the rest of the tour and had to cancel his interview with Stanford.

The medical staff put his leg in plaster, ordered him to use crutches and made arrangements for him to make the 30-hour journey from Toronto to Melbourne, via Chicago, as soon as possible. The diagnosis he received soon after he landed was not good: he had torn the plantaris muscle in his left calf and would not be able to run for four or five weeks. This meant he would certainly miss the Victorian Championships on 19 February and probably the Australian Championships in Perth on 24–26 March. The Australian Championships, of course, were effectively selection trials for the Munich Olympic Games.

While Doubell was undergoing treatment for his calf injury, including plenty of time in the Beaurepaire Pool at the University of Melbourne, he received the notification that he had been accepted by Harvard University to study for a two-year Master of Business Administration degree, starting in September. The Munich Olympic Games would open on 26 August, meaning a virtual clash with the beginning of his studies. Doubell knew that the chances of him qualifying for Munich were increasingly remote, and the letter from Harvard made the decision about his future extremely clear. In an interview with Ron Carter that was published in *The Age* on 29 February, Doubell said:

This is the end for me. I've devoted enough of my life to running and from now on I'm concentrating on my career and studies. I can't keep on running all my life. The life of a competitor is nine or 10 years and I've had nine years.

Doubell's focus for the next stage of his life was not just on his course at Harvard. Jennifer Walker had gone travelling with a girlfriend 'to assert my independence', but Doubell had been writing to her almost daily as well as booking the occasional international telephone call. She recalls:

> When Ralph got into Harvard he asked me if I would come home and get married. I held out for a while but then Ralph had to fill out a form which asked if you wanted single dormitory accommodation at Harvard or an apartment for a married couple. He asked me to help him fill in the form, but I said it was up to him. He filled it in, but he didn't tell me what he'd written. That was sort of the proposal! Not very romantic, but he is a romantic. For most of our married life he has brought me flowers every week, and he still does.

Jennifer flew home to Melbourne and agreed to marry Ralph — they had to be married if she was going to go to Harvard with him — because 'when you love someone you want to live in their best interests, and he really wanted to go to Harvard'. Strangely, Doubell's mother, who was so ambitious for her children's education, was not in favour of him studying and working in America. 'She thought he had a perfectly good job with Shell and wondered why he would leave it,' Jennifer explains. 'It was the security.'

Soon after she returned, Doubell told his fiancée over lunch that he had seen a ring that she might like at Kozminsky, a renowned jeweller in Bourke Street that closed its doors in February 2017 after 165 years of operation:

> I met him there later and they brought out tray after tray after tray. He told them which ring he was interested in, it was an amethyst ring, and then he asked: 'Does it come in any other colours?

Jennifer's parents were living in New Zealand. Her father was a senior executive with AMP and he had been posted there, and they were surprised to learn that their daughter was not marrying her doctor boyfriend but an Olympic athletics champion instead. There was not much time for the Walkers to come to terms with the news, because the young couple had only about five weeks until they would travel to Europe for a brief honeymoon before the groom began his studies. The wedding took place on 19 August 1971 at the Kew Presbyterian Church, where Jennifer's parents and maternal grandparents had been married, and the reception was held at the Hotel Windsor, a Melbourne institution which had been established in 1883. Stanley Spittle, Doubell's long-time training mate, was best man.

As a married couple, the Doubells had to show Harvard that they had $9000 to support themselves for a year. Ralph sold his car and they scraped together every cent they could. 'We had about $9,001', Jennifer says with a laugh. Their honeymoon involved a drive down the Rhine Valley and through the Black Forest, and also a visit to the Munich Olympic Games. Dave Wottle of the USA came from last with 300 metres to go to win the 800 metres from Yevgeniy Arzhanov of the Soviet Union, with Kenya's Mike Boit third. Franz-Josef Kemper of West Germany, whom Doubell had beaten at the Universiade in Tokyo in 1967, finished fourth and Robert Ouku, the British Commonwealth Games champion from 1970, was fifth. Wottle's time was 1:45.86, one-and-a-half seconds slower than Doubell's winning time in Mexico City.

CHAPTER 20

Harvard and Beyond

During his two years at Harvard Business School, Doubell was completely focused on his studies. He did not join the university athletics team and he did not speak to fellow students about his achievements in international track and field. He had moved on to the next chapter in his life. Doubell did, however, continue to run regularly in order to keep fit. He did plenty of track work at the university's excellent facilities and one day a man approached him at the end of his workout. The man said he had been watching him for a few weeks and thought he might have some potential.

He asked whether Doubell had ever thought about taking up athletics seriously. 'I used to do quite a bit but I don't have the time any more,' Doubell replied.

The man persisted, offering to introduce Doubell to the university track coach and saying he thought he had a chance of getting on to the team. Doubell declined politely, repeating that he just didn't have the time because of his studies. A few days later, the weather had turned cold and Doubell turned up for training in his Australian Olympic tracksuit. The friendly talent scout was extremely embarrassed.

Ralph and Jennifer spent two years at Harvard, living in an apartment in the basement of a house in Belmont, a suburb of Boston. While Ralph studied full-time, Jennifer quickly secured a job as a criminologist with the Massachusetts Department of Correction. 'It was an amazing time,' she says. 'The Department of Correction had its first black Commissioner and he was very liberal in his ideas, including education and work programs for the prisoners. I was very busy and I absolutely loved it.'

The Doubells also enjoyed meeting new friends in Boston. 'We had an absolute ball,' Jennifer says. 'We had great company and there was wonderful collegiality among the students.'

Apart from the mental stimulation, the money Jennifer earned was vital in supporting the couple as Ralph focused on getting through the challenging MBA course. 'We didn't have a penny to spare,' Jennifer recalls fondly:

We used to shop at the supermarket on Friday nights for the week. I knew exactly how much to budget for each meal, including slices of deep frozen lamb from New Zealand. We would sometimes entertain, and a friend reminds me to this day that I once said I would never serve a dessert that cost more than 15 cents a head. The price of a half bottle of wine would fluctuate between 98 cents and $1.02. If it went over $1.01 we wouldn't buy it!

Their student budget was strained when Ralph graduated. 'He needed to buy some new clothes and a suit for the interviews,' Jennifer explains. 'We actually went into debt to buy those clothes, and we were very nervous about that.'

As a Harvard MBA graduate, Doubell was never going to have a problem securing a job and paying off the debt for his new suit. It was really a matter of which job to choose, as recruiting firms came onto campus and tried to convince the graduates to join their client. Jennifer remembers being flown to Chicago by one bank, where they were wined and dined and Jennifer was introduced to a leading criminologist. 'They certainly did their homework,' she says.

Doubell ultimately decided to accept an offer from Citibank. He spent four months training in the bank's New York headquarters before spending 13 years working in their San Francisco, Melbourne and London offices. He then worked for nine years at Goldman Sachs, first in London and then in New York and Sydney, before moving to Deutsche Bank for the last five years of his career in investment banking. Later, he was — at different times — chairman of two tech startups, national marketing manager for Rushton Valuers and CEO of Artez Pacific, a software company that provided on-line fundraising assistance for charities.

Throughout this time, Jennifer continued to pursue her career while also raising three children. She used her social work and criminology skills in San Francisco and then Melbourne, where Anna (1978) and Andrew (1981) were born. When Ralph was posted to London in 1982, she began studying for an MBA at London Business School. Their third child, James, was born in London in 1985. Later, when they moved to Sydney with Goldman

Sachs, Jennifer began a new career. She was thinking about doing a PhD in organisational behaviour at the Australian Graduate School of Management, but she wasn't entirely sure. The Dean of AGSM, Professor Fred Hilmer, suggested she should work for him a few days a week until she decided what she wanted to do. She was soon working five days a week managing AGSM's donors and alumni. It was the beginning of what would become a 30-year career in fundraising that has seen her work for the Wesley Mission and the Heart Foundation. Since 2008, Jennifer Doubell has been Executive Director of the Peter MacCallum Cancer Foundation in Melbourne. In 2016 she was named Arthur Venn Fundraiser of the Year.

As was the case at Harvard, Doubell did not initiate conversation about his athletic achievements with his colleagues during his years with some of the world's leading investment banks. Over the decades, a handful of journalists tracked him down. They wrote stories about his successful business career and how he was almost unknown in his home country despite being one of only three Australian men to have won a gold medal on an Olympic athletics track. A number of those stories noted that there were no medals or photos from his athletics career in his office.

While at a dinner party during one of his stints in London, a lawyer was boasting about his son's performances in middle-distance athletics at Cambridge University. The father described how difficult the training was and how much commitment was required, but it didn't sound too daunting to Doubell. After the lawyer had finished his stories, Jennifer suggested that the lawyer and his son might want to speak to her husband. The lawyer rolled his eyes and asked incredulously: 'What would Ralph know about it?'

When he was told who Doubell was, the lawyer was stunned. 'He was sort of like a goldfish in a bowl. His mouth was moving but no words were coming out,' Doubell remembers with a wry smile.

Cholmondeley 'Chum' Darvall was at Deutsche Bank in Australia at the same time as Doubell. They were in different divisions of the bank and so didn't work together on a day-to-day basis, but Darvall was well aware of Doubell's achievements on the running track. Darvall attended The King's School in Sydney and was Australia's junior 800-metres champion in 1976. He won a gold medal as a 19-year-old representing Australia in the 800 metres at the Pacific Conference Games in 1977, beating then Australian champion John Higham and NCAA champion Mark Belger to the tape. Darvall finished fourth in the final of the 800 metres at the 1978 Commonwealth Games in Edmonton, Canada, and took home a bronze medal as a member of Australia's 4 x 400-metres relay team.

Adriaan Paulen, a three-time Olympian for the Netherlands from 1920 to 1928 and President of the IAAF from 1976 to 1981, was in the stands at the 1977 Pacific Conference Games and observed that Darvall had the potential to be 'Australia's best 800-metres runner since Ralph Doubell'.

'I didn't live up to the prediction,' Darvall points out, 'but it was an inspirational comment.' He regards Doubell as an Australian sporting icon:

His was one of the great achievements in Australian athletics, especially as he won the Olympic gold medal and equalled the world record in the same race, but it wasn't accompanied by the sort of fanfare one would have expected. My recollection is that Ralph never initiated any reference to his gold medal or his world record at work and I don't remember him having any memorabilia around his office. He didn't trade off it. There was a rumour that when he was at Citibank he kept his gold medal in one of his desk drawers, but I don't know whether that was true or not! I do remember that when we went to a conference, Ralph was still going out and doing a morning run with a few of the younger staff.

Asked what Doubell was like in an office environment, Darvall says that 'Ralph is very much his own man. He isn't typical of any stereotype. It's a bit like his running, I suppose. He had his own view of things and was quite independent.'

As with athletics, Doubell was a late bloomer when it came to success in the academic and business worlds. He says the primary reason for this was essentially the same:

Once I found an interest in something and found that I was reasonably good, I would go like hell at it. I hadn't found anything to interest me as a teenager until I found running. That's when the competitive spirit kicked in. I did that in business too.

Doubell has no doubt that his athletics training and achievements influenced his life tremendously and helped his business career:

One of the most important lessons is that you learn how to handle pressure and to perform under pressure. When you are on the starting line of a race, there is no one to help you. It's pretty brutal. At the Olympics level, the whole world is watching and if you succeed, everyone is your friend. If you fail, however, everyone can tell you why you failed. You have to learn to withstand the pressure of putting yourself to the test every time, in front of the whole world.

DOUBELL DID FIND HIMSELF in the public eye in Australia during his time as Chairman of Athletics NSW, a position he took on in 1995 at a time when the organisation was in financial difficulties. This was one of a number of forays Doubell took into sports business and administration in the late 1990s and the early years of the 21st century — he was also a founding director of Stadium Australia, the principal venue for the Sydney 2000 Olympics and the 2003 Rugby World Cup, a director of Athletics Australia and CEO of the New South Wales Institute of Sport. Doubell remained Chairman of Athletics NSW until 2004. The situation he was confronted with when he started in the role was front and centre of Athletics NSW's report that appeared in Athletics Australia's *Annual Report* for 1996–97:

Our financial condition continues to be extremely serious. The situation was formally recognised in October last year [1996] when the Board appointed an administrator to independently review the operations of the company. The administrator's appointment was triggered by the approximate $80,000 loss on the Sydney Marathon. Even before this loss, ANSW had in each of the past two years experienced a cash loss of over $100,000.

During this two-year period, costs had been built up well in excess of revenue, but one-off accounting entries and reversals allowed the company to report profit.

The start of the men's 800-metres final in Mexico City. Tom Farrell (USA) is closest to camera in lane eight, Doubell in lane four …

A lap to go. Wilson Kiprugut (566) leads from Ben Cayenne (773) and Dieter Fromm (66), with Doubell moving to fourth, Josef Plachý inside him and Walter Adams on the kerb. Farrell is behind Doubell, with Thomas Saisi wide and out of picture …

'Kiprugut is now four, five yards clear and trying to go away again,' is how the great commentator David Coleman called it for the BBC. 'What an astonishing piece of front running!' But then, 80 metres from the finish, Doubell made his decisive move …

'I'm going to win! There's the tape. Keep pushing, Kiprugut's still there …'

'That's it, that's the tape, I'm holding the tape. I've won!'

The medallists — Wilson Kiprugut (silver), Tom Farrell (bronze) and Doubell (gold) immediately after the final.

Doubell ponders what happens next ... and then he and his great rival seek shelter from the storm.

The medal ceremony took place in front of a drenched and almost deserted stadium.

Back in Melbourne, Doubell's mother Beryl and sister Barbara shared their joy with press photographers.

The homecoming … Doubell was interviewed by Channel Nine's Ron Casey (left) at Sydney airport, and then a week later was at the Melbourne Cup with fellow gold medallists Maureen Caird, Michael Wenden and Lyn McClements (far right).

Doubell in his Australian Olympic tracksuit, jogging on the fairways and around the greens of Melbourne's Yarra Yarra Golf Club.

Right: Doubell in Los Angeles in 1970, on his way to victory in a 1000-yards indoor event against Kenth Andersson (left), Naftali Bon (centre) and Juris Luzins (behind).

Below left: Doubell with his wife Jennifer, pondering a post-athletics career that would take them to Harvard Business School, then New York and London, and eventually back home.

Below right: In July 2018, 20-year-old Joseph Deng broke Doubell's Australian 800-metres record, which had survived almost 50 years. The Olympic champion, content with his many achievements on and off the track, applauded the young man's effort and expressed surprise that his record had lasted for so long.

In January 2017, Doubell revisited Mexico City, where with the help of Dr David Engel, Australia's Ambassador to Mexico (at right in top photo), he returned to the Estadio Olimpico and stood again in lane four. Then he and Jennifer walked the track, Doubell never leaving his lane, as he described in minute detail how he ran the race of his life.

> With the change of the organisation to a company status, our loss from the Sydney Marathon and the impending action of various creditors, our directors had no choice but to appoint administrators.
>
> The administrator's principal objectives were to solve the immediate cash shortfall and satisfy the existing creditors ...

Gordon Windeyer was one of Doubell's fellow board members during these years at Athletics NSW. Windeyer was born in Sydney in 1954 and, unlike Doubell, grew up in an affluent family. His father was a specialist medical practitioner and young Gordon went to Barker College, a private school at Hornsby in Sydney's north. He was a good all-round sportsman, but he did particularly well in athletics. He consistently won the high jump at the Barker carnival and also at the Combined Associated Schools championships, but he didn't start taking sport seriously until he was 16. His father then took him to Helen Firth, an Olympian who was coaching at Beauchamp Park in Chatswood, and Firth then sent Gordon to Jack Pross, a devotee of Percy Cerutty and the coach of many Australian athletics representatives. Pross was known mostly for his expertise in middle-distance running, but he also coached long, high and triple jumpers as well as pole vaulters.

'After a short while, Jack said to my father: 'I don't think he'll make it as a high jumper,' Windeyer recalls with a laugh. 'But I stuck with it and Jack had a huge influence on me.'

Windeyer broke the Combined Associated Schools high jump record in 1971 and, when he finished high school, he continued training with Pross's squad at the University of Sydney, where he was studying Economics:

I was fervent about athletics. It was the main thing in my life. I remember standing on the side of the No. 1 oval at Sydney University and this friend was telling me about his latest female conquest. I was not interested as I had already met my now wife and was very focused on athletics. I knew this was the time to really achieve something significant. My friend couldn't believe it. He stood up and shouted: 'What are you, a man or a mouse, Gordon?!'

Windeyer, like Doubell, had discovered a rare inner drive to succeed in athletics during his first year at University. Two years later, aged 19, Windeyer won the gold medal at the 1974 British Commonwealth Games in Christchurch, clearing 2.16 metres (7ft, 1in). This height set a new Games record and pushed his team mate, Lawrie Peckham, into second place. Peckham had won the high jump gold medal at the two previous British Commonwealth Games and represented Australia at the 1964, 1968 and 1972 Olympic Games, finishing eighth in the final in Mexico City.

Despite having won a British Commonwealth Games gold medal at the age of 19, being Australian champion in 1976 and achieving that year's Olympic qualifying standard, Windeyer was not selected in Australia's team for the Montreal Olympics. The officials decided not to take a high jumper to Canada. Over 40 years later, he still describes this as 'an enormous blow', adding, 'I was completely deflated and found it difficult to motivate myself during 1977.' However, he did retain his Australian title in 1977 and made it three in a row in 1978. During the year he jumped a personal best of 2.21 metres (7ft 3in), which equalled Peckham's Australian record. Windeyer was selected to represent Australia at the Commonwealth Games in Edmonton but performed below his best and finished fifth in the final.

Windeyer stopped competing after Edmonton and began what became a very successful business career. In the late 1980s, he was a co-founder of Catalyst, a private equity firm that was later acquired by Prudential. Windeyer's financial and business experience and skills were a great benefit to the Athletics NSW board, especially as it attempted to solve problems relating to the staging of the Sydney Marathon. He remembers how awkward things became:

> Over the three years from 1994 to 1996, the event [the Sydney Marathon] got into a financial hole and as a result Athletics NSW was in a financial pickle. Ralph had recently become a director and John Treloar [who won three gold medals as a sprinter at the 1950 British Empire Games and finished sixth in the final of the 100 metres at the 1952 Helsinki Olympics] convinced Ralph to run for Chairman — and then he was elected Chairman by the Board. Within a few months Ralph said to me: 'Gordon, we have to put this thing into administration.' I agreed and so did the other directors.'

Athletics NSW was placed into voluntary administration at the start of October 1996, with Deloitte appointed as the administrator.

In early 1997, as the Board and Deloitte worked to save the situation, there was still hope that a profitable Sydney Marathon could be staged later in the year. However, in late July, just one month before the scheduled date for the event, Athletics NSW announced it had been cancelled. Doubell, as Chairman, explained to the media that because the Sydney Marathon had been endorsed by SOCOG as an Olympic test event, it had to be sponsored by one of SOCOG's official Team Millennium sponsors.

'We have been meeting with various Team Millennium members over the past three months but they all felt a minimum of six to eight months was required to maximise their involvement in a major event such as this, together with Olympic sponsorship,' Doubell told the media. All entrants were refunded their entry fees, including hundreds of Japanese running tourists.

The cancellation of the 1997 Sydney Marathon, and Doubell's handling of it, attracted plenty of criticism, but Windeyer says it was a decisive move that set up the organisation for the future. In April 2000, five months before the Sydney Olympic Games, a marathon was finally run over the Olympics course as a test event. In June 2006, Doubell became a Member (AM) in the General Division of the Order of Australia, 'for service to athletics through administrative roles, particularly with Athletics New South Wales, and as a competitor'.

'When Athletics NSW came out of administration it had about $20,000 in the bank,' Windeyer says. 'Ralph said we should aim to put $30,000 to $50,000 aside each year to build a cash reservoir. This has been achieved and in 2018 Athletics NSW has cash reserves of about $1 million. Ralph was the architect of that. He is a very focused guy and he did a darn good job because he got the thing stabilised and set it on the course to a very solid financial position.'

Windeyer readily admits that not everyone appreciated Doubell's manner in the world of athletics administration. 'He can be quite blunt with people, and that gets a lot of people offside. But I have a very enjoyable relationship with Ralph.'

CHAPTER 21

Only Three Men

In 120 years of competition at the modern Olympic Games, only three Australian men have won a gold medal in a running race on the athletics track. Edwin Flack won the 800 metres and the 1500 metres at the first modern Olympics, in Athens in 1896; Herb Elliott won the 1500 metres in Rome in 1960; Ralph Doubell won the 800 metres in Mexico City in 1968. This three-man club is one of the most elite in Australian sport and Doubell's membership in it reinforces the scale of his achievement. Furthermore, in the half-century since the 1968 Games only one Australian man has won an Olympic track medal of any kind, and only ten Australian men have made an Olympic track final.

Australia's women have completely outshone their male teammates on the athletics track at Olympic Games. Let's examine what has happened since the end of World War II. In 1948, 1952 and 1956 there were only three individual track events for women: the 100 metres, 200 metres and 80-metres hurdles. Women also competed in the 4 x 100-metres relay. In London in 1948, Fanny Blankers-Koen of the Netherlands won all three of the individual track events and ran the final leg of her team's gold medal-winning relay. Australia's Shirley Strickland won the bronze medal in the 100 metres and the 80-metres hurdles, finished fourth in the 200 metres and was a key member of Australia's silver medal-winning relay team.

In Helsinki in 1952, Marjorie Jackson of Australia, known as the 'Lithgow Flash', won the gold medal in both the 100 metres and the 200 metres. Strickland won the gold medal in the 80-metres hurdles and a bronze medal in the 100 metres, while Winsome Cripps finished fourth in the 100 metres and 200 metres. The Australian women should have won the 4 x 100-metres relay, but they dropped the baton in the final.

In Melbourne in 1956, Australia's female running team reached its zenith. It was a clean sweep of the three individual track events, with Betty Cuthbert winning the 100 metres and 200 metres and Shirley Strickland winning her second successive Olympic 80-metres hurdles title. Norma Croker, who finished fourth in the 200 metres, and Fleur Mellor joined Cuthbert and Strickland to win the gold medal in the 4 x 100-metres relay. Marlene Mathews won bronze in the 100 metres and 200 metres and Norma Thrower earned bronze in the 80-metres hurdles.

Four years later, the Australian women were unable to make the finals of the 100 metres, 200 metres or 80-metres hurdles in Rome, but Brenda Jones won the silver medal in a new Olympic event for women, the 800 metres. Jones finished only one-tenth of a second behind Lyudmila Shevtsova of the Soviet Union, whose time of 2:04.3 equalled her own world record. Four years later in Tokyo, Australian women returned to their winning ways. Once again, they benefited from the introduction of a new event with Betty Cuthbert winning the inaugural women's 400-metres Olympic title and her teammate, Judy Amoore, taking home the bronze medal. Marilyn Black won bronze in the 200 metres and finished sixth in the 100 metres, while Pam Kilborn won bronze in the 80-metres hurdles. Australia finished sixth in the final of the 4 x 100-metres relay.

As we have seen, Australian women performed very strongly on the track in Mexico City, winning one gold, two silver and a bronze. As well as winning silver in the 200 metres, Raelene Boyle finished fourth in the 100 metres, her world junior record time equal to that given to the bronze medallist, Irena Szewińska of Poland. There were two other top-six finishes.

Boyle won the silver medal in the 100 metres and 200 metres at the 1972 Munich Olympic Games behind Renate Stecher of East Germany. Boyle's performances would be described as excellent in any circumstances, but even more so given the evidence that later emerged about East Germany's state-sponsored, performance-enhancing drugs program during this period. In the 200 metres, Stecher beat Boyle by just five-hundredths of a second. Pam Ryan (née Kilborn) finished fourth in the 100-metres hurdles, with East Germans finishing first and third. Charlene Rendina finished sixth in the 400 metres, with two East Germans crossing the line before her, and Jenny Orr was eighth in the 1500 metres. The Australian women finished sixth in the final of the 4 x 100-metres relay.

Boyle returned for the 1976 Montreal Olympics and finished fourth in the 100 metres, behind two West Germans and an East German. She was disqualified for breaking twice at the start of the semi-final of the 200 metres, a mistake she could never explain. Australia's Denise Robertson performed well to make the final of the 200 metres, but the first five places were filled by East and West Germans, a Soviet was sixth and she finished seventh. Australia finished fifth in the 4 x 100-metres relay and fourth in the 4 x 400-metres relay.

The USA called for a boycott of the 1980 Moscow Olympics, because of the Soviet invasion of Afghanistan, and about 60 countries supported this action, including West Germany, Japan and Canada. The Australian Government also supported the American boycott but the Australian Olympic Committee voted to send a team. Huge pressure was placed on individual athletes not to compete and some, including Raelene Boyle and swimming world-record holder Tracey Wickham, did stay at home. The AOC made one concession, agreeing that Australia would compete under the Olympic, not the Australian, flag. Denise Boyd (née Robertson) was Australia's only female track finalist in Moscow, finishing seventh in the 200 metres.

The USSR did not forget the American-led boycott of the Moscow Games and four years later it convinced more than a dozen Eastern Bloc countries to join it in boycotting the 1984 Los Angeles Olympic Games. The impact was not as severe as the Moscow boycott, but the competition in many events was still significantly diminished. Glynis Nunn was one of two Australian female track finalists, finishing fifth in the 100-metres hurdles. The other was Debbie Flintoff, who was sixth in a new event: the 400-metres hurdles. On the road, Lisa Martin finished seventh in the first women's Olympic marathon. Nunn also created history in Los Angeles by winning the first ever gold medal in the Olympic heptathlon. The five-event women's pentathlon, which was first staged in 1964, comprised the 100-metres hurdles (80 metres until 1969), 800 metres (200 metres until 1976), high jump, long jump and shot put. From 1984, to make it a seven-event heptathlon, the javelin was added and the 200 metres was reinstated and run in addition to the 800.

At the 1988 Seoul Olympics, Debbie Flintoff-King won Australia's first purely track gold medal since 1968 when she finished 0.01 seconds ahead of Tatyana Ledovskaya of the USSR in the 400-metres hurdles. 'Implicit in any gold medal victory are elements of courage and huge commitment,' wrote the AOC's long-time historian Harry Gordon. 'Debbie Flintoff-King transcended most of the normal boundaries, though, in her passage towards her final hurdles victory by the tiniest sliver of a second ... She flowed with such fluid grace across the obstacles that the great Edwin Moses later described hers as the perfect race.' Maree Holland finished eighth in the 400-metres final and Lisa Martin improved on her performance in Los Angeles to win a silver medal in the women's marathon. Jane Flemming couldn't quite follow in the footsteps of Glynis Nunn, finishing seventh in the heptathlon.

It was lean pickings at the 1992 Barcelona Olympic Games, with the only female track finalists being the 4 x 100-metres relay team, who finished in sixth place, and the 4 x 400-metres relay team, including an 18-year-old named Cathy Freeman, who were seventh. Four years later in Atlanta, Freeman won the silver medal in the 400 metres, Margaret Crowley finished fifth in the 1500 metres and the women's team was seventh in the 4 x 100-metres relay.

Cathy Freeman was given the honour of lighting the Olympic cauldron at the beginning of the 2000 Sydney Games and she carried enormous expectation from an adoring public as she raced one lap of the track for two rounds of heats, a semi-final and then the final of the 400 metres. Given the huge pressure on her shoulders, Freeman's magnificent victory in the final was one of the greatest performances by any Australian athlete in any competition. Freeman also finished sixth in the 200-metres final, one place behind her teammate Melinda Gainsford-Taylor, and both were members of Australia's 4 x 400-metres relay team that was fifth in the final.

For the next three Olympic Games, Australia's best performing women were hurdlers. Jana Pittman, who was the reigning world champion in the 400-metres hurdles, was Australia's only female track finalist in Athens in 2004, finishing fifth. Four years later, at the 2008 Beijing Olympics, Sally McLellan won the silver medal in the 100-metres hurdles. At London in 2012, now world champion and married, Sally Pearson won the gold medal in Olympic record time.

At the 2016 Olympics, in Rio de Janeiro, three Australian women qualified for the final of the 5000 metres: Eloise Wellings (ninth), Madeline Hills (tenth) and Genevieve LaCaze (12th). Wellings finished tenth in the 10,000 metres and LaCaze ninth in the 3000-metres steeplechase. Hills was seventh in the final of the 3000-metres steeplechase. The women's 4 x 400-metres relay team was eighth in the final.

AUSTRALIA'S WOMEN RUNNERS HAVE a proud record of achievement on the athletics track in the 18 Olympic Games that have been held between 1948 and 2016. In all, they have 13 gold, nine silver and 10 bronze medals (including Glynis Nunn's heptathlon gold in 1984 and Lisa Martin's marathon silver four years later). How do Australia's men compare?

At the 1948 London Olympic Games, only two men made a track final and both finished fifth: Morris Curotta in the 400 metres and Peter Gardner in the 110-metres hurdles. Australian men didn't win any medals on the track in Helsinki four years later either, but John Treloar finished sixth in the 100 metres, Ken Doubleday fifth and Ray Weinberg sixth in the 110-metres hurdles, Don MacMillan ninth in the 1500 metres, and Les Perry sixth in the 5000 metres.

In Melbourne in 1956, Australia's male runners didn't match the extraordinary success of their female teammates, but they did climb the dais on four occasions. There were three bronze medals in individual events — Hector Hogan in the 100 metres, John Landy in the 1500 metres and Allan Lawrence in the 10,000 metres — while the 4 x 400-metres relay team won the silver medal behind the USA. A number of other Australian men made the final of their track event: David Lean finished fifth in the 400-metres hurdles; Bill Butchart eighth in the 800 metres; Neil Robbins seventh in the 3000-metres steeplechase; Albie Thomas fifth in the 5000 metres and Dave Power seventh in the 10,000 metres. Kevan Gosper was fourth in his semi-final of the 400 metres, with only the top three in each of the two semi-finals going through to the final. The 4 x 100-metres relay team also finished fourth in their semi-final, with only the top three qualifying. While it was hoped that Landy and Hogan would do better than third, overall it was a very creditable performance by the Australian men.

Herb Elliott's dominating performance to win the gold medal in the 1500 metres was the clear highlight for the Australian team at the 1960 Rome Olympic Games, and one of the greatest Australian performances in Olympic history. Dave Power also performed extremely well, improving on his results in Melbourne to win the bronze medal in the 10,000 metres and finish fifth in the 5000 metres. Four years later in Tokyo, Ron Clarke won the bronze medal in the 10,000 metres and was ninth in the 5000 metres. Tony Cook finished eighth in the 10,000 metres, Peter Vassella seventh in the 400 metres and Gary Knoke fourth in the 400-metres hurdles. As we have seen, the Australian men's track team achieved outstanding results at the 1968 Olympic Games, highlighted by Doubell's gold medal in the 800 metres and Peter Norman's silver in the 200 metres. There were four other top-seven finishes.

But in the Olympic Games held since Mexico City, Australian men have struggled to reach the final or finish in the top ten of the 5000 metres or 10,000 metres, let alone earn a medal. It was a reality noted as early as 1988 by the great Sebastian Coe, who wrote of Australasia's post-war runners in his book, *The Olympians*:

After Snell, there was a lull down under, and a period of Olympic disappointment ... Australia's women still sprinted valiantly, but Australian long-distance running leant so heavily on the record-breaking genius of Ron Clarke that only when he bowed out of Olympic competition with such scant reward was it clear how great was the void he left behind. Her middle-distance running too, apart from an exceptional victory in the Mexico 800 metres by Ralph Doubell, went into similar decline, and Australia has since shown signs of real revival only among her marathon men.

Rick Mitchell and Darren Clark made the final of the Olympic 400 metres twice, but they are each counted only once on the list of Australian finalists from 1972 to 2016, which does not include marathon runners. The ten athletes are: Rick Mitchell, Graham Crouch, Bill Scott, Darren Clark, Kyle Vander Kuyp, Rohan Robinson, Craig Mottram, Youcef Abdi, Steve Solomon and Ryan Gregson.

At Munich in 1972, no Australian men qualified for a track final while Derek Clayton finished 13th in the marathon. Four years later, in Montreal, Rick Mitchell finished sixth in the 400 metres and Graham Crouch eighth in the 1500 metres. Chris Wardlaw and David Fitzsimons ran in the 10,000-metres final, with Wardlaw finishing 12th and Fitzsimons 14th.

The only individual medal won by an Australian man on the track since Doubell's gold in Mexico City was Rick Mitchell's silver medal in the 400 metres at the Moscow Games in 1980. Australia's only other male track finalist that year was Bill Scott, who finished ninth in the 10,000 metres, while a 23-year-old named Robert de Castella was tenth in the marathon. Australia's only male track finalist at the 1984 Los Angeles Olympic Games was Darren Clark, who finished fourth in the 400 metres. De Castella, who was now the reigning world record holder, was fifth in the marathon. It was a similar story in Seoul in 1988, with Clark again finishing fourth in the 400 metres and de Castella finishing eighth in the marathon, three places behind his teammate Steve Moneghetti.

No Australian man made a final for an individual track event at the Olympic Games held in Barcelona in 1992. At Atlanta in 1996,

Kyle Vander Kuyp finished seventh in the 110-metres hurdles and Rohan Robinson fifth in the 400-metres hurdles, while Moneghetti was seventh in the marathon. In Sydney in 2000, Mizan Mehari finished 12th in the final of the 5000 metres and Moneghetti tenth in the marathon. Australia's 4 x 400-metres relay team of John Steffensen, Mark Ormrod, Patrick Dwyer and Clinton Hill made headlines when they won a surprise silver medal in Athens in 2004. This was the fourth Olympic silver medal won by Australian men on the athletics track since the war, to go with the golds of Elliott and Doubell and five bronze medals. Australia's only individual male track finalist at the 2004 Games was Craig Mottram, who finished eighth in the 5000 metres. Mottram would win a bronze medal at the 2005 World Championships in Helsinki, but he was unable to progress from his heats at the Olympics Games held in Sydney in 2000, Beijing in 2008 and London in 2012.

A point that needs to be made here, which was emphasised by the respected athletics writer Len Johnson in a column he wrote for the *Runners Tribe* website in 2014, is that the decline in Australia's athletics performances was not confined purely to Olympic competition. Johnson studied the annual rankings published by *Track and Field News*, the self-proclaimed 'Bible of the Sport', and bemoaned the dearth of Australian track athletes at or even near the head of these lists. Sally Pearson was the only Australian track athlete, male or female, to be ranked in a top ten in 2014. Johnson continued:

> Summing up, Pearson is our only current ranker in a track event, and there are only six track events in which we have had a ranked athlete in the past 10 years (2005–14, inclusive). In only

10 of the 22 men's and women's track events has Australia had a top-10 ranker since the turn of the century, a number which drops to nine if we exclude the Sydney 2000 Olympic year.

Australia's only male track finalist at the 2008 Beijing Olympics was Youcef Abdi, who finished sixth in the 3000-metres steeplechase, and four years later in London the sole Australian male track finalist was 19-year-old Steve Solomon, who was eighth in the final of the 400 metres. Ryan Gregson finished ninth in the 1500-metres final in Rio de Janeiro in 2016, with Brett Robinson finishing 14th in the 5000 metres and David McNeill 16th in the 10,000 metres.

THERE ARE MANY THEORIES as to why only one Australian man has won an individual medal on the track, and only ten have qualified for a final or finished in the top ten of the 5000 metres or 10,000 metres, in the 50 years since the 1968 Olympic Games. Much has been written about the dominance of athletes with West African heritage in the 100 metres and 200 metres, and it would be a very pleasant surprise if any Australian man qualified for the final of one of these events in the future. Athletes with West African heritage also fill most of the lanes in the finals of the 400 metres at major championships, though not to the same extent as the shorter sprints. Steve Solomon proved it is possible for an Australian to make an Olympic final with his excellent performance in London in 2012.

Similarly, athletes with East and North African heritage now take home most of the medals in middle-distance and long-distance events at major championships.

It is not the intention here to seek a definitive explanation for this African dominance, but to acknowledge the reality of it. As

Matthew Syed, the author of *Bounce: the myth of talent and power of practice*, noted in an article for *BBC News* in 2011, 'The 100m final at the World Athletics Championships this weekend will be won by a black athlete. Every winner of the 100m since the inaugural event in 1983 has been black, as has every finalist from the last 10 championships with the solitary exception of Matic Osovnikar of Slovenia, who finished seventh in 2007.'

Syed argued that to conclude this was a matter of genetics was presumptuous:

Assuming that this success is driven by genes rather than environment, there is a rather obvious inference to make — black people are naturally better sprinters than white people. Indeed, it is an inference that seems obligatory, barring considerations of political correctness.

But here's the thing. This inference is not merely false — it is logically flawed ... To see how, let us examine success not in the sprints but in distance running, for this is also dominated by black athletes. Kenya has won an astonishing 63 medals at the Olympic Games in races of 800m and above, 21 of them gold, since 1968. Little wonder that one commentator once described distance running as 'a Kenyan monopoly'.

But it turns out that it is not Kenya as a whole that usually wins these medals, but individuals from a tiny region in the Rift Valley called Nandi. As one writer put it: 'Most of Kenya's runners call Nandi home.'

Seen in this context, the notion that black people are naturally superior distance runners seems bizarre. Far from being a 'black' phenomenon, or even a Kenyan phenomenon, distance running is actually a Nandi phenomenon. Or, to put it another way, 'black' distance running success is focused on the tiniest of pinpricks on the map of Africa, with the vast majority of the continent underrepresented.

The same analysis applies to the sprints, where success is focused on Jamaicans and African-Americans. Africa, as a continent, has almost no success at all. Not even West Africans win much ...

Syed argues other factors are at play, among them the fact that many regions renowned for producing exceptional distance runners are located at altitude, and that once countries start producing sporting heroes, the youth of that country aspires to replicate that success. The influence of champions such as Wilson Kiprugut and Kip Keino in Kenya cannot be underrated. Furthermore, in some nations, athletics offers an opportunity unlike any other. 'I started out without any big dreams that one time I would become a world beater,' said David Rudisha, Kenya's Olympic 800-metres champion in 2012 and 2016. 'When I became serious, I found athletics was almost a business. If I ran well, I could achieve well.'

Ethiopia's Abebe Bikila won the Olympic marathon in 1960 and 1964, and Wilson Kiprugut won Kenya's first Olympic medal in Tokyo, but African middle-distance and long-distance athletes arrived *in force* for the first time in Mexico City. It was only the beginning of the continent's love affair with athletics. Since then, a number of African and other 'third world' countries have vastly improved their economic and social circumstances and this has allowed them to invest in sport and the training of young athletes. Many more countries are competitive today than was the case half a century ago and the quality of the fields in elite competitions has become increasingly deep. Beyond the 'Kenyan monopoly', runners from countries such as Ethiopia, Morocco, Algeria, South Africa, Eritrea, Botswana and Burundi claimed Olympic medals in distances from 800 metres to 10,000 at the 1996 to 2016 Games. The strength of today's African running teams is intimidating. With some countries, if one well-known runner is injured there seems to be an inexhaustible supply of younger runners able to step up and take their place. Furthermore, African nations are often able to qualify several runners for a final in major championships and they run as a group. This show of force boosts their own confidence and can overwhelm competitors from other countries.

Doubell recognises that the strength and depth of African competitors in the middle-distance and long-distance events is intimidating, but he stresses that a coach of the calibre of Franz Stampfl can give an athlete the mental strength required to perform at their best in a major championship against any competitor — and aim to win. Australia's Peter Bourke, who was also trained by Stampfl, won the gold medal in the 800 metres at the 1982 Commonwealth Games in Brisbane. He beat Kenya's James Maina Boi in that race and says Stampfl's advice was straightforward:

> Athletes get intimidated by the teams of Kenyans, and other African athletes, in the major competitions. Franz always said: 'Just you worry about yourself and don't worry about anyone else.' Franz gave you great self-belief.

The critical importance of mental strength, in addition to rigorous training, is a recurring theme when Doubell discusses athletics. As we have seen, Stampfl believed the psychological aspect of his role was more important than the physical: 'The coach's job is 20-per-cent technical and 80-per-cent inspirational,' he said frequently. And nowhere is mental strength more vital than at an Olympic Games, particularly in events such as the 800 metres, where an athlete competes not just in one race after weeks of preparation, but in three races on three consecutive days.

Stampfl's succinct advice to Doubell on the eve of the Mexico City Olympic Games was, 'Go out and win the next three races.' For Doubell, this was a clear and concise articulation of a fundamental element of Stampfl's approach to racing at major championships. Doubell wanted to win his semi-final because it would be a psychological as well as physical victory over Kiprugut. He wasn't focused on his time, but he set a new Australian record in winning the race. Peter Bourke states emphatically:

> Some athletes aren't mentally prepared to run three hard races at a major championship. Franz conditioned you to the fact that you had to run three races. I didn't go to the Commonwealth Games to run one race. I knew I had to get through my heat and semi-final in order to race in the final — and then I had to be ready to win the final. My body was conditioned, and my mind was conditioned, to do that. Franz said he could make me as tough as old boots but ... [Bourke puts his index finger to his forehead] ... it's the polish up here that's the thing.

Like Doubell, Bourke was instructed to stamp his authority on his heat and semi-final:

Franz always said to me: 'Go out to win'. Let the others know that you mean business. That was Franz's way. Every race was important, a stepping stone to the gold medal. The same principles applied and worked in 1982 as they did in 1968.

Bourke won his heat, semi-final and final at the 1982 Commonwealth Games. His winning time of 1:44.78 was less than half-a-second outside Doubell's national record and made him the second fastest Australian in history over 800 metres. As at 1 August 2018, it remains the fastest 800 metres run by an Australian in Australia and only four other Australians have run faster than Bourke in the past 25 years: Jeff Riseley in 2012, Alex Rowe in 2014, and Peter Bol and Joseph Deng in 2018.

Chum Darvall also highlights the difference between running one good race and winning at an Olympic Games or major championship:

There is a group of Australians who have managed to run PBs at major events. Ralph is one, Herb Elliott is, of course, another, Peter Bourke won the Commonwealth Games in Brisbane in 1982 and I would include Noel Clough, who won the 880 yards in Jamaica in 1966. They rose to the occasion.

Some Australians have run fast times in Europe, or occasionally in the US college system, sometimes with pacers. But they cannot repeat that in a three-race format at a major competition. They can't win a final after two races at that level. While they have been able to run a time that is close to Ralph, they haven't been able to replicate that on the big stage at a major event. The ability to run sub-1:45 or even sub-1:46 three times in a row versus being able to do it just once is really, really tough.

When I ran in the 800-metres final at the Commonwealth Games, the officials held us in a room for half an hour, an enclosed space with little air, and then they sent us into the bright sunshine in front of 60,000 people. That's just a rehearsal compared with the Olympics.

The preparedness for the occasion is an aspect of Ralph's achievement that I hugely admire. He was able to transcend that, partly due to his inner strength and self-belief and partly because he had arguably the finest middle-distance coach that ever coached in Australia. Weaker people wouldn't have been able to produce it — first because it was the Olympics and second because it was at altitude.

Stampfl wrote in his 1955 book, *Franz Stampfl on Running*, that the preliminary rounds of a major competition are tough and should be taken as seriously as the final, and Doubell learned this basic but very important lesson as soon as he started training with the Austrian. Stampfl could not only optimise the physical aspects of running but also the mental aspects of competing. It was an intrinsic part of Doubell's preparation for Mexico City. He says:

Stampfl was a master of this, but very few other Australian coaches have had the ability to impart on an athlete the competitive desire to overcome every barrier that is thrown at you when competing in an Olympic final.

It is no surprise, therefore, that Doubell is critical of athletes who do not progress beyond their heat at an Olympic Games or World

Championship after failing to run the time that they achieved to qualify for the competition. He has even advocated that if an athlete does this at two successive Olympics, he or she should not be selected again. It is a proposal that has failed to gain traction with the authorities.

'I firmly believe that we perform to expectation,' Doubell says. 'If we do not teach our athletes to expect to win, we will remain a nation of competitors, not a nation of champions. We must teach our athletes to raise their game and demand more.'

Doubell believes that many of today's runners focus too much on achieving a qualifying time for a particular competition and don't spend enough time racing regularly and learning how to compete and win, or to at least strive to win at a major championship. He believes today's runners are too satisfied if they run a qualifying time behind a pace-setter, even if they finish back in the field. Chum Darvall has a similar view:

> It sounds uncharitable, and it is unfashionable to say it, but at its worst there is a kind of Olympic tourism in Australian athletics. It looks to the observer like the aim for a few is to get into the Olympic team rather than be highly competitive when they get there.

Doubell is often criticised for being too harsh on Australian athletes who have come after him, particularly since he hasn't been involved in any coaching since he retired from running. But he is not the only former champion to make tough observations about Australian athletics. Rick Mitchell represented Australia at three Olympic Games, winning a silver medal in the 400 metres at Moscow in 1980. He won gold in the same event at the 1978 Edmonton Commonwealth Games and silver at the Brisbane Commonwealth Games four years later. Asked to report on Australia's Commonwealth Games trials in 2002 for the Fairfax newspapers, he did not hold back:

Dear Australian track athletes (Cathy Freeman excepted),

Let me slap you in the face. What an overrated lot most of you are! ... [We] often defend Australian athletics performances relative to other sports in the country, in particular swimming, on the basis that the whole world turns up to compete in athletics at Olympic Games and World Championships, while only about a third of the world contests events in the pool. That defence has logic, but unfortunately it has become a crutch for many of our present crop of runners. By hiding behind such concepts, you are avoiding direct measurement of your achievements against your predecessors. There are numerous Australian performances, some of them more than 20 years old, which if reproduced at this year's trials would have embarrassed most of you ...

Men's 400 and 800 metres. Boy, would I have liked to race you lot! ... Ralph Doubell's national record for 800 metres is now 34 years old! Peter Bourke's second-best Australian time ever was set in 1982. One of you should set an alarm clock to wake you up to the world of modern 800-metres running. As a group you are simply embarrassing ...

All of you now receive full Institute of Sport support, sophisticated sports science and sports medicine, and better access to international opportunities than any one before your time. Some of you are handsomely sponsored although, given your achievements, I wonder why. You have had the benefit of hometown Olympic and Goodwill Games. With all of these things in your favour, why are you unable to better the performances of those who long preceded you? The performances of my contemporaries were of a high standard at the time, but they should be mediocre compared with what you produce now.

In the 40 years I've been around athletics, I've never seen a medal presented to a pair of sunglasses or a lycra suit. I've only seen them presented to talented, tough, focused athletes who were prepared to do whatever it takes to get to the top; athletes who lay it on the line time after time. It's time the lot of you stopped worrying about image and pretending to be good, and actually went about the process of raising the bar for yourselves.

Mitchell's harsh words make Doubell's views seem tame! Some believe the criticisms from runners of another era are naïve given the amount of money and resources ploughed into athletics by many countries around the world, including the African nations that have made middle-distance and long-distance running a source of national pride. However, even if this counter-argument is true, there is one men's track event in which athletes with no African heritage are regular finalists and medal winners at Olympic Games and World Championships.

It is the 800 metres.

CHAPTER 22

Open Opportunity

While male athletes from Africa, or with African heritage, dominate most track events at major championships, the 800 metres consistently features finalists and medallists from a variety of countries and backgrounds. Ross Tucker, who writes regularly for *The Guardian* and for his *The Science of Sport* website, reflected on this in a preview he wrote during the 2007 World Championships:

> Tonight, in Osaka, the IAAF World Champs concludes with some potentially great races. One of them, the 800m men's final, which is one of our most anticipated races, could be won by any one of the eight finalists. There are few events that are more open and competitive than this race …
>
> The 800m distance is a fascinating one, and well worth discussing further, because it straddles the divide between

what people usually refer to as 'sprinting' and 'middle-distance' running. To some, it is the first of the middle-distance events, whereas to others, it's the last of the sprints. Of course, using such jargon can pose challenges, but generally, when people refer to a sprint, they refer to an event where the athlete goes 'flat out'. This is, of course, never true, because even in a 200m race, there is some pacing, as evidenced by people who go out a little too fast and end up faltering in the final 40 to 50m!

However, the fact remains that the 800m is a unique distance, requiring a combination of sprint ability and endurance ability ...

At the 1964 Tokyo Olympic Games, Wilson Kiprugut finished third in the 800 metres behind Peter Snell and Bill Crothers. Four years later, Kiprugut had to settle for the silver medal in the same event behind Ralph Doubell, with Tom Farrell taking bronze. Behind them came runners from West Germany, Czechoslovakia, East Germany, Kenya and Trinidad.

At the 1972 Munich Olympics, the 800 metres was won by the white American Dave Wottle ahead of the USSR's Yevgeniy Arzhanov and Mike Boit of Kenya. The fact Wottle is white is mentioned because the African heritage of athletes is regularly cited as a key reason why European and 'Western' athletes don't win more medals in middle-distance races at major championships. The other athletes in the 800-metres final in Munich included another Kenyan and four Europeans with apparently no African heritage: two Germans, an Englishman and a Pole. Wottle, who had equalled the 800-metres world record of Snell and Doubell at the US trials two months before the Olympics, was described as 'an army boy from Ohio in the mid-west' by Chris Brasher in his book *Munich 72*. 'They take things very seriously there,' Brasher added.

African countries boycotted the 1976 Montreal Olympic Games because the IOC refused to ban New Zealand from the competition after the All Blacks agreed to tour South Africa that year. Alberto Juantorena of Cuba broke Doubell's Olympic record when he crossed the line in first place ahead of Ivo Van Damme of Belgium and Rick Wohlhuter of the USA. The other finalists included a German, an Englishman, a Yugoslav and an Italian, while Sriram Singh made an extremely rare appearance for India in an Olympic athletics final.

Kenya and a number of other African countries did not compete in the 1980 Moscow Olympic Games. They joined the mass USA-led boycott of those Games because of the Soviet invasion of Afghanistan. Great Britain's Steve Ovett upset his teammate and huge rival Sebastian Coe to take the gold medal, with the USSR's Nikolay Kirov finishing third. Like Australia's athletes in Moscow, both Ovett and Coe competed under the Olympic flag. The other finalists included four Europeans – an Englishman, two Germans, and a Frenchman – as well as a Brazilian.

Brazil's Joaquim Cruz won the 800-metres gold medal in Los Angeles in 1984 with Sebastian Coe taking the silver medal for the second successive Olympiad. The field, in the words of *Sports Illustrated*'s Kenny Moore, was 'one of the most powerful and complete of the Games, unaffected by the boycott', and it captured the diverse character of the event. Cruz grew up 'poor' (his own word) in Taguatinga, near Brasilia, in circumstances that were hardly luxurious, though not as dire as was sometimes painted by journalists who liked to write that he was a product of the favelas. Coe, now Lord Coe and president of the IAAF, then the world 800-metres record holder, was born in London and raised in Sheffield in the north of England. Cruz had seen Coe win the Olympic 1500 on television in 1980 and vowed then that he'd do the same in four years' time. Earl Jones of the USA, an African American, finished third. There were two Kenyans unplaced in the final, as well as an Italian, an Englishman and an American.

A Kenyan won the gold medal in the men's 800 metres at five of the next eight Olympics, those held from 1988 until 2016. Kenyan 800-metres runners also won a silver medal and three bronze medals in that period. In addition, athletes born and raised in Kenya but competing for other countries won two silver medals and a bronze medal.

Paul Ereng won Kenya's first gold medal in the 800 metres at the 1988 Seoul Olympic Games, with Joaquim Cruz winning the silver medal to go with the gold he won in Los Angeles. Said Aouita of Morocco, who had won gold in the 5000 metres four years earlier and hadn't been defeated in a flat race at any distance between 800 and 10,000 metres in three years, took home the bronze, with Britain's Peter Elliott, a carpenter from Rotherham in South Yorkshire, fourth. The other finalists in Seoul were a second Kenyan, a second Brazilian, an American and an Italian.

Ereng had been a 400-metres runner in Kenya, but switched to the 800 after he enrolled at the University of Virginia a year before Seoul. In the Olympic final, he stayed near the back until the final 130 metres, from where he weaved through to take the lead with 40 metres to go and win by nearly half a second. After he returned home to a hero's welcome, there were disputes in Kenya as to the new champion's background. Ereng's parents were of the nomadic Turkana tribe. 'But he was raised Nandi,' Mike Boit, bronze medallist in the 800 in 1972, told Kenny Moore. 'So Ereng seemed to affirm that it is culture, not some gene, that makes the difference,' Moore concluded. 'And in Kenya the racing culture is making converts of even the nomads.'

William Tanui and Nixon Kiprotich won gold and silver for Kenya in Barcelona in 1992, while African American Johnny Gray finally climbed an Olympic dais after securing bronze. Gray had made the final in LA and Seoul but had not been able to win a medal, finishing seventh and then fifth. Three athletes from outside Africa were in the final: a Brazilian, an Italian and an Englishman.

Vebjørn Rodal of Norway was the surprise winner of the 800 metres in 1996, finishing ahead of Hezekiél Sepeng of South Africa and Fred Onyancha of Kenya. Sepeng was the first black South African to win a medal at the Olympics. Rodal's time of 1:42.58 would remain an Olympic record until 2012. The other finalists were a Cuban, a German, a Kenyan, an American (Johnny Gray again, in his fourth successive Olympic 800-metres final) and a Moroccan. As if to prove 800-metres stars could come from anywhere, the official Olympics website began a profile of the new champion this way:

Vebjørn Rodal honed his skills as a middle-distance runner in somewhat unconventional surroundings. While others trained in sunshine, the Norwegian found his home town of Berkak under snow and ice for much of the year, which made maintaining a regular training regimen difficult to impossible.

Salvation came from an unlikely source. A nearby power station had built a tunnel through a mountain that was just under 400 metres long. And so, with the wind howling and snow swirling outside, Rodal was able to hone his running skills, dreaming of competing at the Olympic Games.

Eventually, in 1994, he left his power station behind and started training at more conventional facilities. Within a year, he had won a bronze medal in the 800m at the World Championships …

Another European, Nils Schumann of Germany, stunned the pundits to win the 800 metres in 2000. Wilson Kipketer, born in Kenya but representing Denmark, was the clear favourite, as he had won the 800 metres at the World Championships in 1995, 1997 and 1999, but Schumann beat him by 0.06 seconds with Djabir Saïd-Guerni of Algeria 0.02 seconds behind in third place. Three other Europeans featured in the final — André Bucher of Switzerland, Yuriy Borzakovskiy of Russia and Andrea Longo of Italy — with Atlanta silver medallist Hezekiél Sepeng of South Africa finishing just out of the medals and Glody Dube of Botswana rounding out the field.

Borzakovskiy used his fantastic finishing kick to win the 800-metres gold medal in Athens in 2004, making it three Olympic victories in a row for Europeans. He passed Kipketer, who was leading in the straight, shattering the Kenyan-born Dane's Olympic dreams once again. Kipketer was so affected by Borzakovskiy's move that South Africa's Mbulaeni Mulaudzi edged past him to win the silver medal. All the other finalists were from African countries: Morocco, Kenya, South Africa, Algeria and Sudan.

Borzakovskiy's upbringing in a village on the outskirts of Moscow was, in the words of the IAAF's official website, 'far from being a holiday':

He was born into a family of workers who shared rooms in a so called 'communal flat'. If you do not know what that means, please just count yourself lucky. Imagine several families living all their life in a flat with one kitchen, one bathroom and a single toilet.

His mother Ekaterina worked at a factory, then became a street cleaner. She woke up at 4 or 5 o'clock in the morning each day and it was Yuriy, the elder son, who at 7.30am each morning had to accompany his younger brother to his kindergarten and then make his way to his own school. He also had to prepare the meals for his brother and sister, for his father who worked at a factory had absolutely no time for things like cooking. To say the least, the family was far from being rich.

Africans, including those who had been born in Africa and were now representing other countries, dominated the final of the 800 metres in 2008 and 2012. Wilfred Bungei and Alfred Kirwa Yego of Kenya were first and third in Beijing and Ismail Ahmed Ismail of Sudan finished second. Four years later, Kenya's David Rudisha broke the world record by almost a second to win the gold medal in London, ahead of Nijel Amos of Botswana and Timothy Kitum of Kenya. The final also included two Americans, an Ethiopian, an Englishman and a Sudanese. In 2016, Rudisha made it two gold medals in a row when he won the 800 by nearly half a second, ahead of Taoufik Makhloufi of Algeria and Clayton Murphy of the USA.

Not long after the Rio Games, the world's greatest sprinter, Usain Bolt, and the planet's best long-distance runner, Mo Farah, were sitting in a hotel room in Jamaica discussing who would win a 600-metres race between the two of them. The conversation was recorded by journalist Sean Ingle:

> 'I think I'd have a good chance,' says Farah. 'Just because of my endurance.' Bolt throws him a look of mock-horror. 'So what about me, you and David Rudisha?' Farah laughs. 'That completely changes it,' he replies, chuckling. 'Rudisha is strong. He has run 1min 40sec for 800m. He could jog and still have us.'

There were two other Kenyans as well as Rudisha in the 2016 Olympic 800 final, but also two Europeans: Pierre-Ambroise Bosse of France, who was fourth, and Poland's Marcin Lewandowski, who finished sixth.

BOSSE FOLLOWED UP HIS outstanding run at the 2016 Olympics with a gold-medal performance in the 800 metres at the 2017 World Championships in London, epitomising the success that Europeans have had in the 800 metres at these championships since 1983. At those inaugural World Championships, in Helsinki, the gold medal in the 800 metres was won by Willi Wulbeck of Germany with Rob Druppers of the Netherlands finishing second and Joaquim Cruz third. Kenya's Billy Konchellah won the 800 metres in Rome in 1987, with Great Britain's Peter Elliott securing the silver medal and José Luiz Barbosa of Brazil the bronze. Three other Europeans featured in the final: a Scot, a Pole and a Yugoslav. Konchellah successfully defended his title in Tokyo in 1991, with Barbosa improving on his performance in Rome to take the silver medal and Mark Everett of the USA claiming bronze. Three Europeans were unplaced in the final: a Pole, a Russian and a Spaniard.

The World Championships now moved to a two-year cycle. At Stuttgart in 1993, Paul Ruto won the gold medal for Kenya and his teammate Samson Kitur took bronze. Giuseppe D'Urso of Italy won the silver medal and an Englishman and a Scot were the other Europeans in the final. Wilson Kipketer won the gold medal in 1995 in Gothenburg, ahead of Burundi's Arthémon Hatungimana and Vebjørn Rodal. A German and an Italian also competed in the final. Kipketer made it two world titles in a row when he won in Athens in 1997, with Norberto Téllez of Cuba second and Rich Kenah of the USA third. Rodal made his second World Championship final, finishing fifth, with Marko Koers of the Netherlands sixth. Kipketer completed his World Championship 800-metres hat-trick in Seville in 1999, ahead of Hezekiél Sepeng and Djabir Saïd-Guerni. The Italian Andrea Longo finished sixth while Nils Schumann was eighth.

Europeans thoroughly enjoyed the 800-metres final in Edmonton, Canada, in 2001 with André Bucher of Switzerland winning the gold medal and Pawel Czapiewski of Poland the bronze. Kenya's Wilfred Bungei claimed the silver medal, while Nils Schumann made another major championship final, finishing fifth. 'In Europe, maybe most youngsters think it is safer to go to university and then get a high-paying job,' Bucher said after his victory. 'After all, there are easier ways to earn a living than as an 800-metres runner.' He was just the second Swiss athlete to win a world title, and when he flew home from Canada he was greeted by 5000 fans at the airport. Sebastian Coe, writing in the London *Daily Telegraph*, noted that Bucher had taken up skiing when he was three. 'Only by breaking the 800m world record next year and combining it with an Olympic title in the men's downhill in Salt

Lake City [where the next Winter Olympics would be held] could he be any bigger in Switzerland,' Coe wrote.

Algeria's Saïd-Guerni won the World Championship gold in Paris in 2003, 0.03 seconds ahead of Russia's Yuriy Borzakovskiy with Mbulaeni Mulaudzi third. Andrea Longo again qualified for the 800-metres final at a major championship. Rashid Ramzi, born in Morocco but competing for Bahrain, won the gold medal in 2005 in Helsinki. Ramzi also won the 1500 metres at these Championships, a triumph he would repeat three years later in Beijing, but he would be stripped of his Olympic title after he was found guilty of doping. Borzakovskiy won his second successive World Championship silver medal in 2005 and Kenya's William Yiampoy finished third. Kenya returned to the top of the dais at Osaka in 2007 through the victory of Alfred Kirwa Yego, with Gary Reed of Canada taking home the silver and Borzakovskiy the bronze.

Mbulaeni Mulaudzi of South Africa, who won the silver medal in the 800 metres at the 2004 Athens Olympics and bronze at the 2003 World Championships in Paris, won gold at the 2009 World Championships in Berlin ahead of Yego and Yusuf Saad Kamel of Bahrain. Mulaudzi had carried the South African flag at the Olympic opening ceremony in 2004, and would be tragically killed in a car crash, aged just 34, in 2014. Kamel was born in Kenya and is the son of Billy Konchellah, who won the 800 metres at the 1987 and 1991 World Championships. Europeans were well represented in the final, with Borzakovskiy finishing fourth, Bram Som of the Netherlands seventh and Marcin Lewandowski eighth.

David Rudisha won his first major championship gold medal at the 2011 World Championships in Daegu, South Korea, ahead of Abubaker Kaki of Sudan, with Borzakovskiy third. The Russian now had two silver medals and two bronze medals from the past five World Championships as well as his gold medal from the 2004 Olympics. Lewandowski finished fourth and his Polish teammate, Adam Kszczot, was sixth. Mohammed Aman of Ethiopia won in Moscow in 2013 ahead of the USA's Nick Symmonds and Ayanleh Souleiman of Djibouti. Lewandowski finished just out of the medals in fourth place and Frenchman Pierre-Ambroise Bosse was seventh.

Rudisha won his second 800-metres World Championship in Beijing in 2015, with Kszczot claiming the silver medal for Poland and Amel Tuka from Bosnia and Herzegovina earning the bronze. Bosse was fifth, and then first in London in 2017, after which he quipped, 'I'm not the best in the world, I just won a race at the right time.' He won from Kszczot and Kipyegon Bett of Kenya. Another European, 22-year-old Kyle Langford from Watford, 25 kilometres north of central London, finished fourth.

It is clear that while Kenya has a particularly awesome record and many other African countries are extremely competitive in the men's 800 metres, a number of nations contribute finalists and medallists in this event when it is contested at the highest level. Fifteen Europeans have won medals in the 800 metres at the World Championships since 1983 and another 25 have appeared in a final without finishing on the podium. This includes athletes with no African heritage from France, Germany, Great Britain, Norway, Poland, and Russia. Other athletes with no African heritage, including some from the USA, have been finalists at the World Championships.

No Australian man has qualified for the 800 metres final of an Olympic Games or World Championships since Doubell's victory in Mexico City in 1968. Yet this analysis of the finalists in the 800 metres at the two major championships over the half century since Mexico City indicates that this is the track event that offers a real opportunity for an Australian man to compete in the final, or even win a medal.

CHAPTER 23

A Record for Half a Century

Doubell said consistently during his running career that he was not concerned about recording a particular time, whatever the distance, but that his prime focus was running the race he needed to in order to win. He has reiterated this position many times since his retirement in 1972. If the race was fast, as it was at the Olympics, so was his time because he was racing to win. When Tom Farrell told Doubell after the finish in Mexico City that he had equalled the world record, Doubell's brief response was, 'Well, that's nice.' The main aim for Doubell was to cross the line first and win the gold medal, not to run a world-record time.

Remarkably, however, for the next 49 years and 278 days no Australian man ran faster than Doubell did that night in Mexico

City. Finally, on 20 July 2018, 20-year-old Joseph Deng followed his race plan and held his form down the final straight at the Diamond League meeting in Monaco to cross the line in 1:44.21 and set a new national record. Deng was born in a Kenyan refugee camp in 1998 after his mother fled the civil war in South Sudan. His family moved to Queensland in 2004 when Deng was six and his athletics ability soon became apparent. When Deng was 17 years old he was selected in the Australian team for the 2016 IAAF World Under-20 Championships and he represented Australia at the 2018 Gold Coast Commonwealth Games, finishing seventh in the final of the 800 metres. After those Games, Deng's coach, Justin Rinaldi, decided that Deng and his training partner, Peter Bol, would try to break the Australian 800-metres record during the high-quality athletics competitions held during the European summer. Rinaldi also coached Alex Rowe, who had equalled Doubell's record on 18 July 2014, almost four years to the day earlier than Deng broke it. Like Deng, Rowe ran his fastest time at the Diamond League event in Monaco. The winner of the race on both occasions was Nijel Amos from Botswana, the silver medallist from the 2012 Olympic Games. Amos ran 1:42.45 ahead of Rowe in 2014 and 1:42.14 ahead of Deng in 2018. Amos' time at the London Olympics of 1:41.73 makes him, as at 1 August 2018, the equal third fastest 800-metres runner in history, behind David Rudisha and Wilson Kipketer and tied with Sebastian Coe.

When the Australian media reported in 2014 that Rowe had equalled the national record, and in 2018 that Deng had beaten it, no mention was made of the fact that Doubell's winning time in Mexico City was recorded and reported as 1:44.3 and that some record books still show 1:44.3 as his time. The reason Doubell's time was changed to 1:44.4 in some reports is because his manually recorded time was 1:44.3, but his electronically recorded time was 1:44.4. In 1968, athletics officials were not yet convinced that electronic timing was more reliable than manual timing. Three separate timekeepers were used to record the times for each runner in a major competition. Almost a decade after the 1968 Olympics, international authorities decided that from 1 January 1977 only electronic times would count as world records. Doubell's world record is still listed by the IAAF in its official world-record progression list as 1:44.3, the hand-timed record, with the auto-time noted. For the purposes of the Australian All-Time List, Athletics Australia considers his auto-time from Mexico City (1:44.40) to be official.

The extraordinary quality of Doubell's performance in Mexico City is highlighted by the fact that it took half a century for another Australian to beat his time by just two tenths of a second — or one tenth of a second when compared with his manual time of 1:44.3. Over the same 50 years, the world record has been lowered to David Rudisha's current mark of 1:40.91. Those three-and-a-half seconds represent a substantial distance in an 800-metres race.

From discussions with a number of prominent former athletes and others with a lengthy involvement in track and field, including Doubell, here is a list of the key elements that are essential for Joseph Deng, or some other Australian athlete, to further reduce the national mark for the 800 metres.

Natural ability
An athlete needs many factors to fall in their favour, including absence of injury or illness, to deliver their best performance and

run a record time. First, the athlete must have extraordinary natural ability and this includes certain physiological factors. Bill Hooker, Doubell's training mate and the father of 2008 Olympic pole vault gold medallist Steve Hooker, remembers how training with Franz Stampfl's squad gave him an insight into part of what made Doubell such a special athlete:

> Everyone in the Stampfl squad used to do time trials on the weekend. It didn't matter whether you were a runner or a shot putter or a javelin thrower, you would do some sort of time trial. Ralph and I would do time trials of a similar distance and Stampfl would come up at the end and take our pulse for five or six seconds and call out what it was. He would then wait a minute or two and take it again. Ralph's resting pulse was very low, about 40, and one day after a time trial Stampfl called out his pulse as over 200. When you have a heart that can cover a range like that, you have a very good engine.

Doubell was undoubtedly blessed with extraordinary acceleration for an 800-metres runner and 'a very good engine', but he and other successful Australian athletes from the 1950s and 1960s have pointed out repeatedly that young Australian men today have the same physical capability as they did. They are therefore bemused why, for example, Doubell's Australian record stood for so long. One explanation is that Australian athletics, and middle-distance running in particular, was a much more popular sport in the 1950s and 1960s. It enjoyed its fair share of front-page and back-page news and young athletes with superior athletic ability were attracted to running tracks around the country, hoping to follow in the footsteps of heroes such as John Landy and Herb Elliott. Bill Hooker points out that the situation today is very different:

> Have a look at what you need to be a good 800-metres runner and have a look at what you need to be a good midfielder in Australian rules football. It's pretty much the same criteria — speed and endurance. Most of the talent pool is more interested in playing Aussie rules, however, because they can make a lot of money. And the AFL [Australian Football League] has excellent talent identification programs.

Paul Jenes makes a similar observation. 'We have a lot of talented athletes but they go off in all different directions. Who knows, a guy playing in the AFL or NRL [National Rugby League] could be a super 800-metres runner.'

This begs the question why Australian athletics organisations don't tap into this talent pool, for example by focusing on some of the athletes who miss out on the AFL draft. Hooker says he has been told that by that stage the young men have been turned into footballers and it's too late to make them elite runners. If this truly is the position of Australia's athletics organisations, surely it deserves closer scrutiny. Of course, as Jenes and others point out, the athlete must not only possess the necessary raw talent, but also the desire to do the hard training to become a track champion.

An inner drive to succeed

After describing Doubell's special physical capabilities, Hooker adds: 'But you need more than just a very good engine. Ralph made the most of what he had. He was always extremely focused at training. He was there to do a job and that's the way he went about his business.'

Hooker, Stanley Spittle and many others highlight Doubell's hunger, his inner drive to succeed, as being an essential part of their friend's success at the elite level. It is not enough just to have the right body shape, lung capacity, resting pulse rate or to live at altitude, although these provide a strong foundation. To be successful at the highest level of competition, athletes must be driven to train extraordinarily hard and with relentless intensity, as Doubell did.

Doubell does not understand fully where his inner drive came from, but he does know that it was essential to his success. He didn't grow up in abject poverty, but the family finances were very stretched, particularly after his father died. Success on the athletics track didn't just give him personal satisfaction; it opened doors to a range of opportunities that he otherwise could not have afforded or enjoyed, such as interstate and international travel. This was a critical driver to finding the motivation to rise before breakfast for early-morning recovery sessions on the local golf course and to push himself through Stampfl's exhausting training programs after a day of study or work.

Arthur Lydiard, the legendary New Zealand coach of Olympic gold medallists Peter Snell and Murray Halberg as well as many other excellent middle-distance runners, does not mince his words on this subject: 'It is my opinion that modern runners are soft,' he told Garth Gilmour for the book *Arthur Lydiard, Master Coach*. 'They want, and expect, to have everything done for them and they have no taste for the hard work that successful conditioning demands. They are satisfied with the shortcuts despite all the evidence that they don't work.'

An inspirational, even eccentric, coach

The third key factor for an athlete to perform at their best at the highest level, challenging themselves and existing records, is for them to have an inspirational coach. Franz Stampfl, Percy Cerutty and Arthur Lydiard were all coaches who challenged the accepted thinking of the time and whose athletes achieved continued success in major competitions. They all attracted strong criticism for their methods and were labelled 'eccentric' and worse. Critically, they were larger-than-life characters who could inspire greatness in the athletes who were fortunate enough to fall under their tutelage. If we concentrate on Australia only, Stampfl and Cerutty were instrumental in the country's success on the track during the 1950s and 1960s because they challenged their athletes *and* the established system.

Doubell has stressed consistently that his relationship with Stampfl was intrinsic to his success. Stampfl prepared him mentally as well as physically. Doubell believes performances by Australian track athletes in recent times have reflected the lack of non-conformist coaches such as Stampfl and Cerutty:

In contrast, Australian swimming has produced coaches who don't bow down to officialdom and are willing to experiment. This willingness to experiment has not been fostered in Australian athletics. Australians haven't changed substantially in the half century since I ran in Mexico City. What is missing is the coach who can inspire athletes to do a bit more training, or a slightly different type of training, and to inspire them to achieve their absolute best.

Doubell adds that Australia's sporting institutes have not kept pace with international expertise in developing middle-distance runners:

> Most theories of management argue that directors should not hold their positions on a board for more than about ten years. Most governments implement this practice in their commercial operations, but not it seems in sport. Some directors have been in place for a quarter of a century. We know that board influence is as crucial in sport as it is in business or government and I think the failure to change directors means the organisation misses new ideas and so it falls behind.

Training with real intensity

The Stampfl regime involved not just timing every distance run during training, but ensuring that athletes had a target time to achieve for each effort. This meant the athletes had to push themselves to achieve their target times, and this required extra effort as the session wore on and the athletes suffered fatigue. Furthermore, the quality of the Stampfl squad meant that sessions were run at a high level of intensity. This is also one of the key elements in the success of Kenya's athletes. Their training sessions are extremely tough. Britain's Mo Farah, winner of four Olympic and six World Championship gold medals over 5000 and 10,000 metres, discovered this when he moved in with some London-based Kenyan athletes in 2005. At the time, he was a good British runner but nowhere near the world's best. In his autobiography, *Twin Ambitions*, Farah wrote:

> The Kenyans went out for their first run early. They'd be up, dressed and out the front door no later than 7am. They believed

it was best to get the first run out of the way nice and early, when your head is clear and your body is nicely rested ... The Kenyans trained hard. And I mean really hard. Those first sessions, I bust a gut trying to keep up with them. By the end of the session I was knackered.

Farah realised he would have to work harder, which included training with more intensity, if he wanted to beat the Kenyans and win. He did, and this was a key factor in his extraordinary future success.

For middle-distance runners, Doubell believes that these intense training sessions must include speed work. Stampfl's regime required his athletes to be timed while running measured distances repeatedly on the track because this is essential for an athlete to improve their speed. Doubell believes strongly that athletes can only build up and improve their speed if they complete speedwork sessions on the track while being timed over every run.

Regular competition

Doubell ran for Melbourne University Athletics Club and competed in interclub competitions week in, week out over many years and over distances from 100 yards to the mile, as well as in team relays. He did this because he loved running and enjoyed contributing to his team's performance. The lasting benefit was that he learned how to compete over different distances and in varying conditions, and deal with situations in an 880-yards or 800-metres race in which the first lap was either too slow or too fast. These experiences strengthened Doubell mentally as well as physically. It undoubtedly helped him to deal with the issues that arose during his races in

Mexico City, such as when Alfredo Cubias cut him off in the heat and the officials wrongly attributed a false start to him in the final.

Peter Bourke also ran regularly in interclub competition. He says:

> I can tell you right now that I would not have won the Commonwealth Games gold medal had I not done interclub. On a Saturday, I could run an 800 metres and after that maybe a 4 x 200-metres relay. The week after, I would run a 400 and a 1500. In the weeks leading up to the Commonwealth Games, I was running PBs for those other distances. Those PBs in those other distances gave me confidence. And when I started to taper, the 800 fell into place.
>
> Young athletes need to understand that interclub is a great part of your training. You get competition, someone to chase, and you get pushed outside your comfort zone if you run a distance that is not your pet event. It gave me the speed and the endurance, it had me primed. And you learn to deal with the flying elbows and getting cut off — it's all part of the mental preparation.

A reasonable balance

In *Franz Stampfl on Running*, the Austrian coach wrote:

> The athlete who believes that all normal social life and entertainment must be abandoned in the interest of rigorous and continuous training is a man devoid of imagination and proper understanding of the value of recreation. A colourless, Spartan life in which all other interests are sacrificed to a single

ideal is no existence for a man intent on achieving physical and mental fitness. Indeed, the relaxation and mental stimulation that hobbies, books, music and the company of friends provide are as necessary to his well-being and athletic ambitions as the two hours of physical effort that comprise his daily program. Nobody, unless he is a complete moron, can eat, drink and sleep athletics without the fun that ought to be there giving way to drudgery.

Doubell was either a student or working at Shell when he achieved his greatest successes on the track. He believes that today's athletes should heed Stampfl's warning:

What I see these days is athletes who have one interest in life: track and field. That's a real danger because you cannot survive and maintain a reasonable balance if that's all you are doing ... I think the whole concept of living in a sporting environment day in and day out would drive me up the wall. Actually, I think it detracts from your performance.

Return to Mexico City

In January 2017, the Doubells were invited to the wedding of a cousin in Mexico City. Ralph decided to contact Dr David Engel, the Australian Ambassador to Mexico, through a Melbourne-based friend who had worked with the Department of Foreign Affairs and Trade, to see if there was any chance a visit could be organised to the Estadio Olympico. Dr Engel, once he understood why the request was being made, was very happy to make the necessary arrangements. While in town for the wedding, Ralph and Jennifer returned to the stadium where nearly 50 years earlier he had enjoyed the greatest day of his sporting life.

As they stood at the edge of the track, Doubell could remember exactly where he was during both laps of the 800-metres final. He remembered the false start he was wrongly blamed for, his conservative start when the gun was fired for the second time, the way he moved his way up through the back half of the field to be ideally placed at the bell, his tracking of Wilson Kiprugut to ensure the metaphorical rubber band between them remained taut, and his perfectly timed finishing burst that saw him break the tape to win the gold medal. He and Jennifer walked the track, and stopped from time to time while he described what had been happening at various stages of the race. He remembered looking up at the scoreboard and seeing his time of 1:44.3 and Tom Farrell confirming he had equalled the world record. He remembered the emotional moment when he saw Franz Stampfl across the room at the media conference, and the wordless gratitude he showed his coach and mentor by hugging him close.

So many things could have prevented him from winning that race on 15 October 1968.

What if his mother hadn't insisted he stay at school after his father died when he was just 14 years old? He would not have benefited from an excellent Melbourne High School education and received encouragement from his first athletics coach, Mike Agostini.

What if Dafydd Lewis hadn't decided to establish a trust to fund scholarships for boys like him who otherwise could not afford to go to university?

What if Hilda Rawlinson hadn't seen a copy of the *Sporting Globe* on the counter of her local newsagency in Eaglemont, inspiring her to suggest to her husband that he approach Sir Frank Beaurepaire to help fund the employment of the famous coach Franz Stampfl at the University of Melbourne?

What if Alf Lazer, who didn't even know him at the time, hadn't decided to anonymously pay for him to travel to the 1963

Intervarsity competition in Adelaide, piquing his interest in travel and allowing him to show he did have some athletic talent?

What if he hadn't been controversially overlooked by the selectors for the British Commonwealth team that competed against the USA in Los Angeles in July 1967, allowing him to travel to Tokyo for the 1967 Universiade and beat the European record holder, Franz-Joseph Kemper, for a confidence-boosting victory?

What if Mark Hines, a club runner he had never met, hadn't agreed to be a 'rabbit' and run a fast first lap that night at Melbourne's Olympic Park in March 1968, allowing him to run a qualifying time for Mexico City at his very last attempt?

What if his Achilles injury hadn't healed in time for the Games?

So many stars aligned to allow him to run the best race of his life and win an Olympic gold medal and equal the world record.

For some reason, Doubell has never experienced the public acclaim in Australia enjoyed by his fellow Olympic middle-distance gold medallist Herb Elliott, whose relatively brief career ended when he retired at the age of 22. A number of athletes who have not won Olympic gold, including some who have not gone close to achieving this feat, have received greater recognition. The fact Doubell remains one of only three Australian men to have won an Olympic gold medal in a running race on the athletics track is not enough on its own to attract adulation at home. Perhaps it is because Doubell's best results were achieved overseas at a time when media coverage was not what it is today. Social media was a phenomenon for the future. Perhaps it has something to do with his personality, which incorporated a combination of shyness and confidence that has sometimes been perceived as arrogance.

'I can't tell you why he didn't capture the public imagination,' said Ray Weinberg, who observed him closely in Mexico City and became friends with him in the following years. 'He was a cool character and he was very confident, but you have to be if you are going to run at that level. He has a reserve about him which you don't always break down. But I have been lucky enough to become close to him.'

For Doubell, his victory in Mexico City is reward enough. An Olympic gold medal is the ultimate goal for any track athlete and he trained extremely hard for years to achieve it, aided by an extraordinary coach and close mates. It was the highlight of his decade-long running career that enabled him to travel the world and make many friends.

When his running career ended, Doubell was ready to move on to the next stage of his life. He married Jennifer within months and 46 years later they remain a devoted couple with three grown children. Here she was now, proudly standing by his side on the edge of the Mexico City track. He enjoyed an extremely successful business career that allowed him to work and live in New York and London, as well as Sydney and Melbourne.

He had come a long way from the working-class suburbs of Melbourne where money was always in short supply, particularly after his father died. In his seven decades on earth he had much to be proud of. There had been many tough times and he had answered each challenge stoically. 'Do not worry, it is only pain,' Franz had told him. Following that doctrine had served him well, both on and off the track.

FOR THE RECORD

Men's 800 Metres at the 1968 Olympic Games

Mexico City, 13–15 October
Entries: 43 athletes from 32 nations
World Record: 1:44.3 (Peter Snell, New Zealand)
Olympic Record: 1:45.1 (Peter Snell, New Zealand)
Australian Record: 1:46.7 (Ralph Doubell*)

Round One (13 October)
First two in each heat, plus four fastest other finishers through to semi-finals

Heat One

Finish	Athlete	Nation	Time (H)	Time (A)
1	Thomas Saisi	Kenya	1:47.0	1:46.99
2	Jean-Pierre Dufresne	France	1:47.6	1:47.61
3	Matias Habtemichael	Ethiopia	1:49.6	1:49.63
4	Papa M'Baye N'Diaye	Senegal	1:51.3	1:51.31
5	Wade Bell	USA	1:51.5	1:51.52
6	Róbert Honti	Hungary	1:53.8	1:53.88

* Doubell ran 1:46.7 at the 1967 Summer Universiade in Tokyo. In 1968, the Amateur Athletic Union of Australia did not recognise performances made outside Australia as national records. It listed Doubell's 1:47.2 achieved at Olympic Park, Melbourne, on 29 March 1968 as the Australian 800-metres record.

Heat Two

Finish	Athlete	Nation	Time (H)	Time (A)
1	Dieter Fromm	East Germany	1:46.9	1:46.98
2	Franz-Josef Kemper	West Germany	1:47.0	1:47.02
3	Ron Kutschinski	USA	1:47.6	1:47.61
4	Ramasamy Subramaniam	Malaysia	1:50.8	1:50.87
5	Gilbert Van Manshoven	Belgium	1:52.3	1:52.32
DNF	Guillermo Cuello	Argentina	–	–

Heat Three

Finish	Athlete	Nation	Time (H)	Time (A)
1	Walter Adams	West Germany	1:48.4	1:48.50
2	Jozef Plachý	Czechoslovakia	1:48.6	1:48.65
3	Noel Carroll	Ireland	1:49.0	1:49.01
4	Ahmed Issa	Chad	1:49.0	1:49.09
5	Roberto Silva	Mexico	1:50.4	1:50.49
6	Gerd Larsen	Denmark	1:51.9	1:51.98
DNF	Neville Myton	Jamaica	–	–

Heat Four

Finish	Athlete	Nation	Time (H)	Time (A)
1	Ralph Doubell	Australia	1:47.2	1:47.24
2	Henryk Szordykowski	Poland	1:47.4	1:47.48
3	Robert Ouko	Kenya	1:47.6	1:47.65
4	John Ametepey	Ghana	1:50.7	1:50.78
5	Gilles Sibon	France	1:50.8	1:50.87
6	Chris Carter	Great Britain	1:52.9	1:52.99
7	José L'Oficial	Dominican Republic	1:55.6	1:55.66
8	Alfredo Cubías	El Salvador	2:08.7	2:08.72

Heat Five

Finish	Athlete	Nation	Time (H)	Time (A)
1	Wilson Kiprugut	Kenya	1:46.1	1:46.17
2	Tom Farrell	USA	1:47.9	1:47.96
3	Tomáŝ Jungwirth	Czechoslovakia	1:48.7	1:48.72
4	Anders Gärderud	Sweden	1:48.9	1:48.99
5	Jun Nagai	Japan	1:51.2	1:51.27
6	Angelo Hussein	Sudan	1:53.4	1:53.43
7	Jacques Pennewaert	Belgium	1:53.8	1:53.81
8	Francisco Menocal	Nicaragua	1:58.9	1:58.96

Peter Snell's world 800-metres record of 1:44.3 was achieved at Christchurch on 3 February 1962. His Olympic record of 1:45.1 was made at Tokyo on 16 October 1964, when he successfully defended the title he had won in Rome four years earlier.

Heat Six

Finish	Athlete	Nation	Time (H)	Time (A)
1	Dave Cropper	Great Britain	1:47.9	1:47.96
2	Benedict Cayenne	Trinidad	1:48.2	1:48.22
3	Yevhen Arzhanov	Soviet Union	1:48.4	1:48.46
4	Byron Dyce	Jamaica	1:48.5	1:48.58
5	Mamo Sebsibe	Ethiopia	1:49.7	1:49.75
6	Gianni Del Buono	Italy	1:50.2	1:50.23
7	Xaver Frick, Jr.	Liechtenstein	1:52.6	1:52.68
8	Carlos Báez	Puerto Rico	1:52.6	1:52.70

Semi-Finals (14 October)

First four in each semi-final through to the final

First Semi-Final

Finish	Athlete	Nation	Time (H)	Time (A)
1	Walter Adams	West Germany	1:46.4	1:46.41
2	Dieter Fromm	East Germany	1:46.5	1:46.54
3	Thomas Saisi	Kenya	1:46.6	1:46.64
4	Ben Cayenne	Trinidad	1:46.8	1:46.83
5	Ron Kutschinski	USA	1:47.3	1:47.39
6	Jean-Pierre Dufresne	France	1:51.8	1:51.89
DNS	Yevhen Arzhanov	Soviet Union	–	–
DNS	Henryk Szordykowski	Poland	–	–

Second Semi-Final

Finish	Athlete	Nation	Time (H)	Time (A)
1	Ralph Doubell	Australia	1:45.7	1:45.78
2	Wilson Kiprugut	Kenya	1:45.8	1:45.84
3	Jozef Plachý	Czechoslovakia	1:45.9	1:45.96
4	Tom Farrell	USA	1:46.1	1:46.11
5	Robert Ouko	Kenya	1:47.1	1:47.15
6	Byron Dyce	Jamaica	1:47.2	1:47.30
7	Franz-Josef Kemper	West Germany	1:47.3	1:47.37
8	Dave Cropper	Great Britain	1:47.6	1:47.67

The men's 800-metres heats were the third event on the track at the Mexico City Olympics, after heats of the men's 100 metres and the men's 400-metres hurdles. Doubell was the first Australian to win a race at the 1968 Games. The only final on day one was the men's 10,000 metres, won by Kenya's Naftali Temu, with Australia's Ron Clarke sixth.

This classic image — taken by Bruce Howard, who was in Mexico City for the Herald and Weekly Times — is Doubell's favourite photograph from the men's 800 metres at the 1968 Olympics.

Final (15 October)

Finish	Athlete	Nation	Time (H)	Time (A)
1	Ralph Doubell	Australia	1:44.3	1:44.40
2	Wilson Kiprugut	Kenya	1:44.5	1:44.57
3	Tom Farrell	USA	1:45.4	1:45.46
4	Walter Adams	West Germany	1:45.8	1:45.83
5	Jozef Plachý	Czechoslovakia	1:45.9	1:45.99
6	Dieter Fromm	East Germany	1:46.2	1:46.30
7	Thomas Saisi	Kenya	1:47.5	1:47.59
8	Ben Cayenne	Trinidad	1:54.3	1:54.40

Notes

1. 'Times (H)' indicates the athlete's time recorded by hand; 'Times (A)' indicates time measured automatically (electronically); 'DNF' indicates Did not Finish; 'DNS' indicates Did not Start.
2. Doubell set a new Australian record in the semi-final. He broke that record, and established a new Olympic record and equalled Peter Snell's world record in the final.
3. Doubell is one of four Australians to reach the men's 800-metres final at an Olympic Games, after Edwin Flack (first in 1896), Gerald Backhouse (eighth in 1936), and Bill Butchart (eighth in 1956).
4. The men's 800-metres final (run at 6.10pm) was the last event on the program for the third day of competition. Other finals completed on this day were the men's discus, in which Al Oerter (USA) became the first athlete to win the same Olympic track-and-field event four times, the men's 400-metres hurdles, won by David Hemery (Great Britain), and the women's 100 metres, won by Wyomia Tyus (USA) with Australia's Raelene Boyle fourth and Dianne Burge sixth.
5. Doubell won Australia's first medal in Mexico City. Australia's other medallists were:

Gold
18 October: Maureen Caird, Women's 80m hurdles (Athletics)
19 October: Mike Wenden, Men's 100m freestyle (Swimming)
21 October: Lyn McClements, Women's 100m butterfly (Swimming)
24 October: Mike Wenden, Men's 200m freestyle (Swimming)

Silver
16 October: Peter Norman, Men's 200 metres (Athletics)
17 October: Women's 4 x 100m medley relay (Swimming)
18 October: Raelene Boyle, Women's 200 metres (Athletics)
18 October: Pam Kilborn, Women's 80m hurdles (Athletics)
19 October: Men's eight (Rowing)
21 October: Men's 4 x 200m freestyle relay (Swimming)
26 October: Men's Hockey

Bronze
17 October: Men's 4 x 100m freestyle relay (Swimming)
18 October: Jenny Lamy, Women's 200 metres (Athletics)
20 October: Karen Moras, Women's 400m freestyle (Swimming)
21 October: Men's three-day event (Equestrian)
26 October: Greg Brough, Men's 1500m freestyle (Swimming)

MEN'S 800 METRES
WORLD RECORD PROGRESSION SINCE 1912

Time	Athlete (Country)	Venue	Date
1:51.9	Ted Meredith (USA)	Stockholm	8 July 1912
1:51.6	Otto Peltzer (Germany)	London	3 July 1926
1:50.6	Séra Martin (France)	Paris	14 July 1928
1:49.8	Tom Hampson (Great Britain)	Los Angeles	2 August 1932
1:49.8	Ben Eastman (USA)	Princeton	16 June 1934
1:49.7	Glenn Cunningham (USA)	Stockholm	20 August 1936
1:49.6	Elroy Robinson (USA)	New York	11 July 1937
1:48.4	Sydney Wooderson (GB)	London	20 August 1938
1:46.6	Rudolf Harbig (Germany)	Milan	15 July 1939
1:45.7	Roger Moens (Belgium)	Oslo	3 August 1955
1:44.3	Peter Snell (New Zealand)	Christchurch	3 February 1962
1:44.3	Ralph Doubell (Australia)	Mexico City	15 October 1968
1:44.3	Dave Wottle (USA)	Eugene	1 July 1972
1:43.7	Marcello Fiasconaro (Italy)	Milan	27 June 1973
1:43.5	Alberto Juantorena (Cuba)	Montreal	25 July 1976
1:43.4	Alberto Juantorena (Cuba)	Sofia	21 August 1977
1:42.33	Sebastian Coe (Great Britain)	Oslo	5 July 1979
1:41.73	Sebastian Coe (Great Britain)	Florence	10 June 1981
1:41.73	Wilson Kipketer (Denmark)	Stockholm	7 July 1997
1:41.24	Wilson Kipketer (Denmark)	Zurich	13 August 1997
1:41.11	Wilson Kipketer (Denmark)	Cologne	24 August 1997
1:41.09	David Rudisha (Kenya)	Berlin	22 August 2010
1:41.01	David Rudisha (Kenya)	Rieti	29 August 2010
1:40.91	David Rudisha (Kenya)	London	9 August 2012

Notes

1. These are the official world records achieved since the establishment of the International Association of Athletics Federations (IAAF) in 1912.
2. The times recorded by Peltzer, Eastman and Robinson were for 880 yards (804.672 metres).
3. Hampson was electronically timed at 1:49.7.
4. The 800-metres world records set or equalled by Meredith (1912), Hampson (1932), Doubell (1968), Juantorena (1976) and Rudisha (2012) were achieved at the Olympic Games.
5. As at 15 August 2018, the only men not on the above list to have run below 1:42.0 are Botswana's Nijel Amos, who ran 1: 41.73 at London in 2012, and Brazil's Joaquim Cruz, who ran 1:41.77 at Cologne in 1984.
6. From 1 January 1977, the IAAF ruled that all world records must be auto-timed, with events beyond 400 metres rounded up to the nearest one-tenth of a second. From 1 January 1981, official timing for all races up to 10,000m was in one-hundredths of a second.
7. Coe's world-record time from Oslo in 1979 was auto-timed at 1:42.33 but, as per the existing IAAF regulations, was rounded up to the next tenth of a second (1:42.4). On 1 January 1981, with the change to the IAAF rules, the record was officially readjusted to the original auto-time.

8. Doubell's world record is listed by the IAAF in its official world record progression list as 1:44.3, the hand-timed record, with the auto-time noted. For the purposes of the Australian All-Time List, Athletics Australia considers his auto-time from Mexico City (1:44.40) to be official.

9. Doubell's long-time Australian record was equalled by Victoria's Alex Rowe at Monaco on 18 July 2014, and finally beaten by 20-year-old Joseph Deng at Monaco on 20 July 2018. As at 1 August 2018, the top 10 on Athletics Australia's All-Time List for 800 metres (compiled by Athletics Australia statistician Paul Jenes, Fletcher McEwen and David Tarbotton) is as follows:

Time	Athlete	Venue	Date
1:44.21	Joseph Deng	Monaco	20 July 2018
1:44.40	Ralph Doubell	Mexico City	15 October 1968
1:44.40	Alex Rowe	Monaco	18 July 2014
1:44.48	Jeff Riseley	Lignano	17 July 2012
1:44.56	Peter Bol	Stockholm	10 June 2018
1:44.78	Peter Bourke	Brisbane	20 March 1982
1:45.03	Brendan Hanigan	Lappeenranta	26 July 1994
1:45.16	Luke Mathews	Melbourne	5 March 2016
1:45.21	Grant Cremar	Seville	27 August 1999
1:45.36	Bill Hooker	London	14 July 1973

10. Doubell's gold medal-winning time from Mexico City was the Australian record for 49 years, 278 days. He first claimed the Australian residents record on 12 February 1966, when he ran 1:47.7 at the Victorian championships at Olympic Park, breaking Tony Blue's record. Fifteen days later, Doubell ran 1:47.3 at the Australian championships in Perth, breaking Peter Snell's open Australian record (the best time achieved in Australia by a local or overseas athlete) by three-tenths of a second. This time equalled Herb Elliott's best for 880 yards — achieved in London on 4 August 1958 — which had been the fastest time for 880 yards or 800 metres ever run by an Australian. At the 1966 British Empire and Commonwealth Games in Kingston, Noel Clough won the 880 yards in 1:46.9. On 3 September 1967, at the Universiade in Tokyo, Doubell won the 800 metres in 1:46.7, which remained the best 800-metres time recorded by an Australian until Doubell ran 1:45.7 in his semi-final in Mexico City. Doubell therefore held the record for best 800-metres time achieved by an Australian on home soil or overseas continuously from 3 September 1967 until 20 July 2018, a total of 50 years, 320 days.

The victorious Australian 4 x 880-yards relay team in Dublin in 1966. *From left*: Keith Wheeler, Ralph Doubell, Ken Roche and Noel Clough. The quartet's time of 7:19.7 remains the Australian record for this rarely run event.

ACKNOWLEDGMENTS

First and foremost, I would like to thank Ralph for giving me his support, his scrapbooks and so much of his time. He was initially wary, but I hope he is pleased with the result.

Ralph is reluctant to talk about himself or his extraordinary achievements, so the assistance of others was vital. Stanley Spittle, Ralph's great mate, made himself available many times despite battling various health issues. Jennifer Doubell, Ralph's wife of 46 years, generously shared some wonderful memories.

Alan Gregory, the Melbourne High School historian, allowed me to sit for hours sifting through the school archives, while Alf Lazer provided important information about the Melbourne University Athletics Club.

Many athletes gave me invaluable insights into their sport and Ralph, including Tom Farrell, Tony Sneazwell, Bill Hooker, Trevor Vincent, Noel Clough, Gordon Windeyer, Chum Darvall, Peter Bourke and Mark Hines. Thanks also to Athletics Australia statistician Paul Jenes, who shared his memories as a spectator in Mexico City, and physiotherapist David Zuker, who recalled treating Ralph in the weeks before the '68 Games.

I interviewed the wonderful Ray Weinberg just a few weeks before he passed away and I send my sincere condolences to his wife, Shirley, and his family.

I am extremely grateful for finding Geoff Armstrong, the publisher, who shared my enthusiasm for this subject as well as his expertise and guidance.

Finally, thank you to my family for your love and support.

Michael Sharp
August 2018

PHOTOGRAPHS

Thanks go to the many people who helped with the photographs that appear in this book, most notably Ralph and Jennifer Doubell. The support of Dr David Engel and Lorena Zapiain at the Australian Embassy in Mexico, Stanley Spittle, Anton Stampfl and Brett Weinberg, and the good people at AAP Photos, Getty Images, the National Archives of Australia, Newspix, Snapper Media and the State Library of NSW is also much appreciated. Some of the photographs come from private collections, with original creators unknown. The known sources are:

Section 1
Page 2, below: courtesy of the Franz Stampfl Trust
Page 3, below left: News Limited, Newspix
Page 5, above: Stanley Spittle
Page 6, below: News Limited, Newspix
Page 7, above: Brett Weinberg
Page 8, above left: State Library of NSW
Page 8, above right: Associated Press/AAP Photos

FURTHER READING

The following sources were consulted during the making of this book:

Books

Roger Bannister, *Twin Tracks*; Robson Press, London, 2014

Neal Bascomb, *The Perfect Mile*; Mariner Books, New York, 2005

Chris Brasher, *Mexico 1968: A Diary of the XIXth Olympiad*; Stanley Paul, London, 1968

Chris Brasher, *Munich 72*; Stanley Paul, London, 1972

John Bryant, *Chris Brasher: The Man Who Made the London Marathon*; Aurum Press Ltd, London, 2012

Ron Clarke, *The Unforgiving Minute*; Pelham Books, London, 1966

Ron Clarke (editor), *Athletics the Australian Way*; Lansdowne, Melbourne, 1971

James Coote, *Olympic Report 1968*; Robert Hale, London, 1968

Sebastian Coe, *The Olympians*; Pavilion Books, London, 1988

Brian Corrigan, *The Life of Brian: Confessions of an Olympic Doctor*; ABC Books, Sydney, 2001

Cleve Dheenshaw, *The Commonwealth Games: The First 60 Years 1930-1990*; ABC Books, Sydney, 1994

Herb Elliott, *The Golden Mile*; Cassell, London, 1961

Gareth Evans, *Incorrigible Optimist: A Political Memoir*; Melbourne University Press, Melbourne, 2017

Mo Farah, *Twin Ambitions*; Hodder and Stoughton, London 2013

Garth Gilmour, *Arthur Lydiard: Master Coach*; Exisle Publishing Limited, Auckland, 2004

Harry Gordon, *Australia and the Olympic Games*; University of Queensland Press, Brisbane, 1994

Bruce Howard, *15 Days in '56: The first Australian Olympics*; Angus and Robertson, Sydney, 1995

Graeme Kelly, *Mr Controversial: The Story of Percy Wells Cerutty*; Stanley Paul, London, 1964

Len Johnson, *The Landy Era*; Melbourne Books, Melbourne, 2009

Rafer Johnson, *The Best That I Can Be*; Doubleday, New York, 1998

Damian Johnstone and Matt Norman, *A Race to Remember: The Peter Norman Story*; JoJo Publishing, Melbourne, 2008

Brian Lenton, *Interviews*; Brian Lenton Publications, Canberra, 1997

Benzion Patkin, *The Dunera Internees*; Cassell Australia Limited, Sydney, 1979

June E. Senyard, *The Ties That Bind: A History of Sport at the University of Melbourne*; Walla Walla Press, Sydney, 2004

Franz Stampfl, *Franz Stampfl on Running*; Herbert Jenkins Limited, London, 1955

Matthew Syed, *Bounce: The Myth of Talent and Power of Practice*; Fourth Estate, London, 2010

Kevin B. Witherspoon, *Before the Eyes of the World: Mexico and the 1968 Olympic Games*; Northern Illinois University Press, Illinois, 2014

Annuals, Official Reports and Record Books

The Amateur Athletic Union of Australia, *Almanacs of Records and Results* (various years)

Athletics Australia, *Handbooks of Records and Results* (various years)

Paul Jenes, Peter Hamilton, David Tarbotton, Fletcher McEwen and Bert Gardiner, *Australian Ranking Lists* and *Australian IAAF World Record Holders and World Best Performances*; athletics.com.au, 2018

Richard Hymans and Imre Matrahazi (editors), *IAAF World Records* (2015 edition); IAAF, Monaco, 2015

Melbourne Olympic Games Invitation; Melbourne Invitation Committee for Olympic Games 1956, Melbourne, 1949

Mexico 68; official report produced by the Organising Committee of the Games of the XIX Olympiad, Mexico, 1969

David Wallechinsky and Jaime Loucky, *The Complete Book of the Olympics 2012 Edition*; Aurum Press, London, 2012

Essays and Radio Presentations

Abraham Abrahams, *On the Subject of Hell-Ships*; Jewish Standard, 1 August 1947

Alastair Aitken, *David Rudisha interview*; activetrainingworld.co.uk, 2 August 2014.

Paul Connolly, *The Forgotten Story of ... Franz Stampfl*; The Guardian, 30 May 2013

Leah McLennan and Andrew Collins, *Former Olympic track athletes recall effects of illness while attending 1968 Mexico Games*; ABC Great Southern, 15 August 2016

Terry O'Connor, *The Mysterious Mentor of Melbourne*; Sports Illustrated, 26 November 1956

Amanda Smith (presenter) and Michael Shirrefs (producer), *Ralph Doubell and Franz Stampfl*; The Sports Factor, ABC Radio National, 28 July 2000

Matthew Syed, *Is it Wrong to Note 100m Winners are Always Black?*; bbc.co.uk, 27 August 2011

Nikko Tanui, *Wilson Kiprugut Chumo: Champion who brought first medal to Kenyan soil*; standardmedia.co.ke, 27 November 2013

John Underwood, *No Goody Two-Shoes*; Sports Illustrated, 10 March 1969

Dave Zirin, *The Explosive 1968 Olympics*; International Socialist Review Issue 61, September-October 2008

Newspapers, Magazines and Websites

The Age (Melbourne), *The Australian* (Sydney), *The Australian Financial Review* (Sydney), *The Canberra Times*, *Chicago Tribune*, *The Christian Science Monitor* (Boston), *The Courier-Mail* (Brisbane), *Daily News* (New York), *The Daily Telegraph* (London), *The Guardian* (London), *The Herald* (Melbourne), iaaf.org (IAAF), independent.ie (Dublin), *Jewish Standard* (New Jersey), *Los Angeles Times*, *New York Post*, *The New York Times*, *The Observer* (London), olympic.org (IOC), racingpast.ca (a history of middle and long-distance running), runnerstribe.com (Runner's Tribe), *The San Bernardino Sun*, scienceofsport.blogspot.com (The Science of Sport), si.com/vault (Sports Illustrated), *The Sporting Globe* (Melbourne), *Sports Illustrated* (New York), *The Sun* (Melbourne), *Sunday Telegraph* (Sydney), *The Sydney*

Morning Herald, *The Times* (London), *Track and Field News* (California), trove.nla.gov.au (National Library of Australia's digitised newspaper collection), *Unicorn* (the magazine of Melbourne High School), *World Sports* (London), youtube.com (for Bud Greenspan's official film of the men's 800 metres in Mexico City and for David Coleman's call of the race for the BBC).

Among the stories consulted were articles by prominent Australian sports journalists of the 1960s and early '70s such as Ron Carter, Robert Gray, Steve Hayward, Graeme Kelly, Ken Knox, Alan Trengove, Jim Webster and Bruce Welch, columns by celebrated American sportswriters such as Frank Litzsky (*New York Times*), Phil Pepe (New York *Daily News*) and Pat Putnam (*Sports Illustrated*), and reports and analysis by former athletes and coaches such as Mike Agostini, Roger Bannister, Chris Brasher, Ralph Doubell, Rick Mitchell and Franz Stampfl.

For Chapter 22, 'Open Opportunity', quotes on specific athletes were sourced as follows:

Kenny Moore (on Joaquin Cruz, page 274–275), *Spinning Straw Into Gold*; Sports Illustrated, 24 December 1984

Kenny Moore (on Paul Ereng, page 275–276), *Sons of the Wind*; Sports Illustrated, 26 February 1990

IOC News (on Vebjørn Rodal, page 276–277), *Resourceful Rodal Reaps Rewards in the 800m*; olympic.org, 31 July 1996

Nickolai Dolgopolov and Rostislav Orlov (on Yuriy Borzakovskiy, page 277–278), *Borzakovskiy: So Many Goals Yet to Achieve*; iaaf.org, 7 December 2004

Sean Ingle (on David Rudisha, page 278–279), *Rudisha feeling fit enough to beat all comers — even Bolt and Farah*; independent.ie, 11 June 2017

Duncan Mackay (on André Bucher, page 280), *Hard work has Bucher battling*; The Guardian, 31 August 2001

Sebastian Coe (on André Bucher, page 280–281), *Quality and precision as Bucher times it to perfection*; The Daily Telegraph, 20 August 2001

INDEX

ABOUT THE AUTHOR

Michael Sharp practised as a lawyer before becoming a journalist with *The Sydney Morning Herald*. He then began a career in corporate communication and has advised several leading Australian companies and organisations. Michael was a mediocre middle-distance runner at school and has been in awe of Ralph Doubell ever since. He decided the 50th anniversary of Doubell's gold medal-winning run at the 1968 Olympic Games was the ideal time to recall Doubell's undervalued achievements and tell the story of his life. Michael is an avid sports fan who has run many fun runs and half-marathons, and a dozen marathons. This is his first book.